Angela Ma

NERO

Homeschooling
by Anna Cestelli Guidi

Over the last decade, Angela Marzullo's production, which the artist developed with her two daughters, Lucie and Stella, has had as its conceptual reference the idea of *Homeschooling*, that is education "at home" understood as an alternative pedagogy opposed to the traditional method. Angela Marzullo's works consist of a series of videos that derive from the analysis of critical texts from the 60s and 70s and their "revitalization" from a feminine point of view, in search of a feminist genealogy in education and art. *

From 2005 to 2015, the artist has reshaped her work around her life as a woman and mother, thus realizing the avowedly feminist slogan of the 70s: "The personal is political." Involving her daughters in her creative process and dialogue with texts that belong to the collective consciousness, Marzullo manages to give form to works that confront, in an unexpected and entirely personal manner, the reflection on issues of responsibility and education, with the aim of awakening the consciousness of women.

From the first video, we see how Marzullo—filmmaker and performer—brings her academic background and personal world together: *Performing* is a low-tech self-produced home video, made with Michael Hofer, who is the artist's partner and the girls' father, and with whom Marzullo has collaborated since then. In this creative and playful homemade film, which is almost a "family business," 5 and 9 year old Lucie and Stella interpret some of the historical video performances of the 70s: the culinary alphabet of *Semiotics of the Kitchen* by Martha Rosler, a cornerstone work of feminism, is staged with small play kitchen utensils; the little brush which Lucie uses in no way diminishes the ferocity of the disturbing *Art Must Be Beautiful* by Marina Abramovič; sitting at a small table like Carole Roussopoulos and Delphine Seyrig, the girls read the

* *Homeschooling* is the title of the 2010 exhibition in which the works realized together with the Starkids were presented for the first time at the Ex Elettrofonica in Rome.

irreverent feminist *S.C.U.M. Manifesto*, written by Valerie Solanas; at the same table they also portray the legendary *Performer/Audience/Mirror* by Dan Graham and *Claim Excerpts* by Vito Acconci, the first to establish the new expressive medium of the video camera as art.

The clash between the radicalism of these performances and their intimate and familiar representation—they are in fact staged as a children's theater show where the "Starkids" play (the artist relies on the semantic complexity of the French word *jouer*) in their bedroom in front of the camera like movie stars—causes a short circuit that resonates in a timeless dimension disclosing new horizons. In this way *Performing* signals, in 2005, the beginning of a re-interpretation, of a dialogic relationship with texts of the past, that is the stylistic and narrative approach of the body of work collected here. From women's perspective, Marzullo selects "minor" texts by theorists and thinkers of the 70s, texts that reflect an unconventional pedagogical approach based on critical thinking, social responsibility and resistance.

On the path from childhood to adolescence Lucie and Stella have voiced the words of Walter Benjamin, Pierpaolo Pasolini, Hannah Arendt, Theodor Adorno and Carla Lonzi: through their voices, these texts are now re-proposed, acquiring new life and becoming part of a familiar and feminine lexicon, as for example *Concettina*, the female version of *Gennariello* from the *Lettere Luterane*. Marzullo's work therefore is not simply a nostalgic return to the paradigms of the 70s: the dialogic relationship Lucie and Stella establish with these texts acquires a new intensity and poetic narrative, strongly characterized by the architectural landscape in which the girls move. With great sensitivity, the mother-artist selects texts that are always connected to her daughters' age. This enables the Starkids to remain "natural," with their words, from time to time, adhering to their body movements, to the playful wondering of children, girls and finally adolescents. So if in the 2005 *Performing*, the girls' performances are almost remakes in miniature, ten years later in 2015, in *Let's Spit on Hegel*, Lucie and Stella, now two teenagers of 15 and 19, two women aware of their feminist standpoint, seem to realize the full correspondence between the meaning of the text, the *Manifesto di Rivolta Femminile* by Carla Lonzi, and their lives.

With the involvement of her daughters in her artistic practice, Marzullo has thus developed her idea of *homeschooling* within a feminist framework, and Lucie and Stella have grown interiorizing the texts which they were asked to recite. Benjamin's words in *Proletarian Theatre for Children* (2006), Pasolini's in *Short Pedagogical Treatise* (2008) and in *Concettina* (2010), Hannah Arendt's in *The Crisis of Education* (2014), Adorno's in *Educating for Autonomy* (2015), and Carla Lonzi's in *Let's Spit on Hegel* (2015): all these texts have been the "heavenly food," so to speak, that has nourished the conscience of these two young women, increasing their awareness of their place in the world. From Pasolinian disobedience as resistance to cultural homogenization, to the idea of difference in opposition to Lonzi's symbolic dominant order of male culture: Marzullo's critique of the dominant western forms of knowledge voiced in *Let's Spit on Hegel* (the final work of the series) expresses the artist's radicalization, openly declaring her feminist line of descent within the history of art and philosophy.

Disowning Culture: Double Notes on Carla Lonzi for Angela Marzullo
by Francesco Ventrella

"We have watched for 4,000 years: now we have seen." [1] This statement from the *Manifesto of Rivolta Femminile* does not look back with nostalgia, but is redolent of the possibilities which can be realized when the subject, after seeing herself, has become conscious of her position in the present. The history that women have watched for 4,000 years is obviously the history that men have told themselves by relegating women to being spectators, while at the same time reproducing images of women which are total fantasy. "Male creativity has another male creativity for its own interlocutor, but relegates women to the position of consumers and spectators excluding them from any form of competition." [2]

The opening scene of Angela Marzullo's *Let's Spit on Hegel* (2015) breaks the boundaries of women's historical invisibility while it envisions a scene of consciousness by staging the encounter of a mythical woman with her own curious young counterpart. Indeed, the Sphinx is a reminder of a double riddle: the one allegedly resolved by Oedipus, and the one which Freud attempted to explain. The certainty of these two men's resolutions is also, as Laura Mulvey pointed out, the other side of their anxiety: "Curiosity and the riddling spirit of the Sphinx activate questions that open up the closures of repression and maintain the force of the 'uncertainty principle'... The story is still in the making. The Sphinx and her riddle are still waiting for a 'beyond.'" [3] For 4,000 years we have been watching Oedipus; now is the time to turn to the Sphinx.

Seen from behind, the cape of the Sphinx shows a concentric-core motif which western visual culture has tried alterna-

1 "Manifesto di Rivolta Femminile" [1970], in Carla Lonzi, *Sputiamo su Hegel e La Donna Clitoridea e la Donna Vaginale*, Scritti di Rivolta Femminile, Rome: 1974, p. 16.

2 "Assenza della donna dai momenti celebrativi della manifestazione della cultura maschile" [1971], in Carla Lonzi, *Sputiamo su Hegel*, p. 63.

3 Laura Mulvey, *Visual and Other Pleasures*, Indiana University Press, Bloomington: 1989, p. 200.

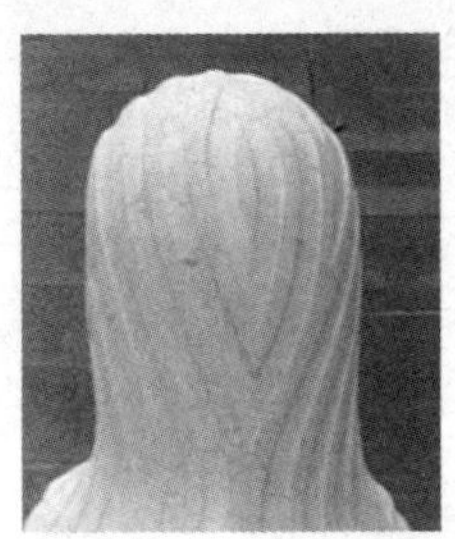

tively to obliterate or sublimate into other iconographies: draperies, conch shells, flowers. Two curious gazes scan the surface, one from the left, the other from the right. One young woman joins her thumbs and indexes together to form the shape of a triangle with her hands: woman is no longer investigated as an image, but is the subject of inquiry. The triangle frames her own eye and it doubles in the eye of the Sphinx. Like the woman with a movie camera, the triangular lens pans out to linger on the ear of the mythological animal first, then on her mouth, her breast, her paw. Inside the triangular frame, the folds and shapes of her body become a morphology investigated by the young woman's curious gaze. The triangle is obviously not an innocent gesture, but one with a genealogy. It was invented by feminists in the 1970s, and is in opposition with its phallic analogous, the communist raised fist. The two hands joined together do not reduce woman to anatomy, but are an expression that comes from the female body, previous to any verbal communication. As Ilaria Bussoni explains, "In that space which is opened out and isolated by the two hands, a piece of the body subtracts itself from being an organ and a function, and an interrogation arises on who is that subject who is free to not occupy the place which was allocated to her by function." [4]

While we witness the identification of the feminist gesture with an imaginary camera we can also hear the voice of these two young women reciting the first paragraph of one of the most radical documents of Rivolta Femminile, which disowns culture as an expression of male creativity. In this text, Carla Lonzi argues that by absenting themselves from the "celebratory moments of male creative manifestation" women refuse to perpetuate man's culture and thus accomplish their most radical goal: "With her absence, woman makes a gesture of self-consciousness, which is liberating and thus

4 Ilaria Bussoni, *E con un gesto le donne si inventarono il sesso*, in *Il gesto femminista. La rivolta delle donne: nel corpo, nel lavoro, nell'arte*, ed. by Ilaria Bussoni and Raffaella Perna, Derive Approdi, Rome: 2014, p. 61.

creative." Therefore, women's creativity cannot be enjoyed within the world of culture that men created for themselves, but only outside it.

One cannot help wondering what Carla Lonzi would have thought of a video that uses her words to make art — a cultural system and a form of expression that she herself disowned when she resigned from the "phony" profession of art criticism in 1969. However, before being shown as art, this video by Angela Marzullo deals with feminist practice. In fact, beyond the mere illustration of Lonzi's ideas, the work is also a documentation of the relation between the artist and her two daughters within their project of homeschooling. As an educational practice opposed to the institutionalized impartation of knowledge professed by the school system, homeschooling gives these three women the chance to unlearn the traditions handed down by male culture. Hence, we see two young women gluing newspapers with commodified images of women onto a bronze female nude outside the Clos Voltaire in Geneva as a practical exercise to understand how culture projects sexualized stereotypes onto women's bodies.

The pedagogical triangulation of mother and daughters may also imply a cultural privilege, not necessarily heteronormative, about another patriarchal institution, which is the family. However, the familial vertical axis of mother and daughters runs parallel to the unfamiliar horizontal axis of siblings through which the philosophy of homeschooling is made legible in the video. Siblings show similarities and likenesses. Still, as Juliet Mitchell has argued, they maintain a difference which implies a sense of vulnerability derived from the consciousness that another so similar to me may survive me (which is also a trigger of the siblings' attachment). [5] We encounter many doubles and doubling in this video, starting from the very recitation of Lonzi's text, which establishes a form of resonance between the two siblings. Lonzi herself embraced voice recording and the transcription of direct quotes in order to capture a relation with the world that was more authentic than the phallic conception of creation *ex nihilo*. Indeed, she turned to resonance in order to find and found feminist creativity and break up with compulsory repetition of four millennia of male culture: "The fact that the artist expects an ever more adequate spectator reveals an impasse when knowledge is confined to one single role. For this reason it is not right to speak of creativity within feminism, unless one understands that it is not a patriarchal type of creativity. The self-consciousness of one woman is incomplete and stuck if it is not reflected in the self-consciousness of another woman." [6] Lonzi's words have a particular resonance today, which she would have found very unsettling. Siblings teach us that the only way to break up with repetition compulsion is by embracing the unfamiliar similarities of repetition itself.

5 Juliet Mitchell, *Siblings. Sex and Violence*, Polity, London: 2003.

6 Carla Lonzi, *Taci, anzi parla. Diario di una femminista*, Scritti di Rivolta Femminile, Rome: 1978, p. 49.

The dialogues which accompany the images are the English subtitles of the videos, translated by Angela Marzullo from the original textual references.

Performing

Claim Excerpts
Semiotics of the Kitchen
Art Must Be Beautiful
S.C.U.M.
Performer Audience Mirror
Relation in Time

2005
16' 45", color, sound, DV
Language: French and English, English subtitles
Format of distribution 16/9

STELLA: Here is my bed. This is my territory. Leave me alone. Leave me alone. Don't get in. It's my bed. This is my territory. Leave me alone. You can't get in. I want to be alone. Leave me alone. Let me think. You are idiots. I don't like you.

Claim Excerpts
from Vito Acconci, 1971

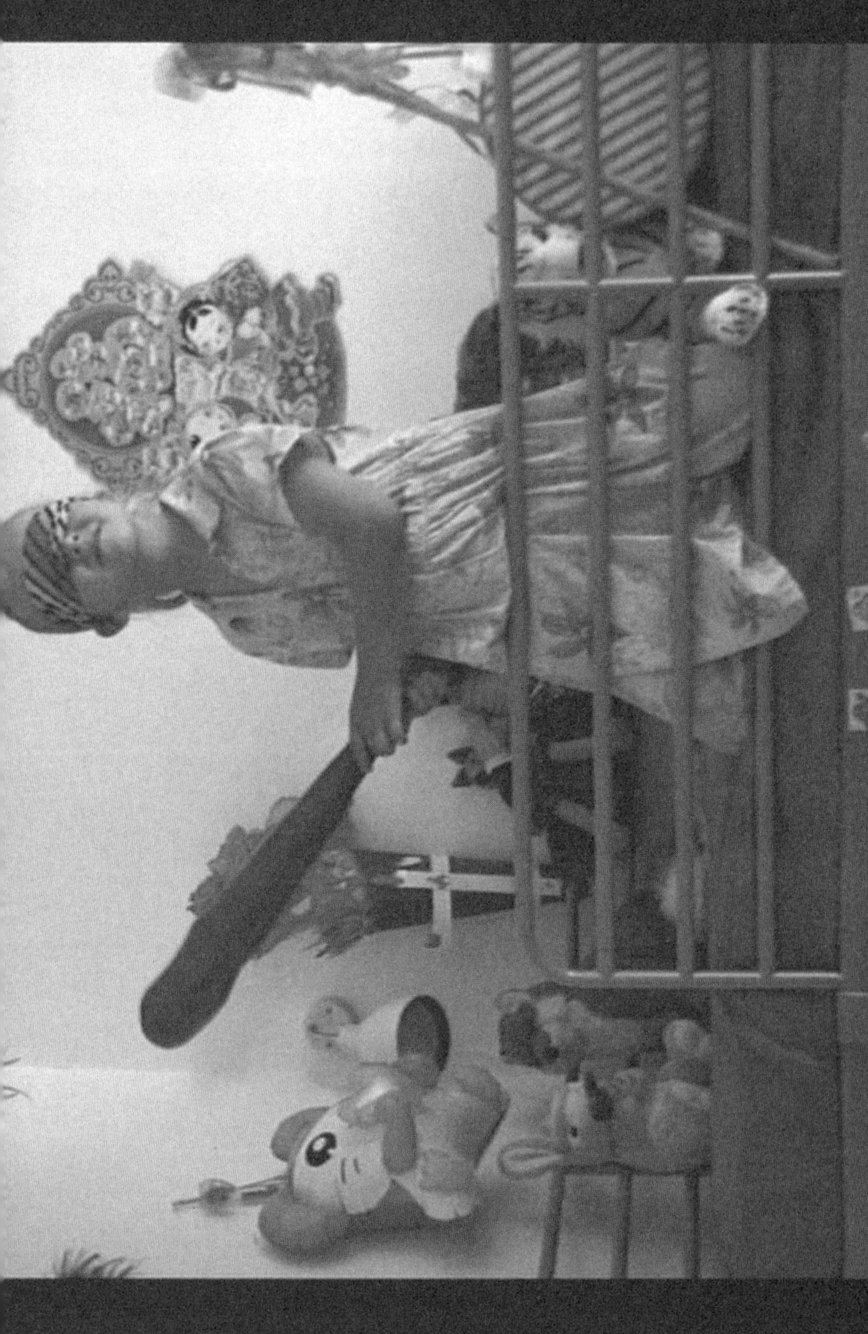

LUCIE: Apron.

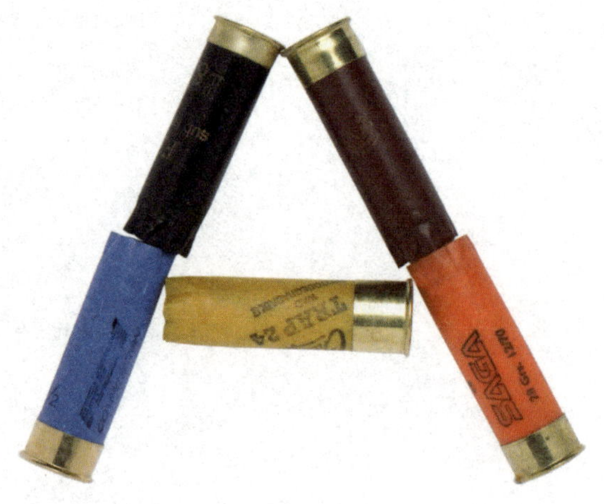

Semiotics of the Kitchen
from Martha Rosler, 1976

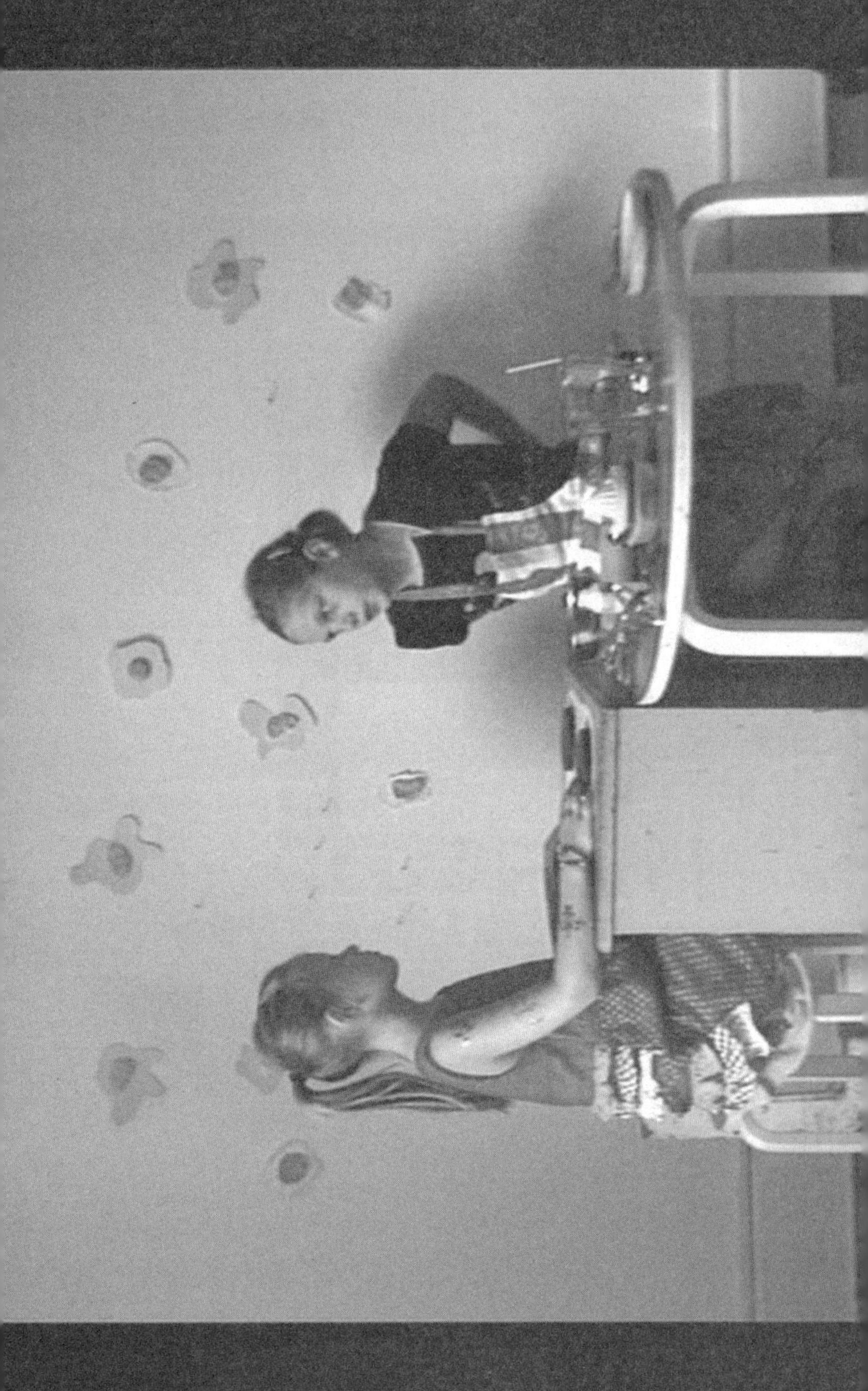

LUCIE: Bowl.

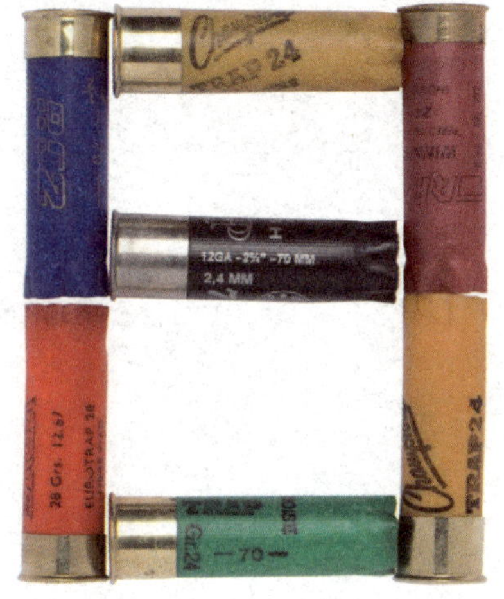

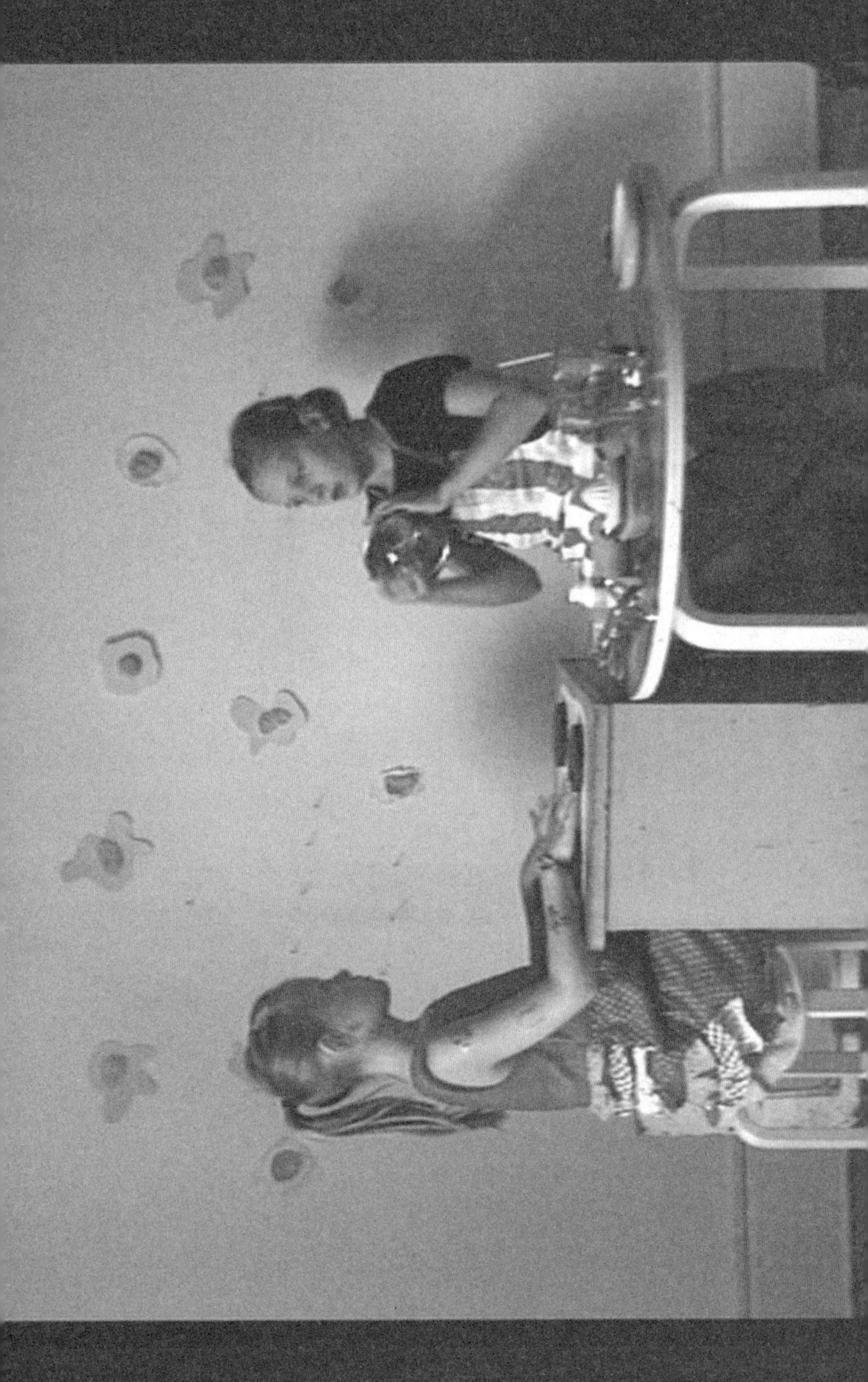

LUCIE: Chopper.

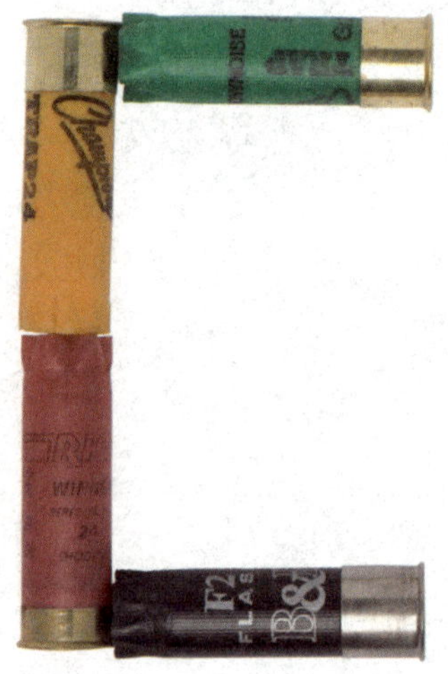

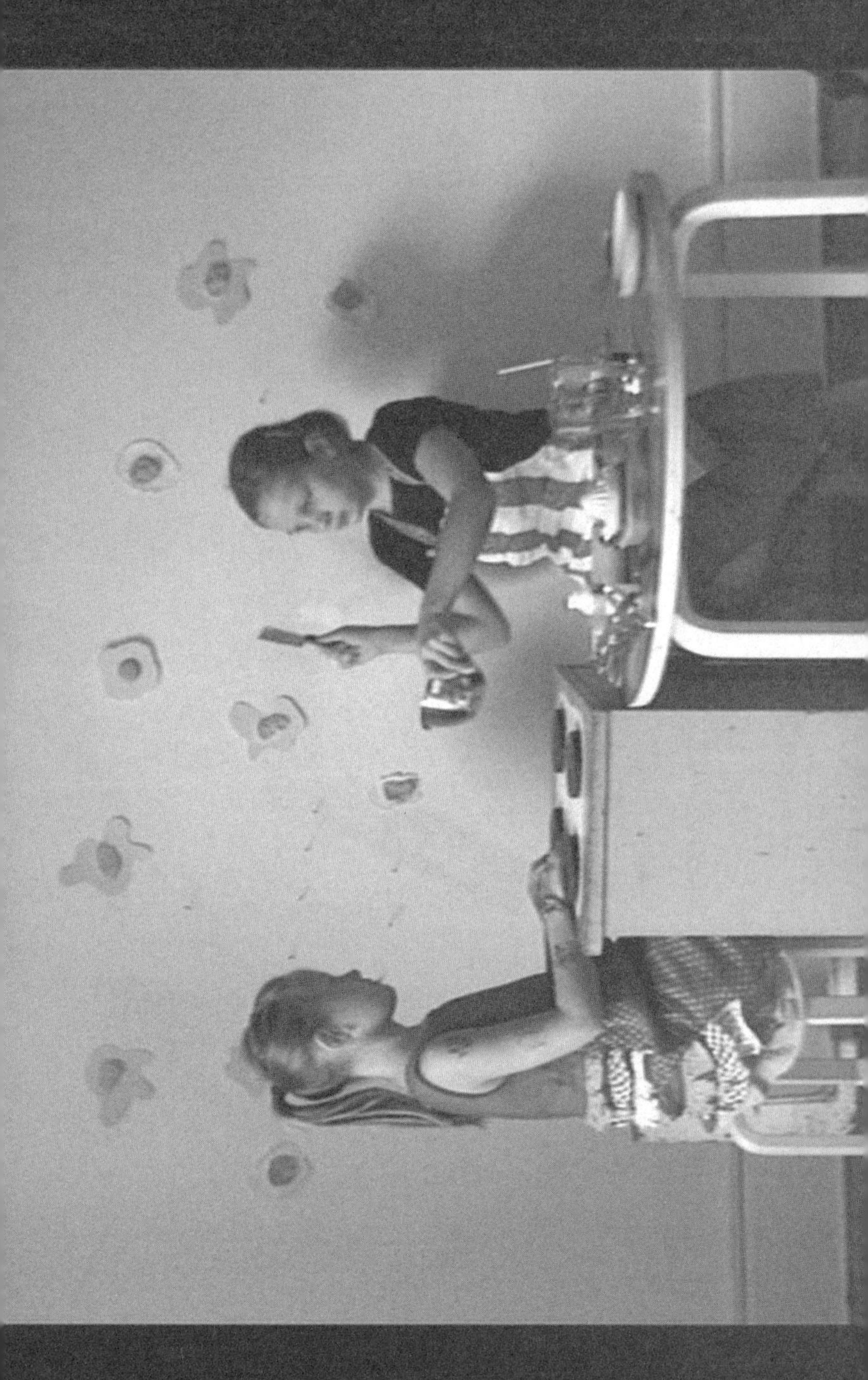

LUCIE: Dish.

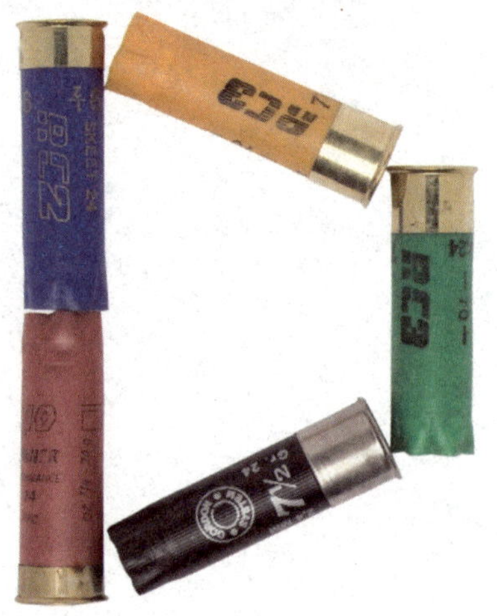

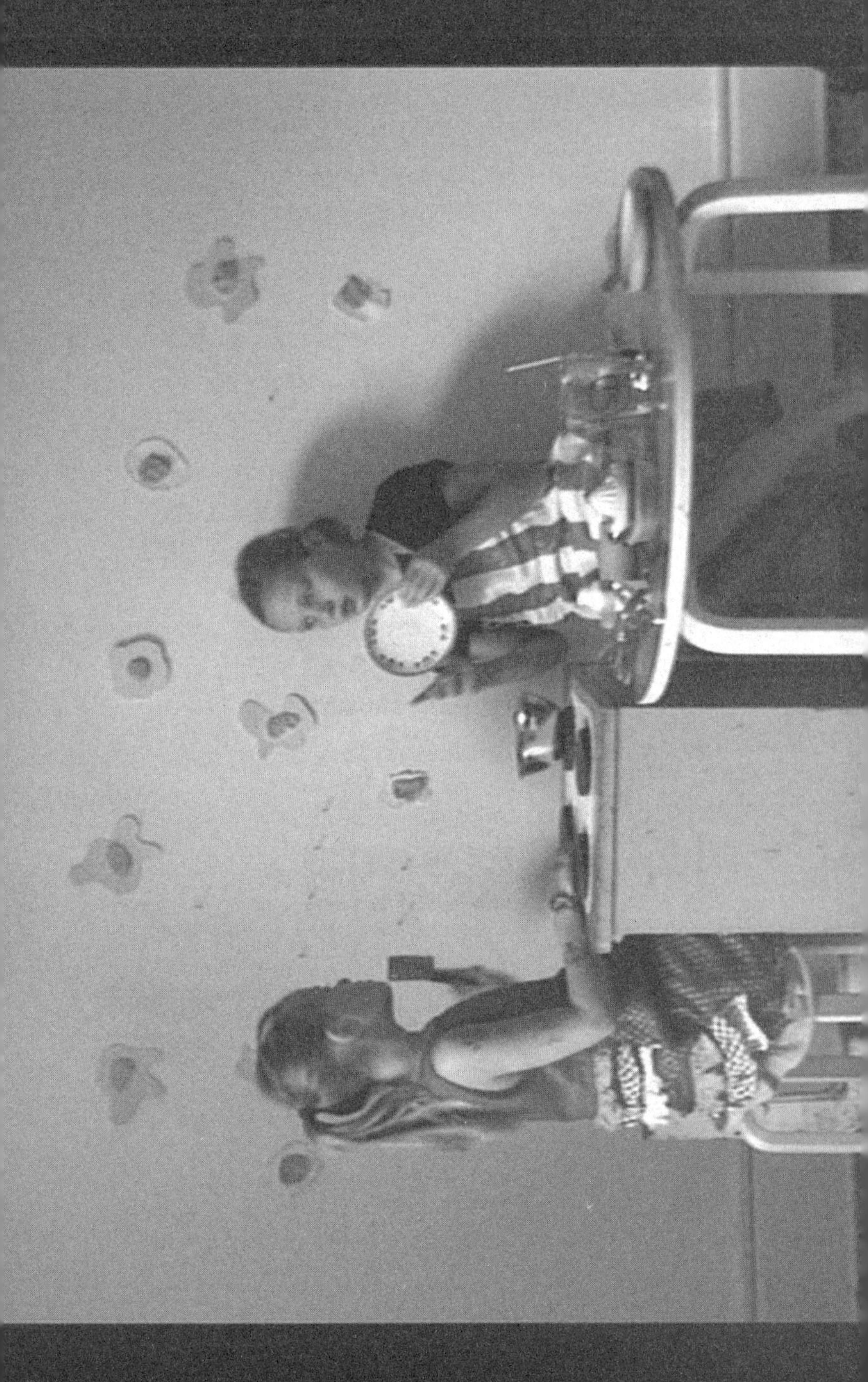

LUCIE : Eggbeater.

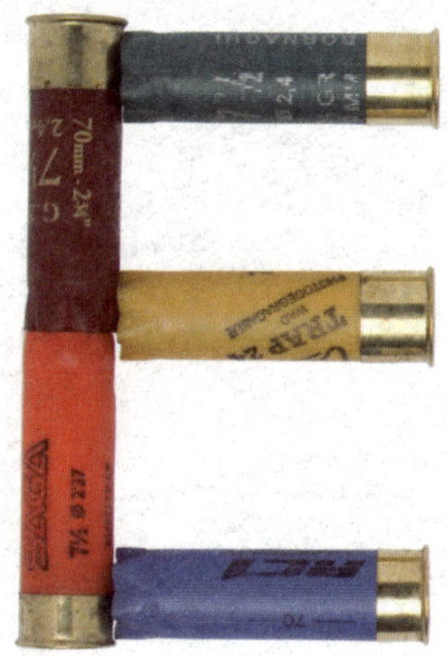

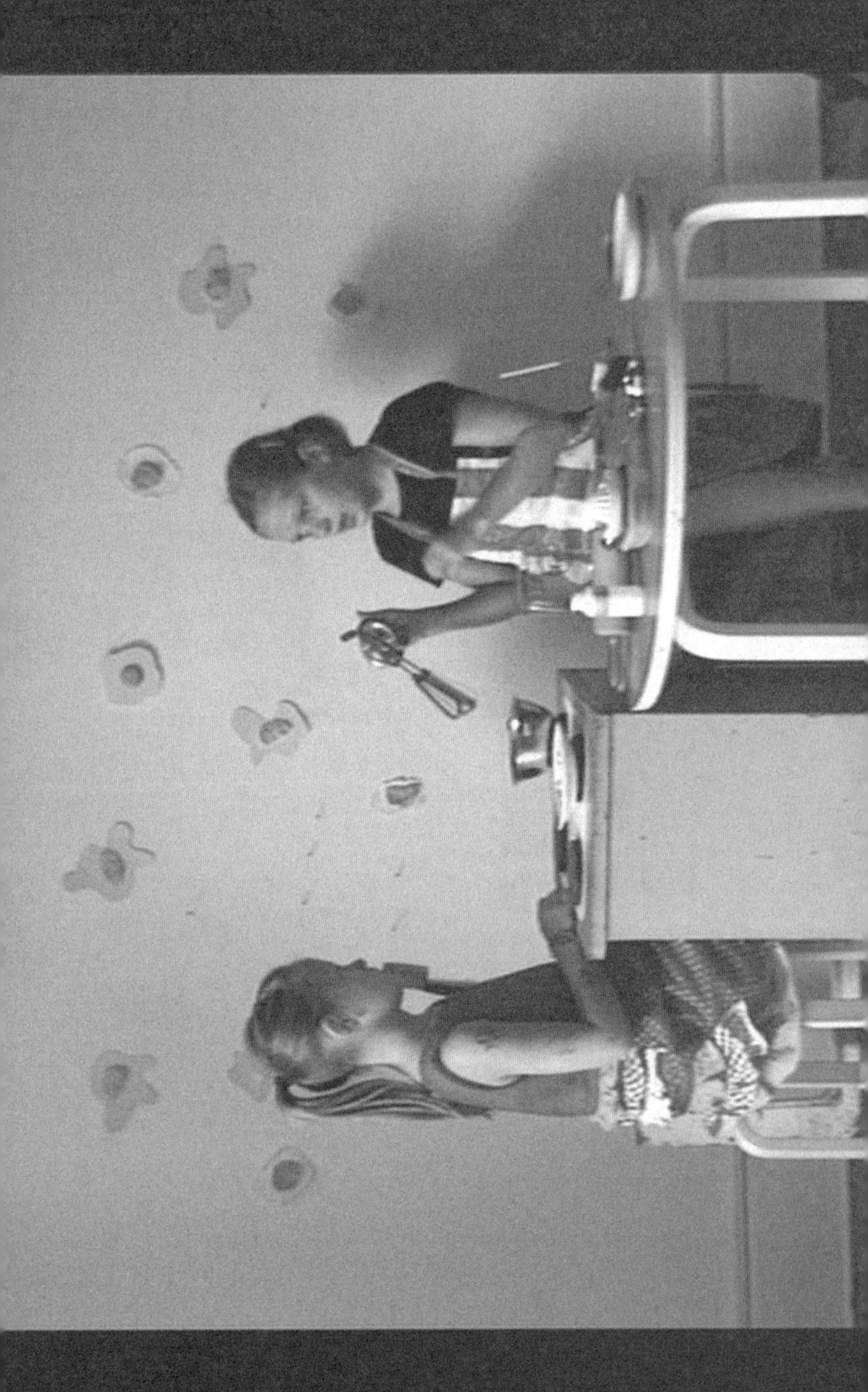

LUCIE: Fork.

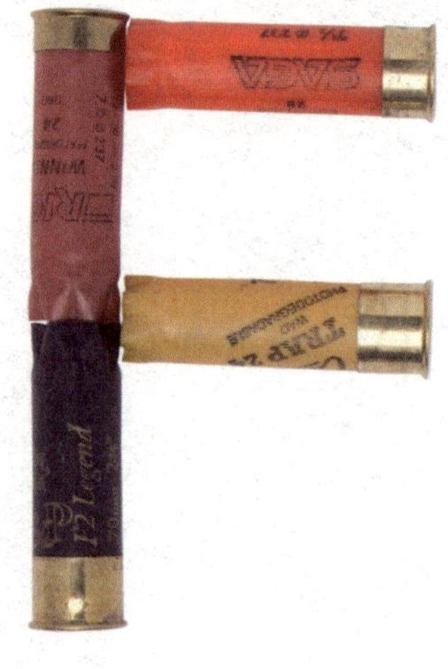

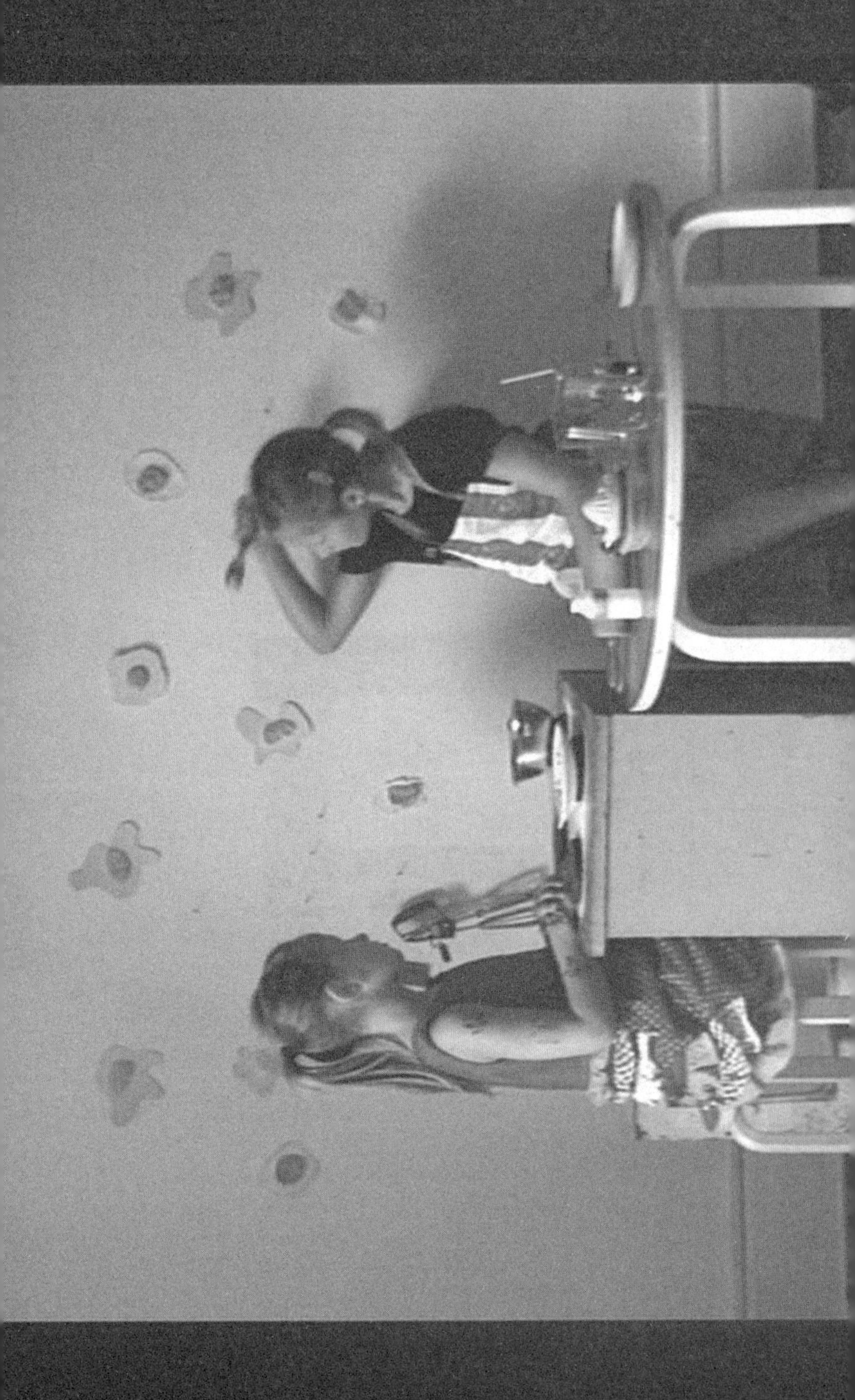

LUCIE: Grater.

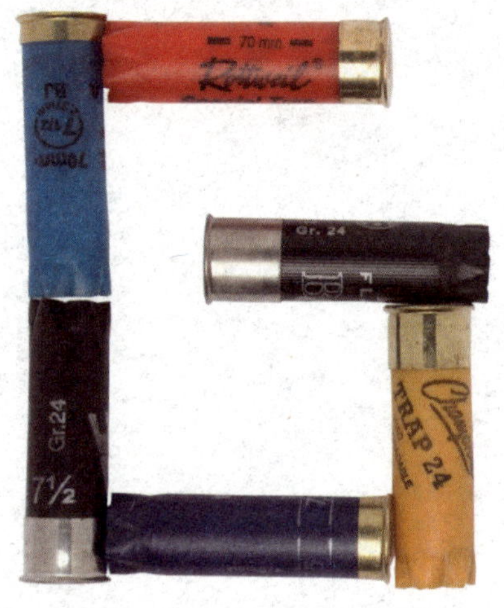

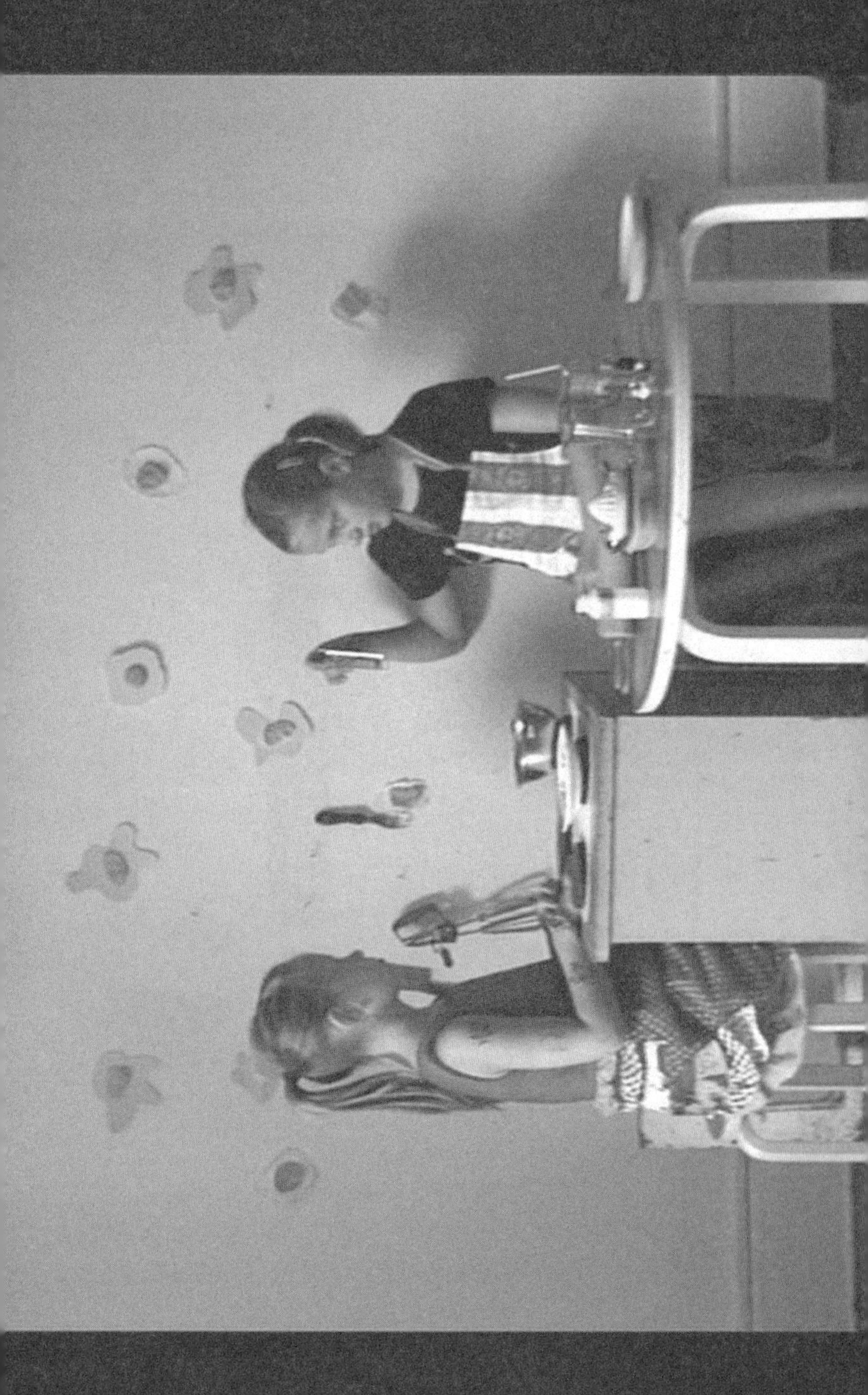

LUCIE: Hamburger press.

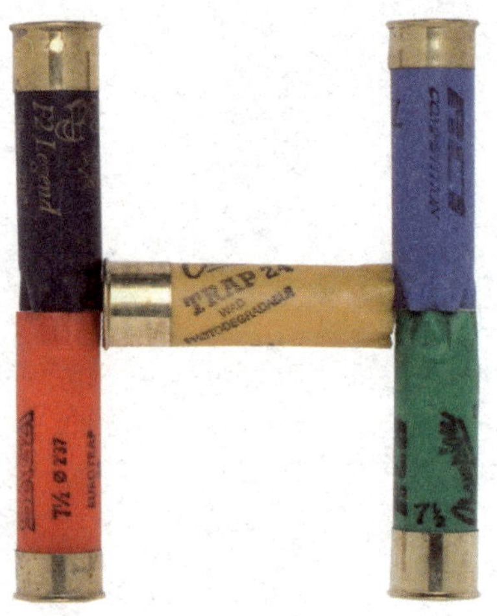

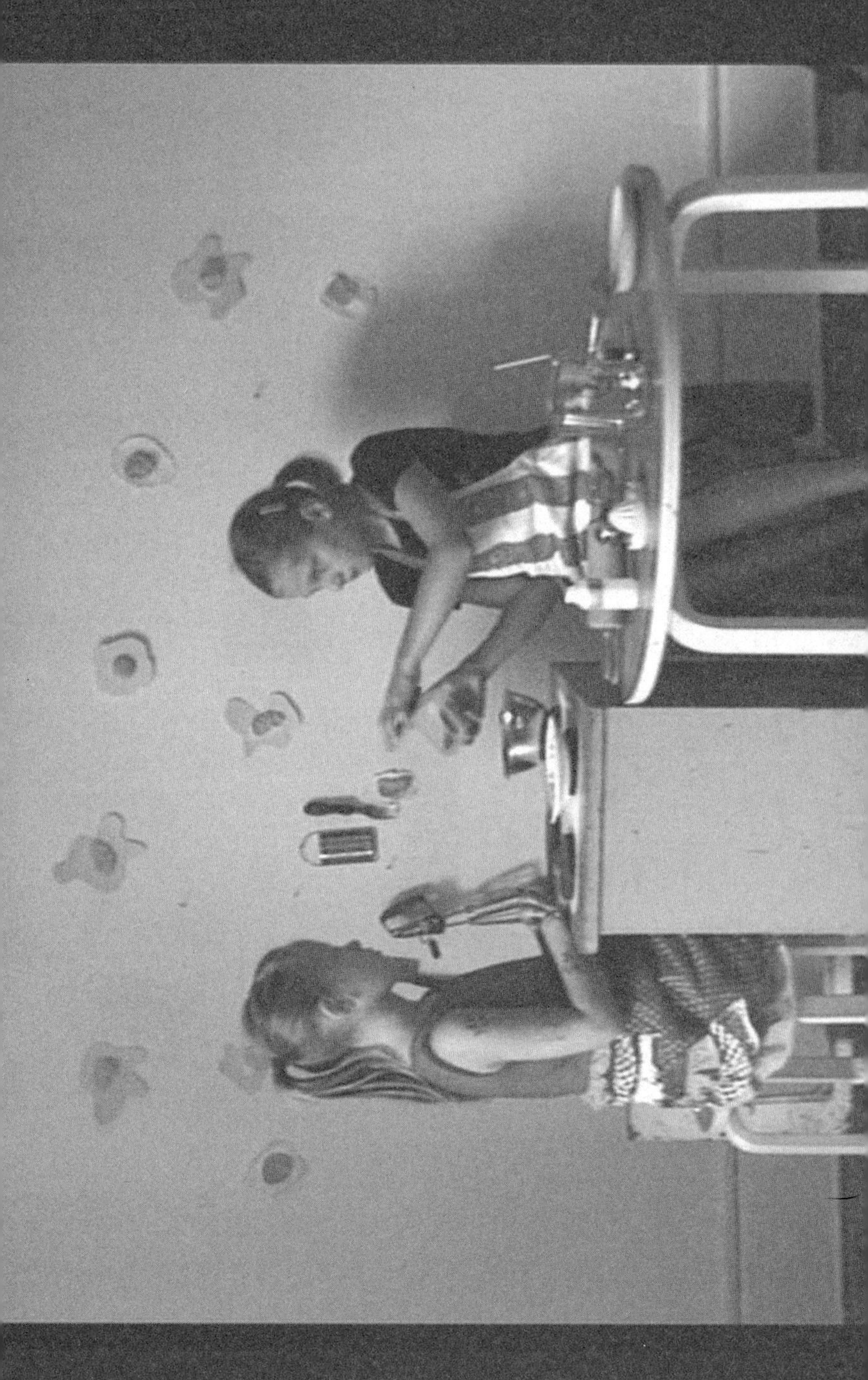

LUCIE: Ice pick.

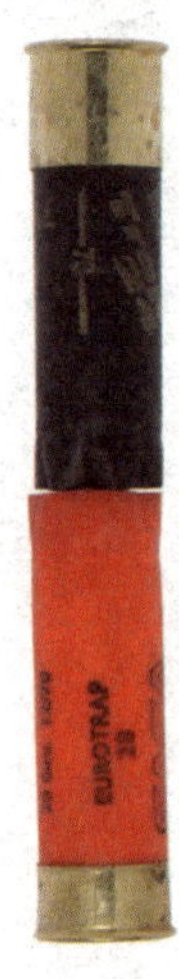

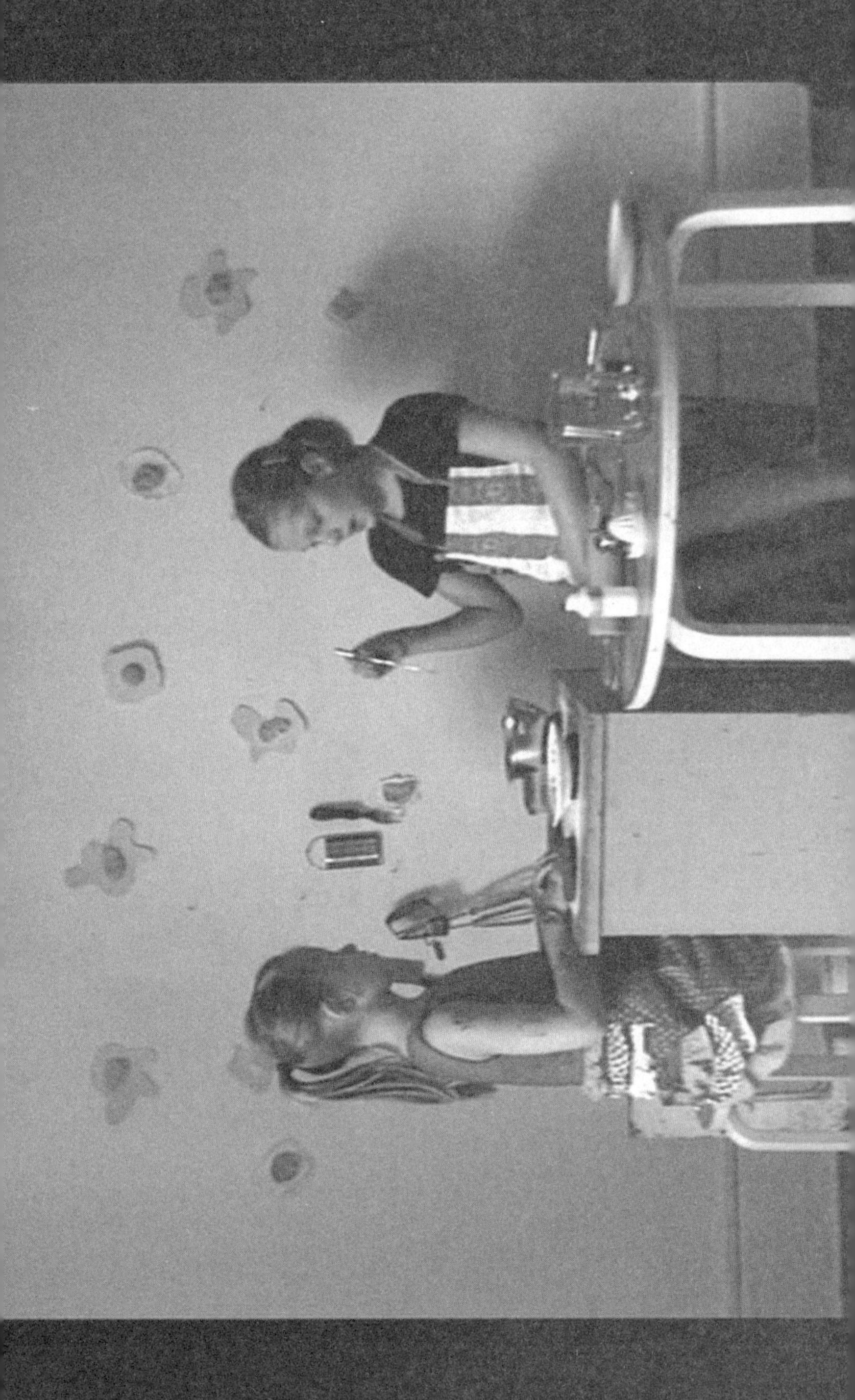

LUCIE: Juicer.

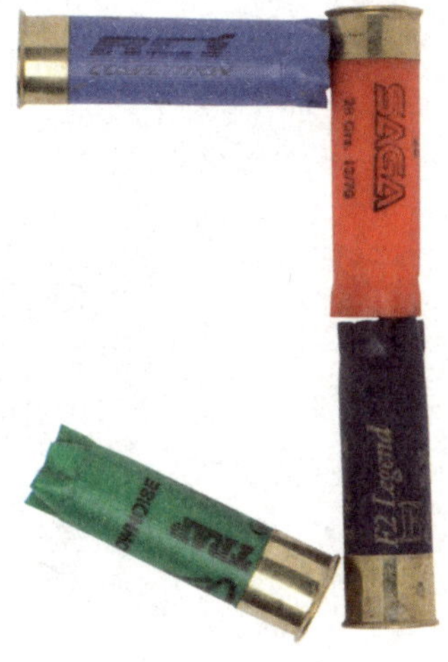

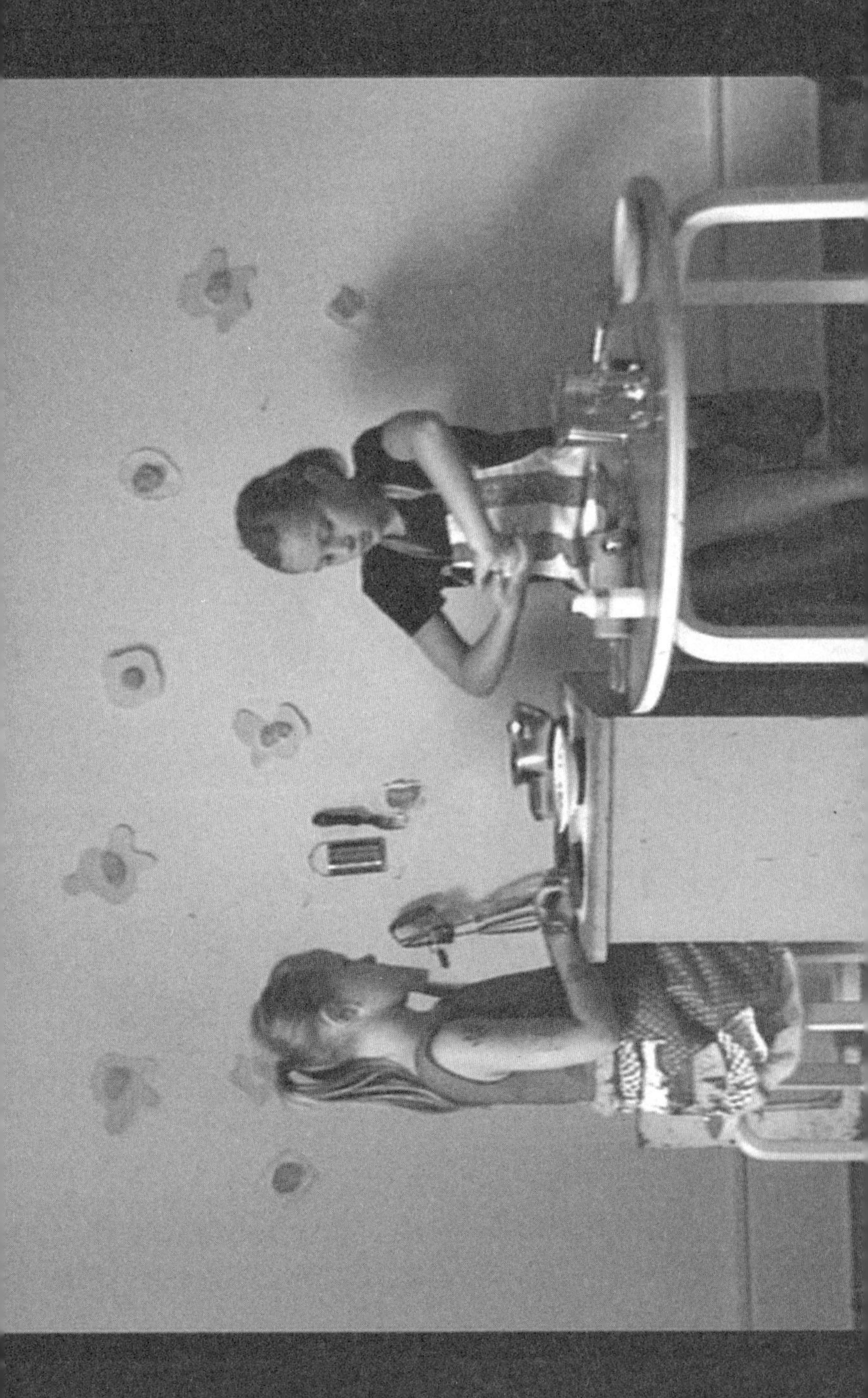

LUCIE: Knife.

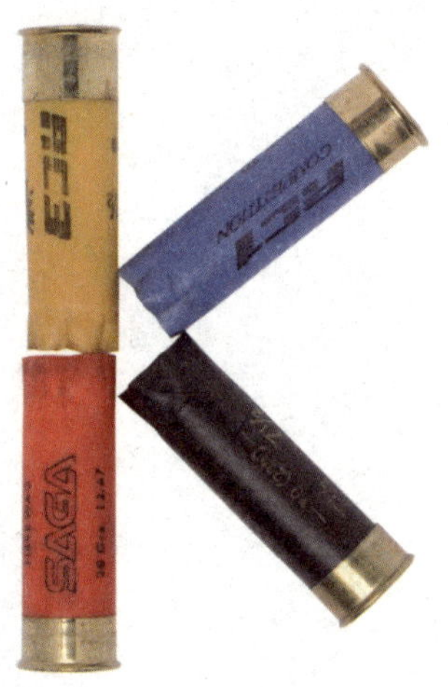

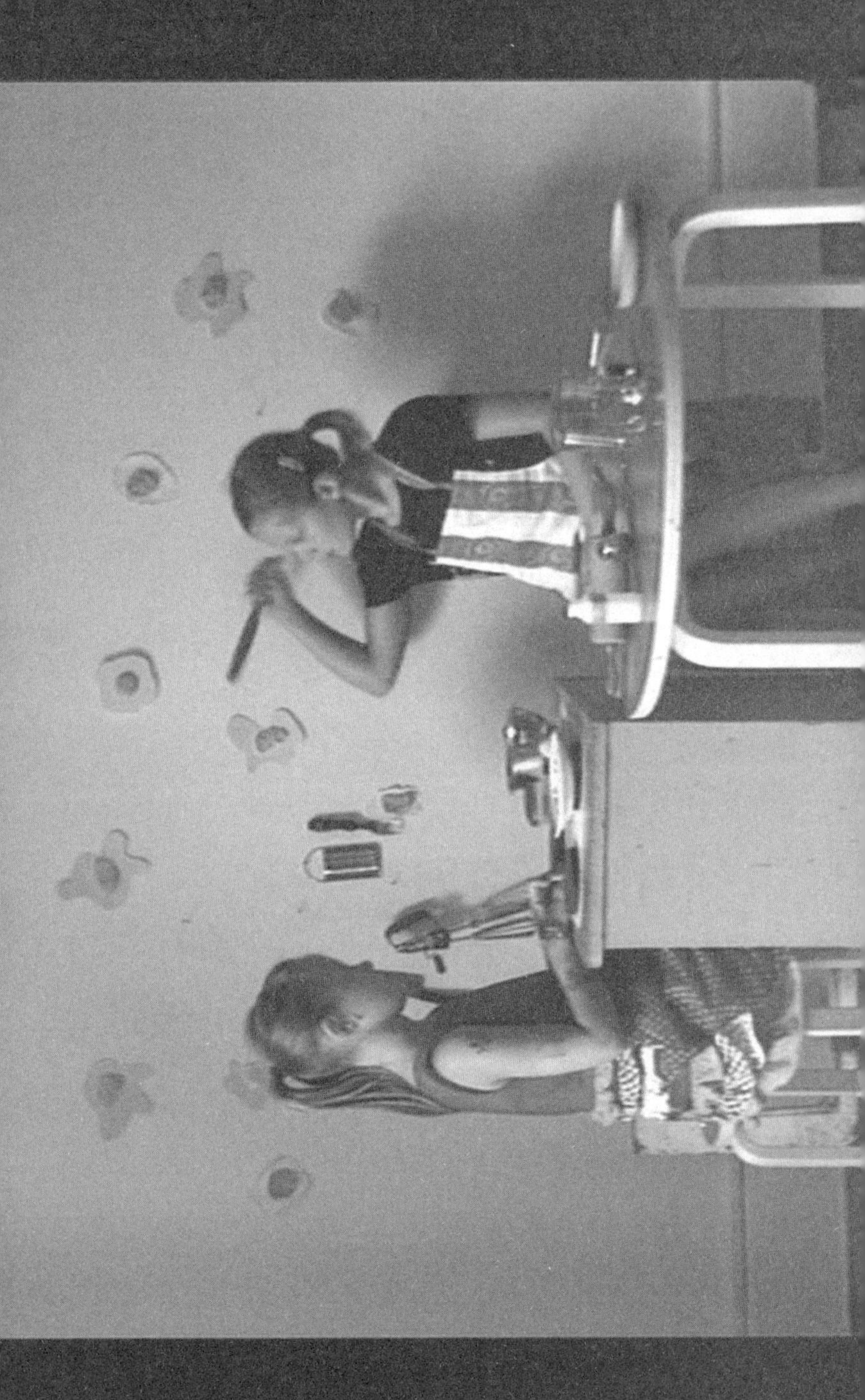

LUCIE: Ladle.

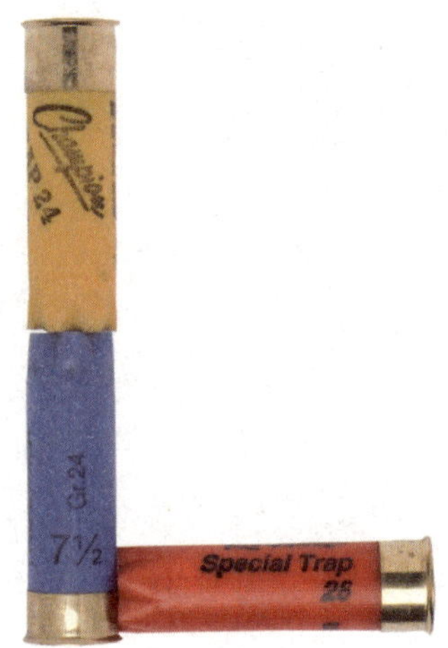

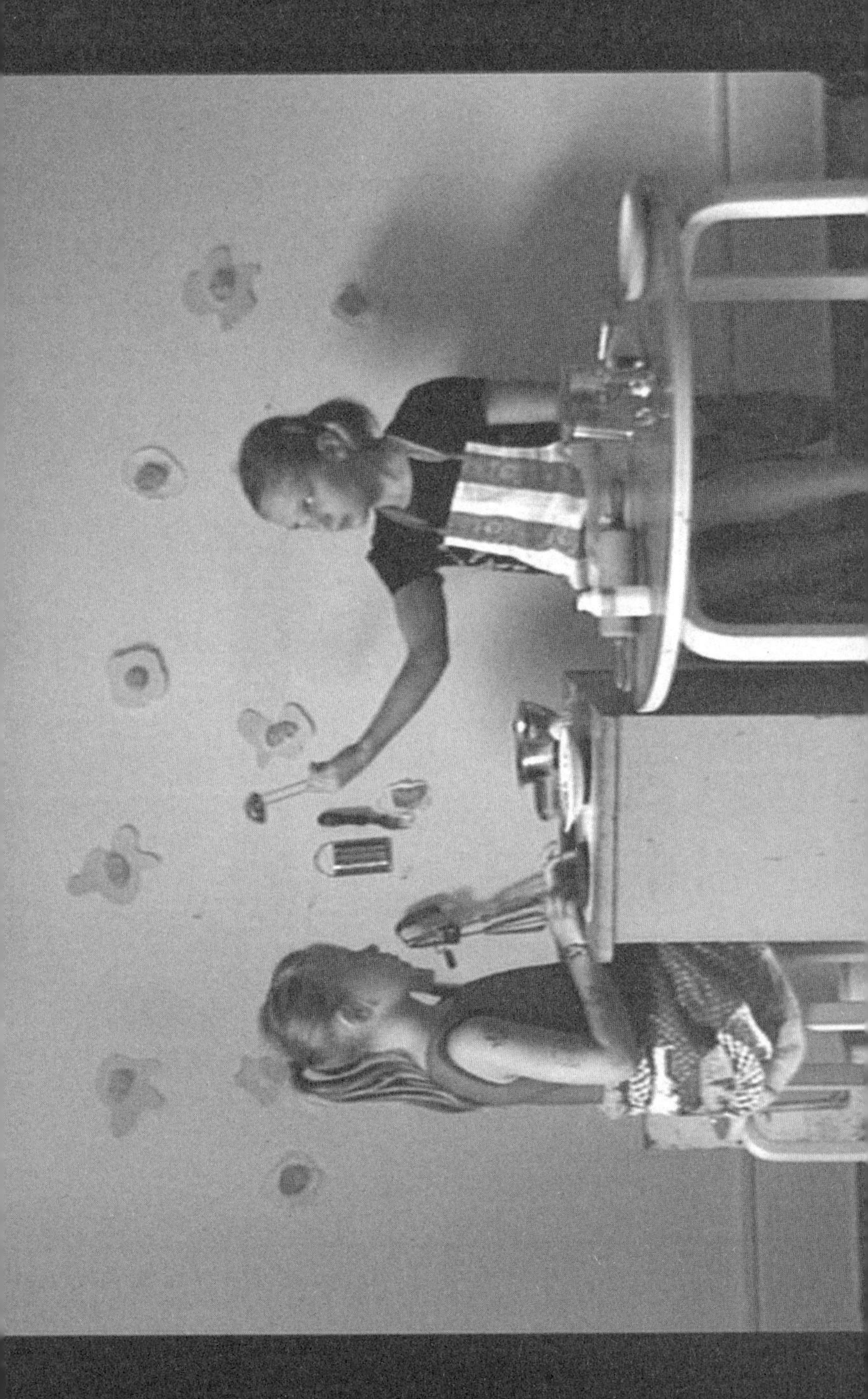

LUCIE: Measuring spoon.

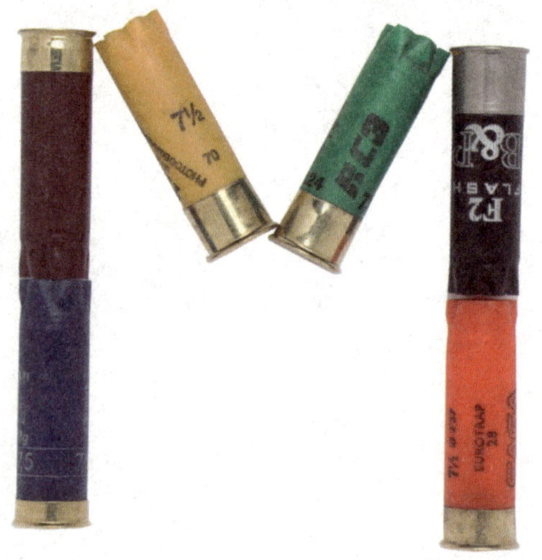

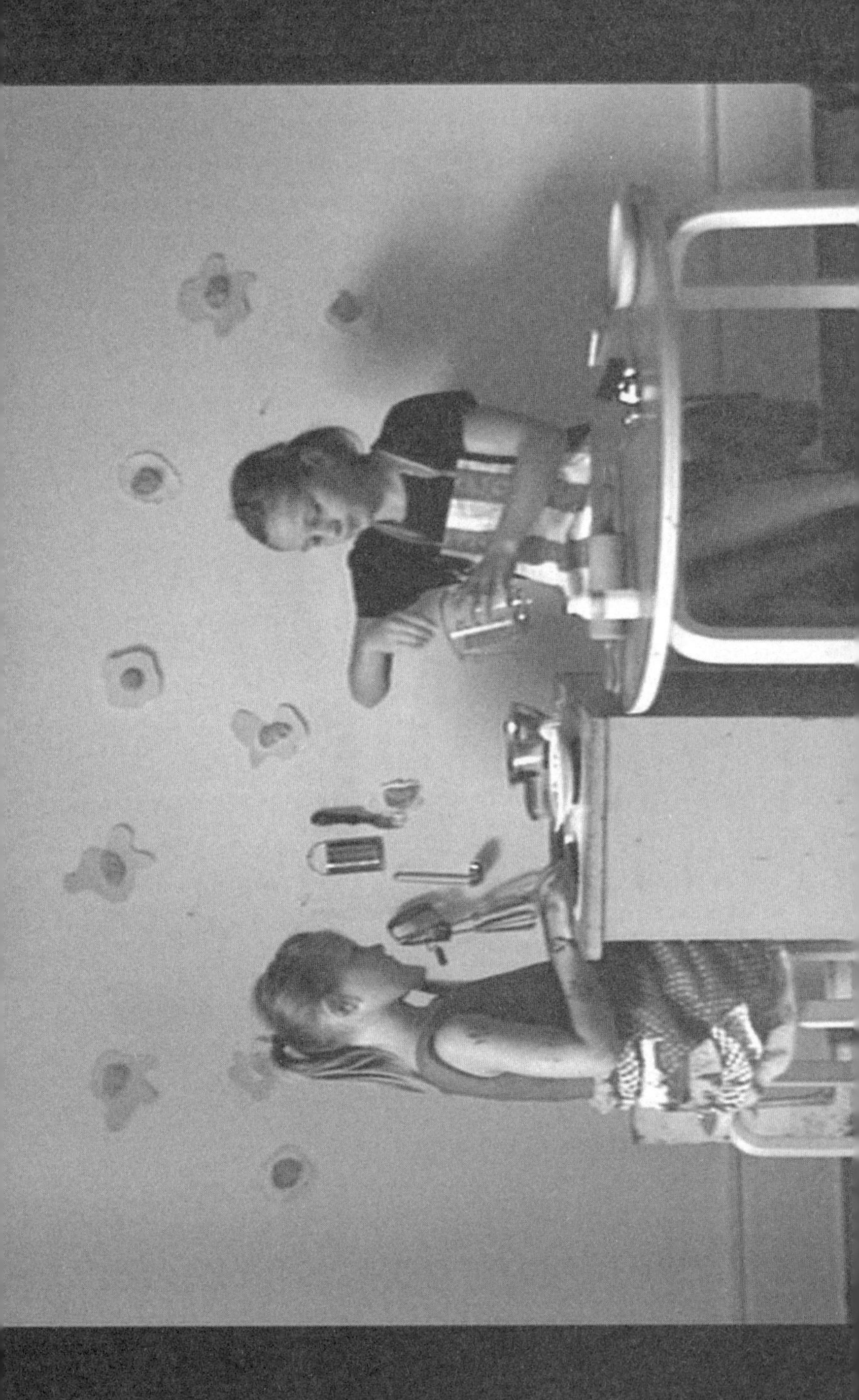

LUCIE: Nutcracker.

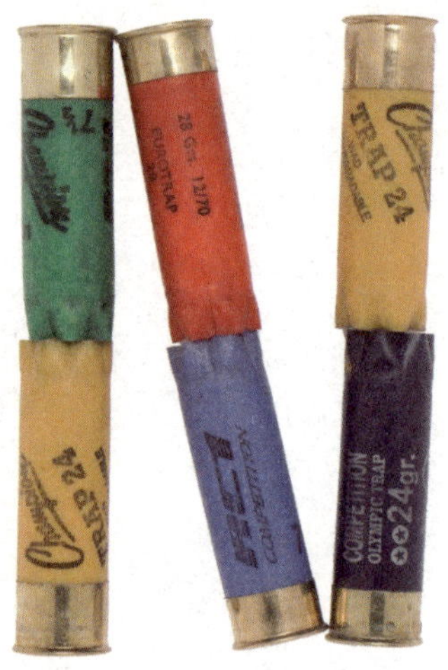

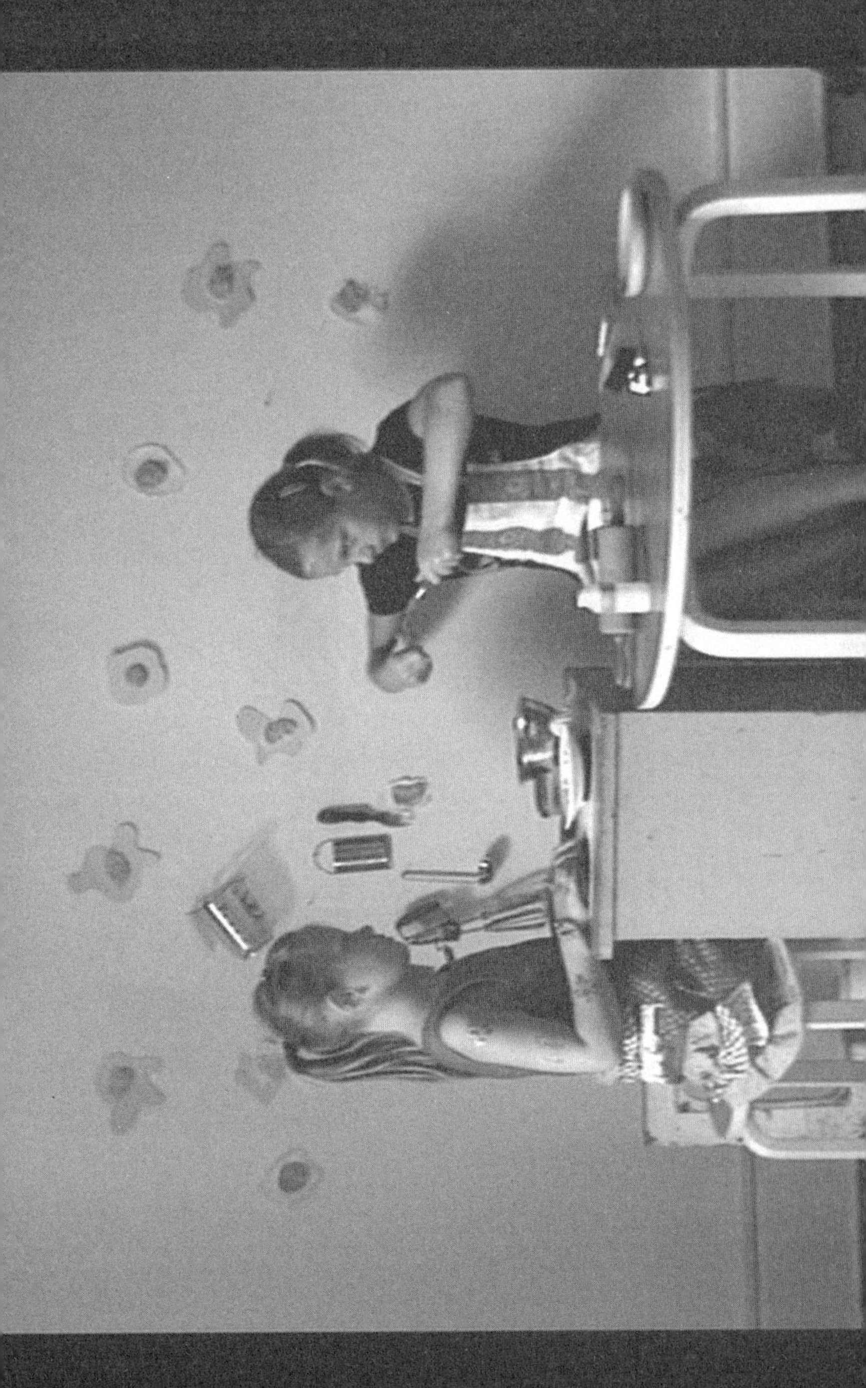

LUCIE: Opener.

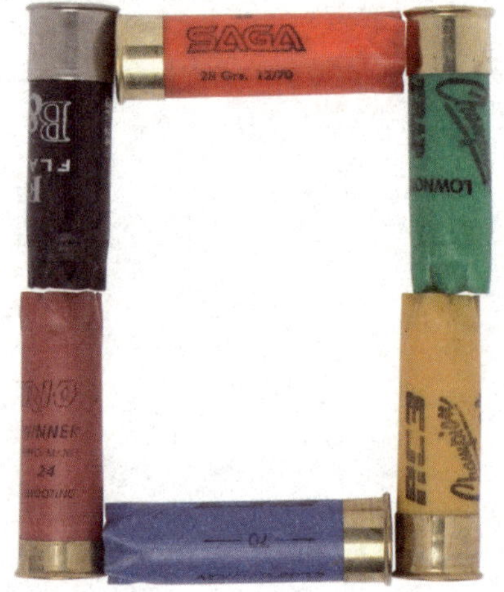

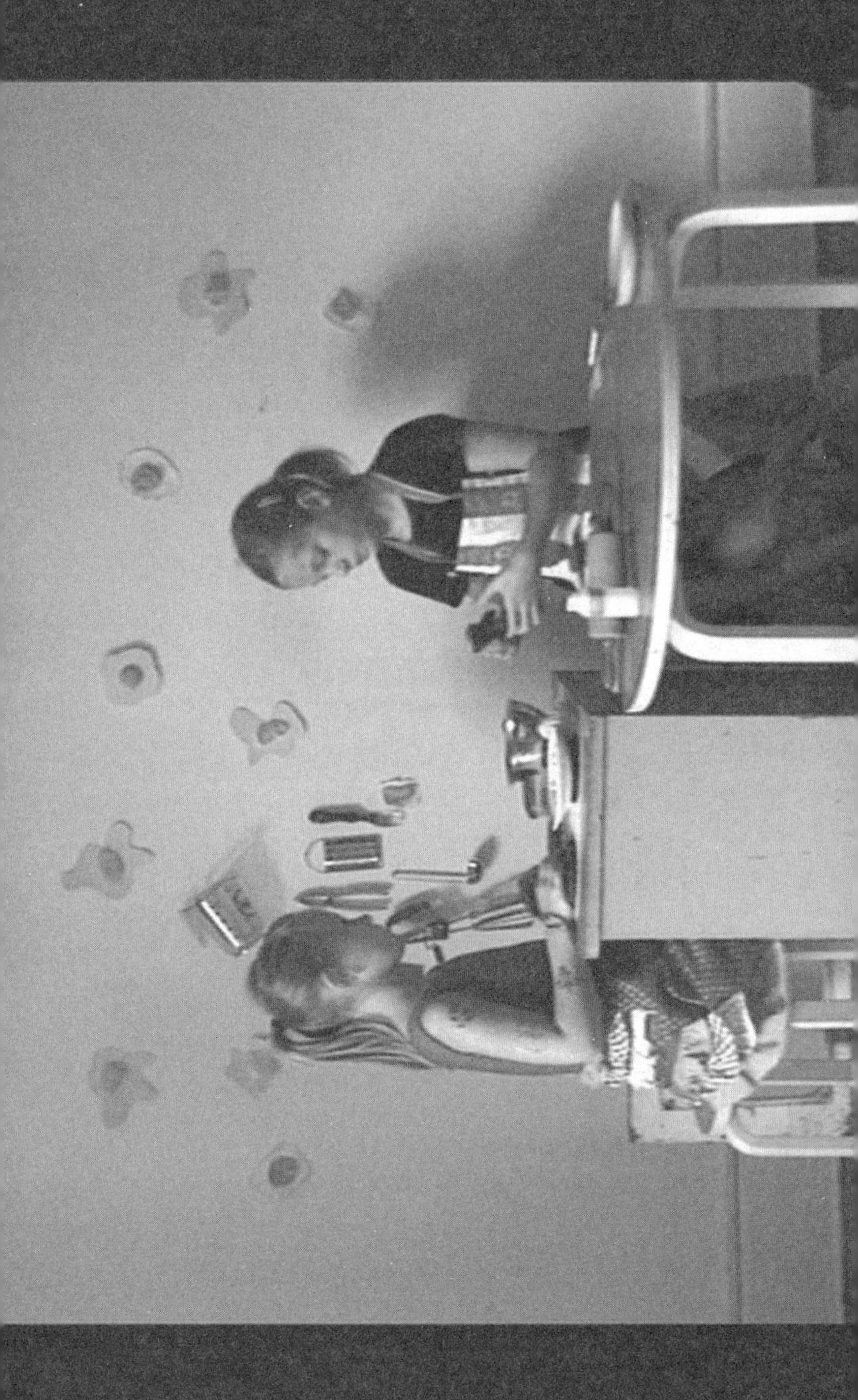

LUCIE: Pan.

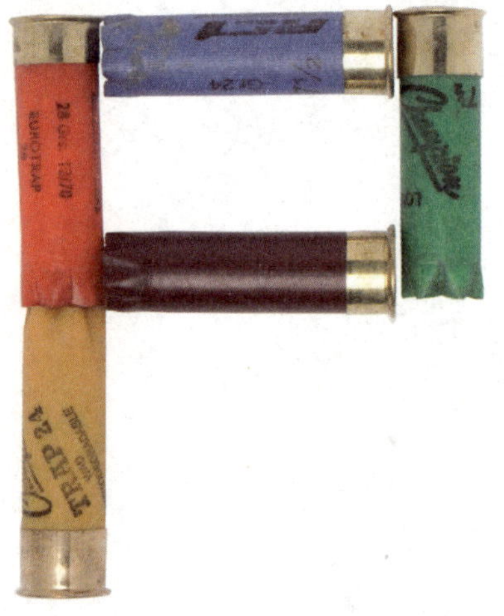

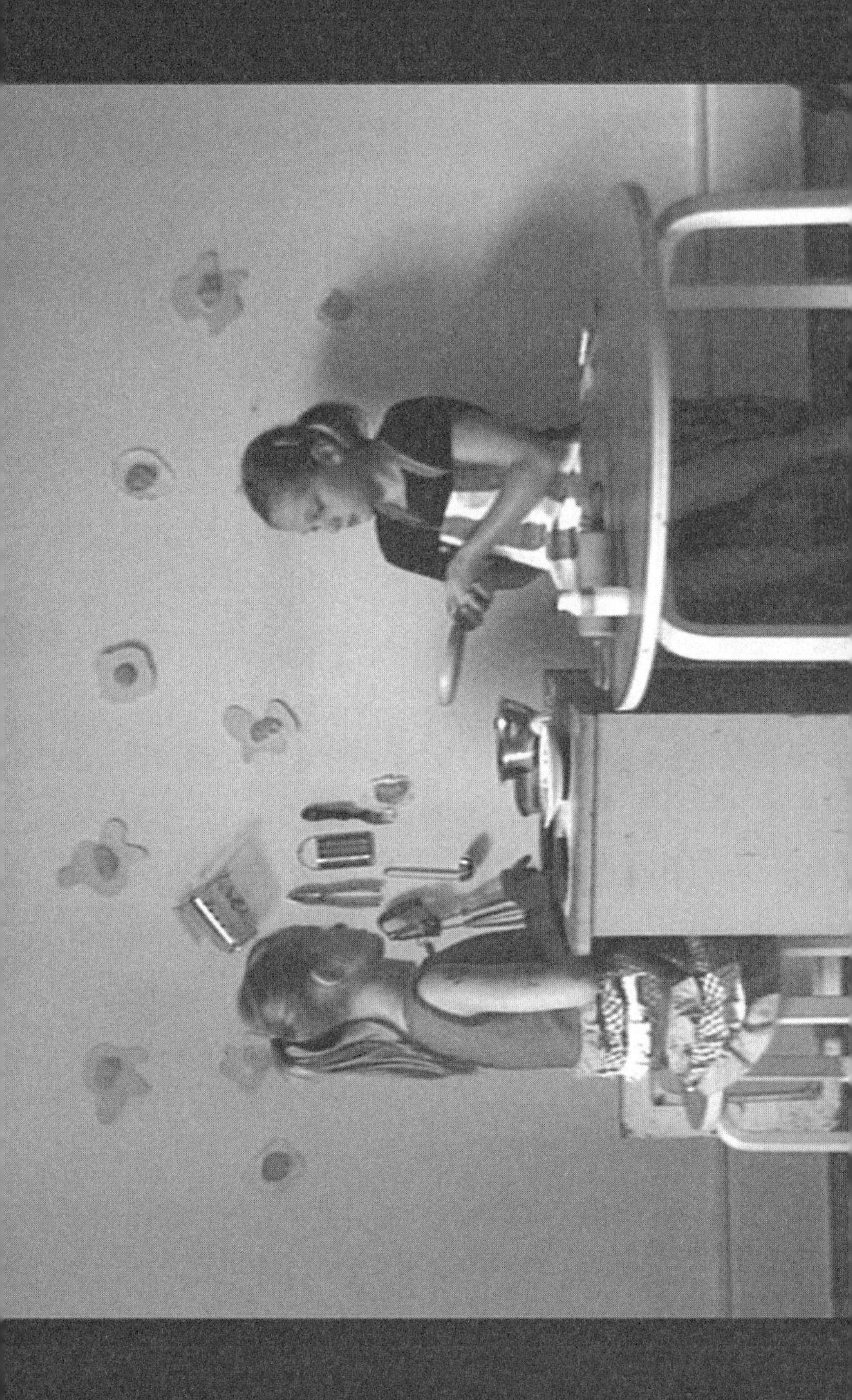

LUCIE: Quart bottle.

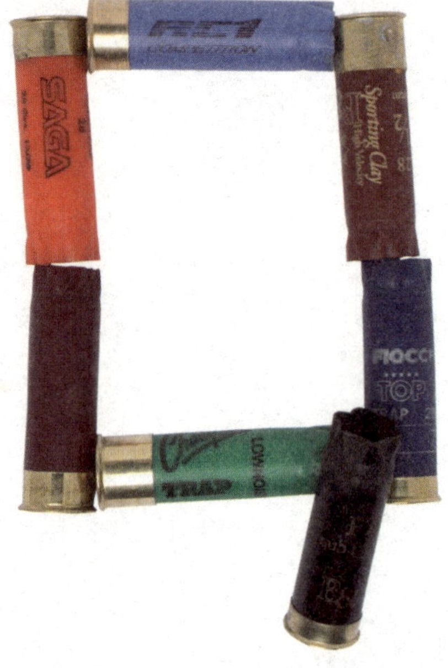

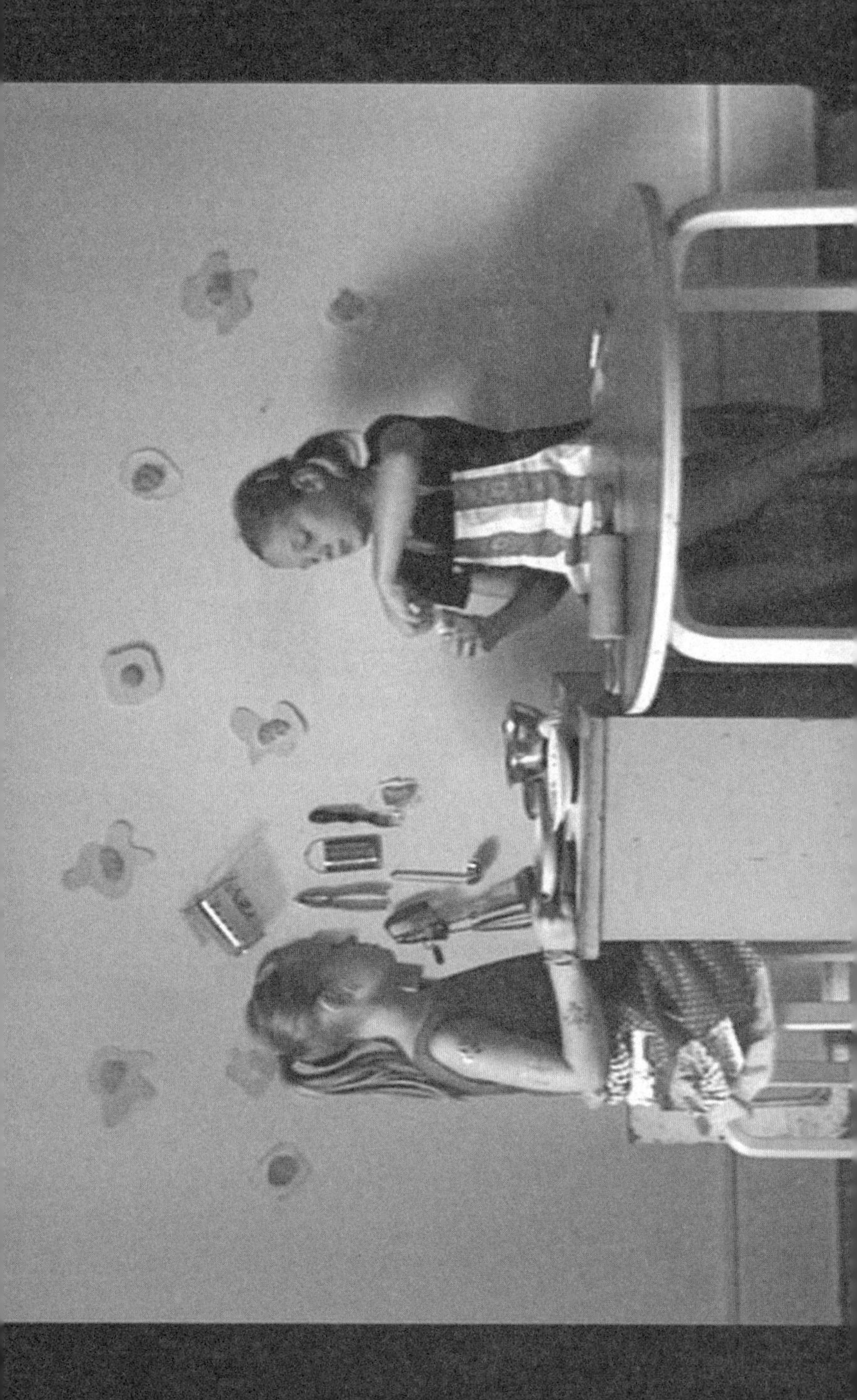

LUCIE: Rolling pins.

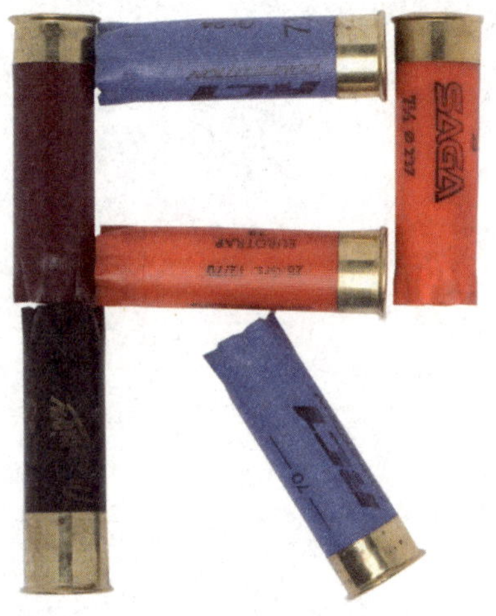

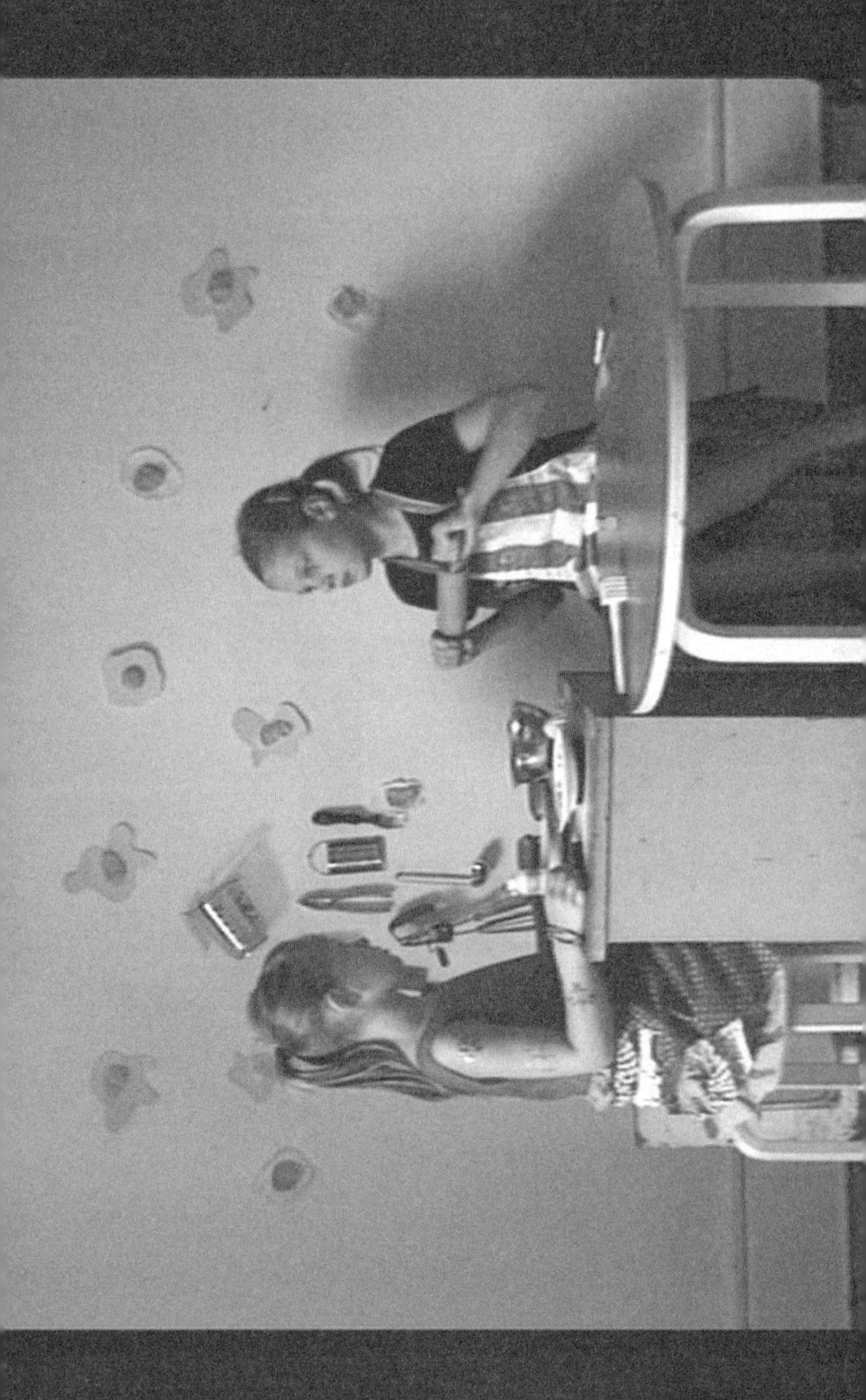

LUCIE: Spoon.

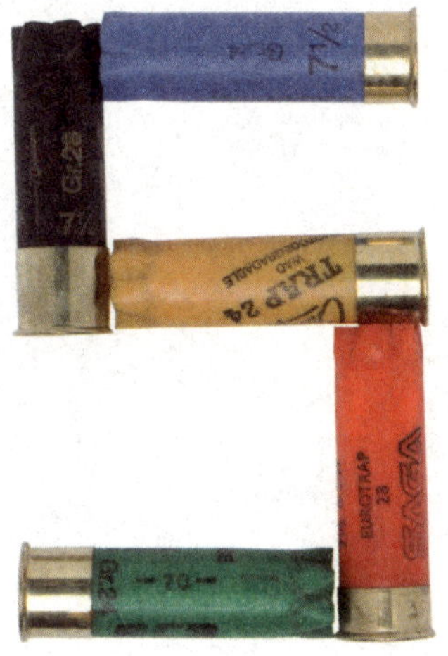

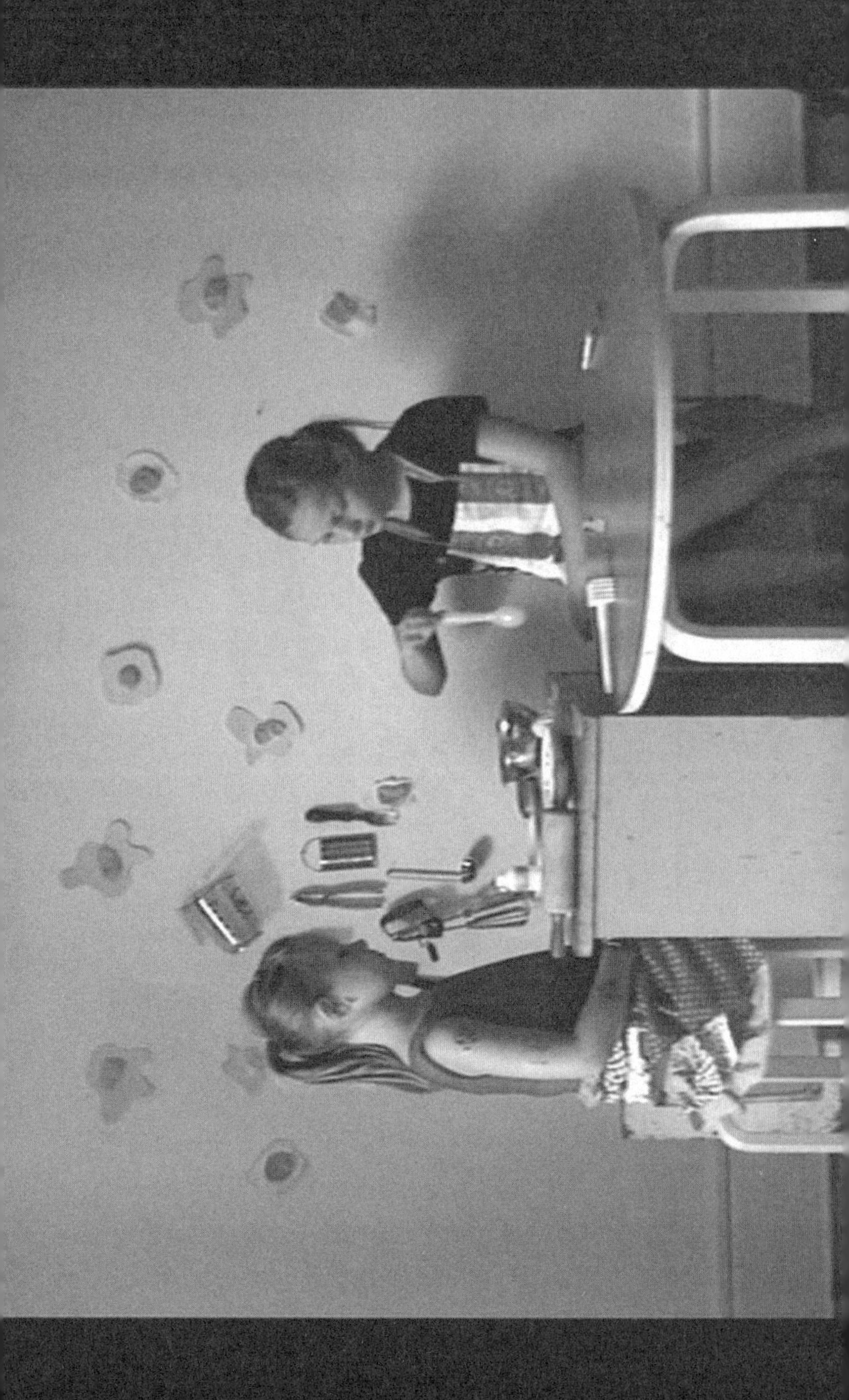

LUCIE: Tenderizer.

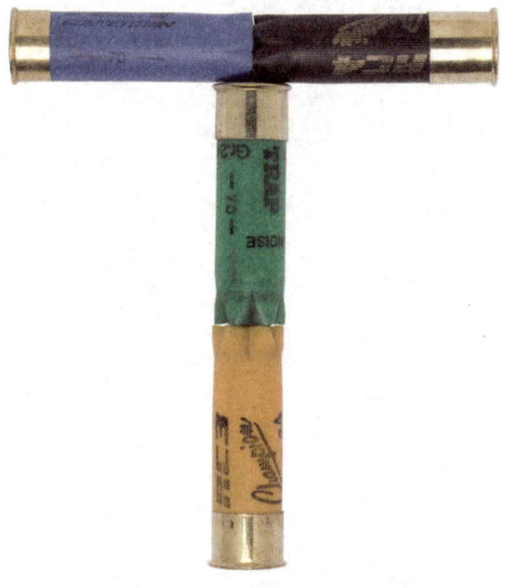

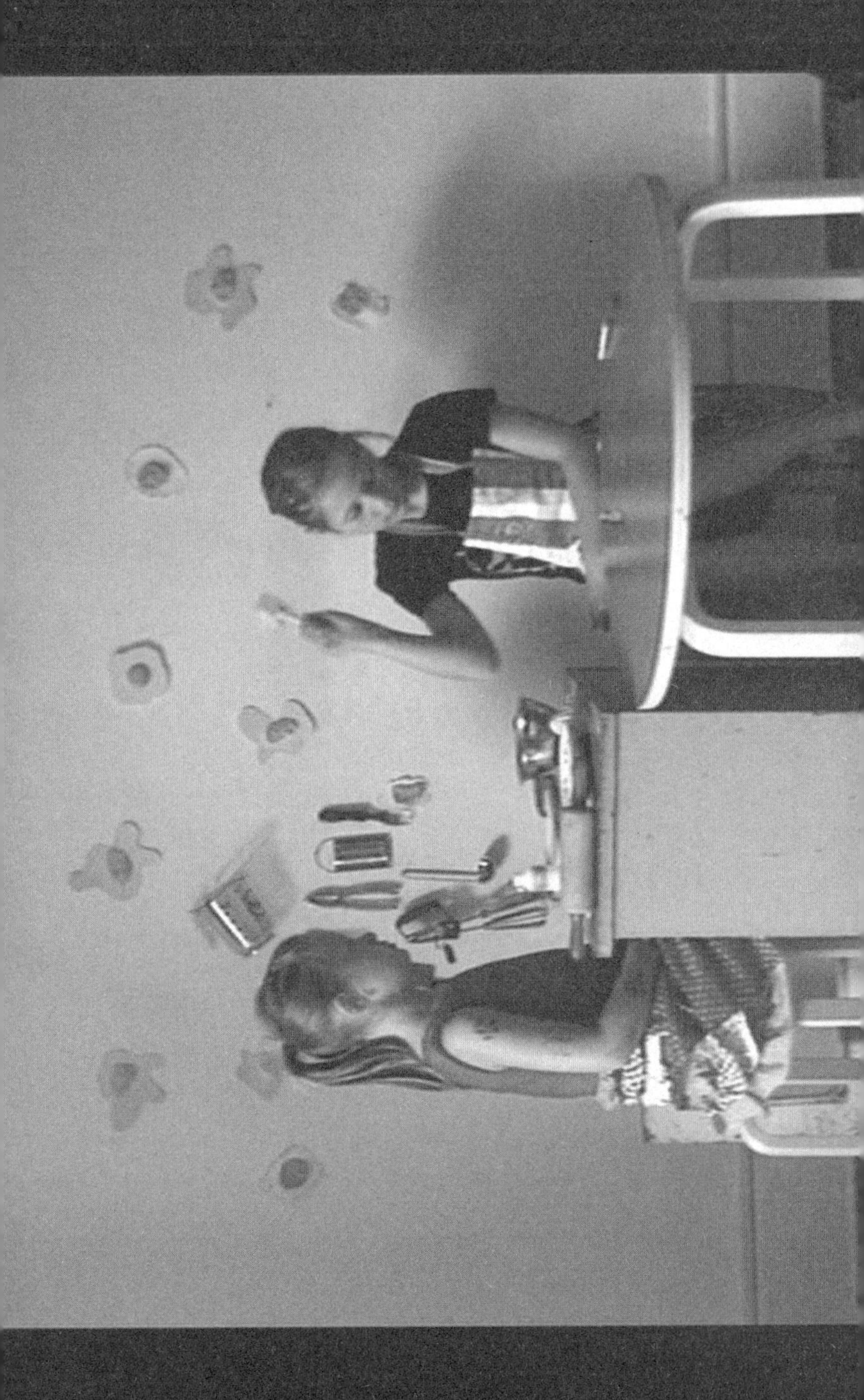

LUCIE: U.

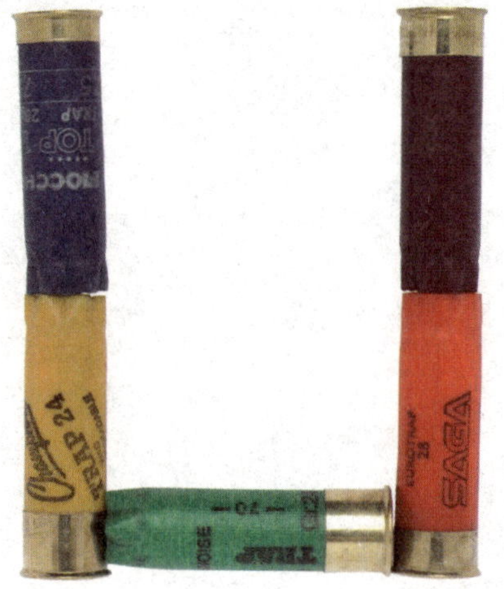

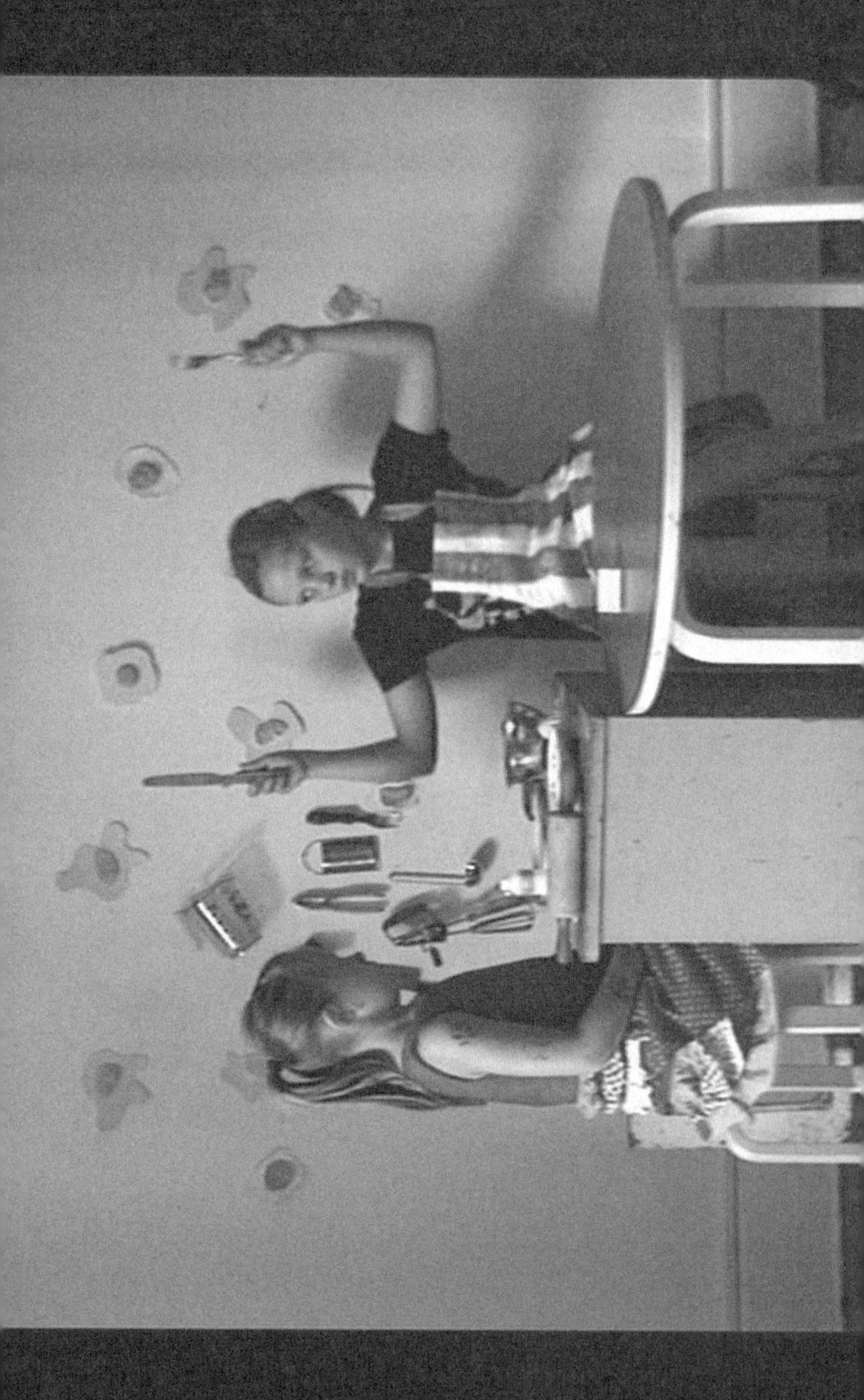

LUCIE: V.

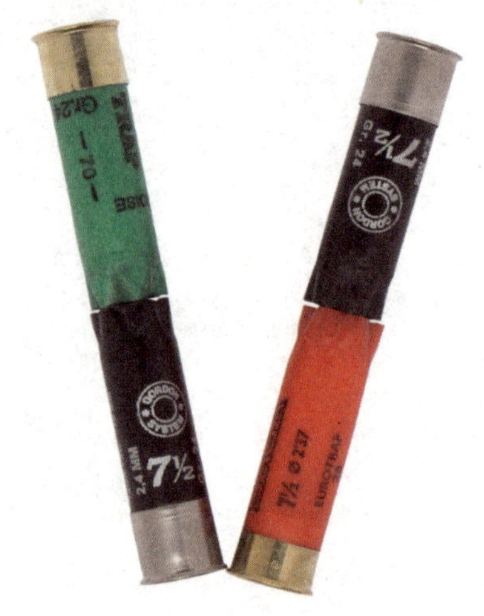

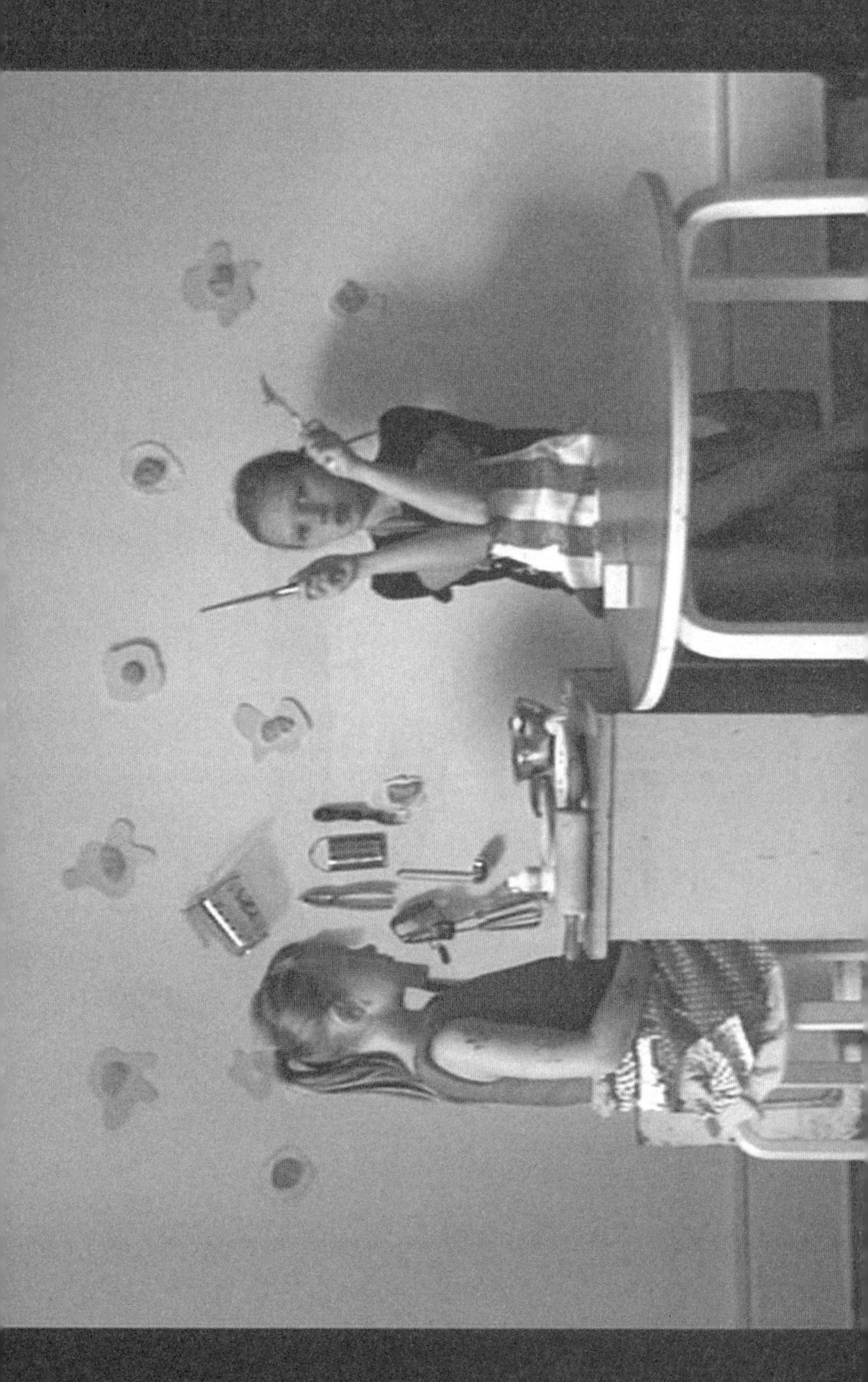

LUCIE: W.

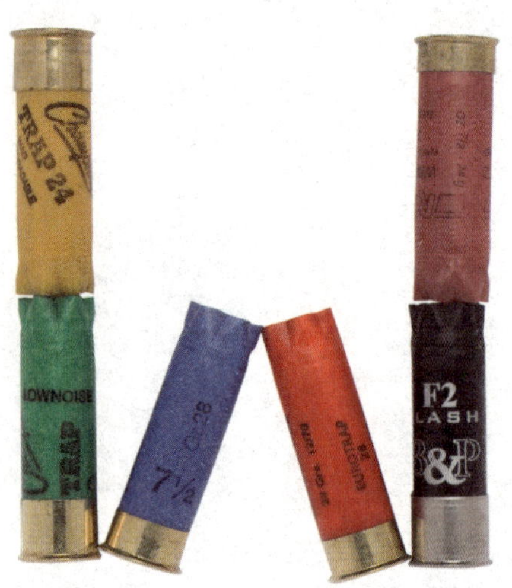

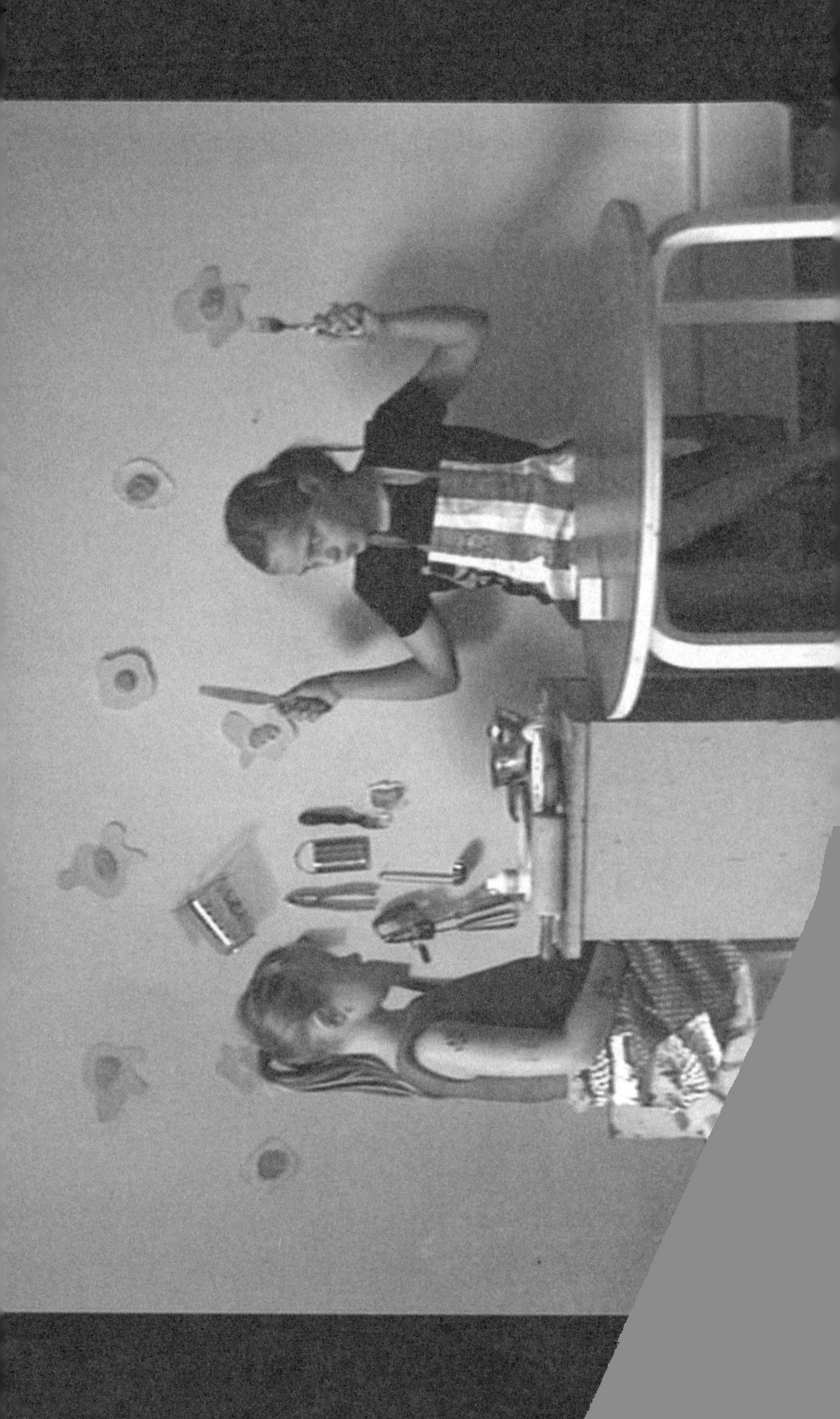

LUCIE: X.

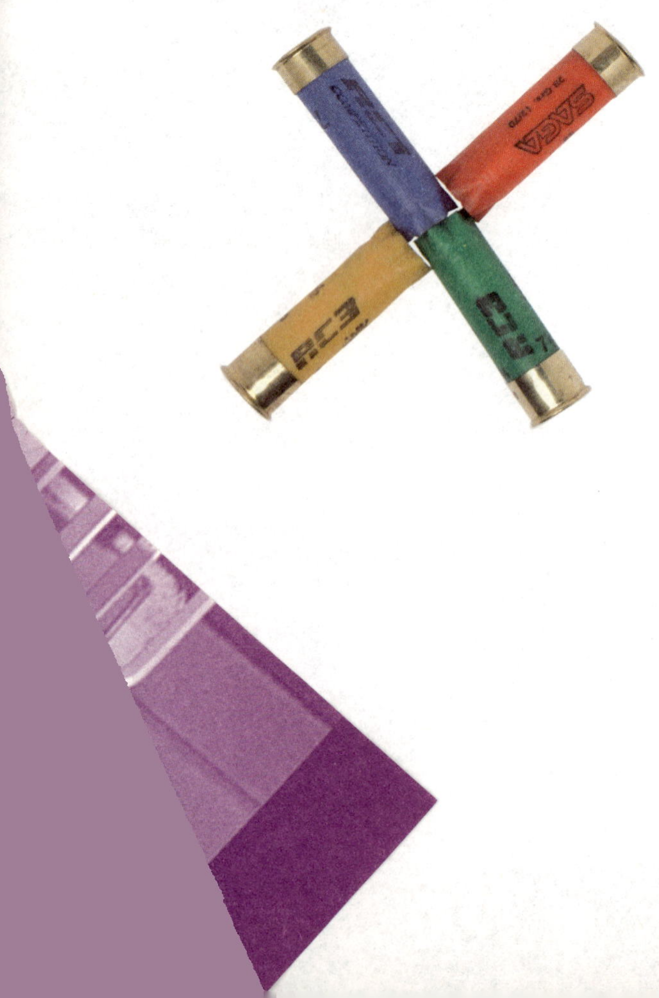

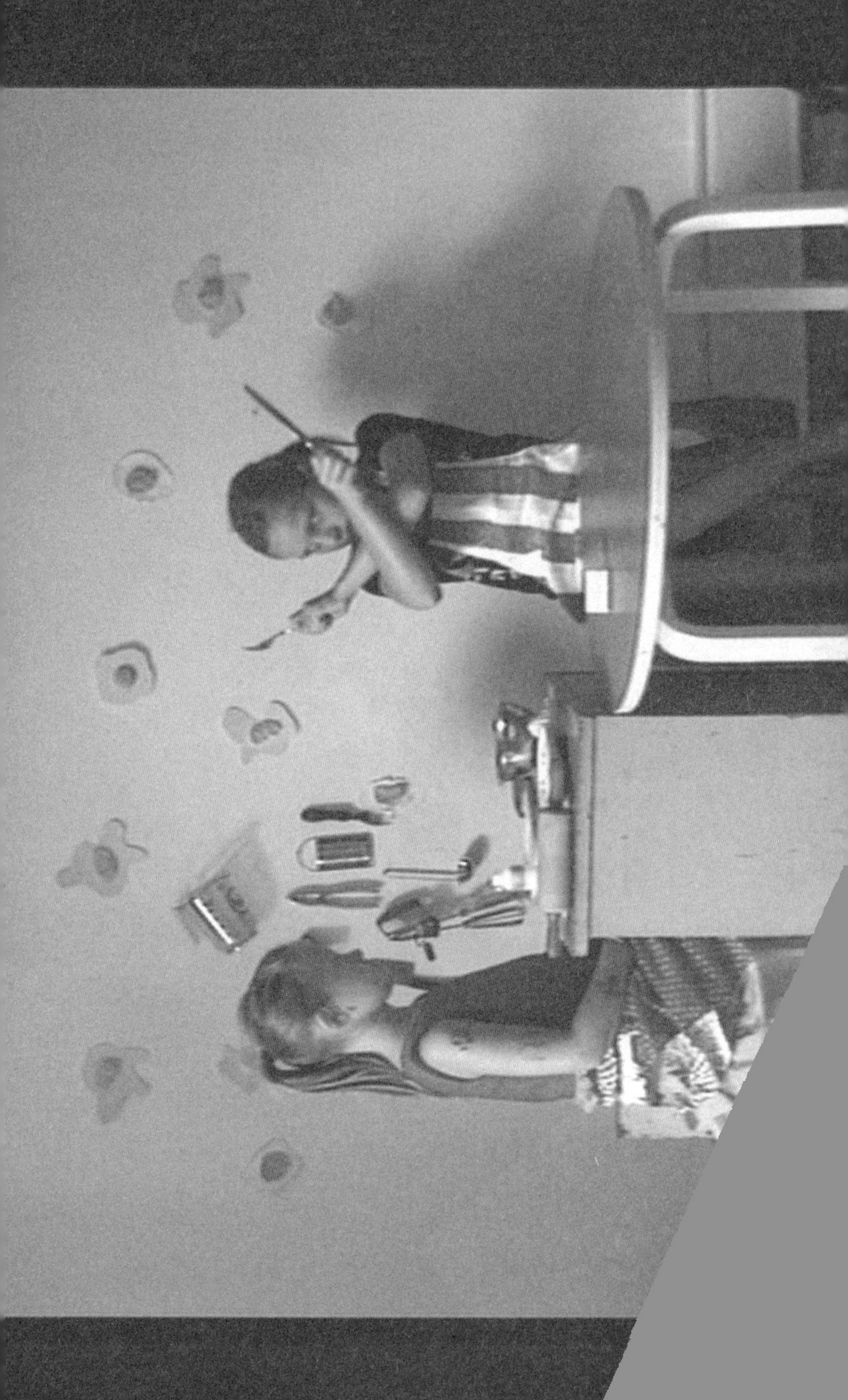

LUCIE: Y.

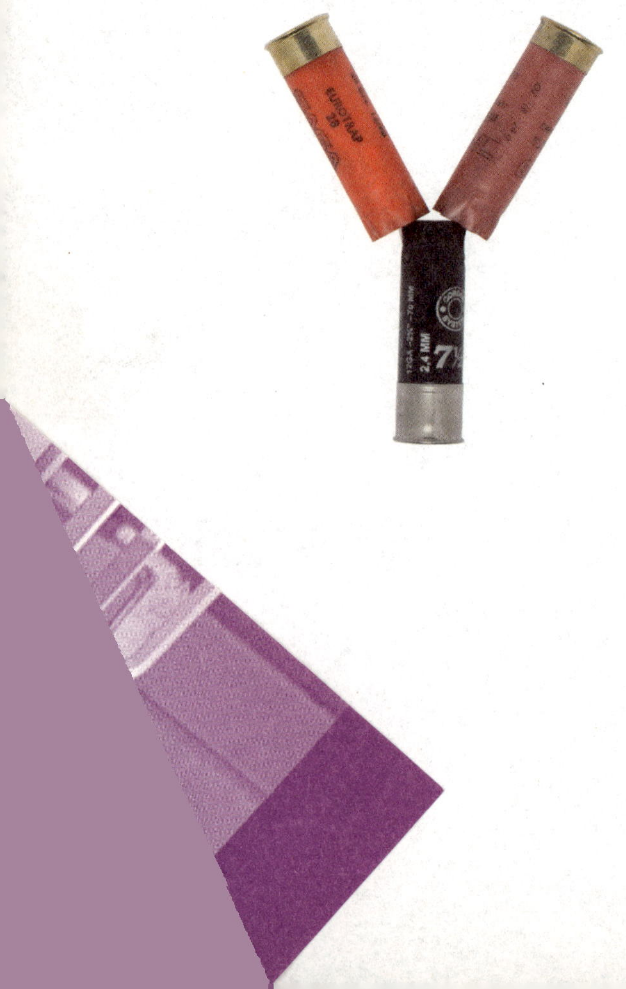

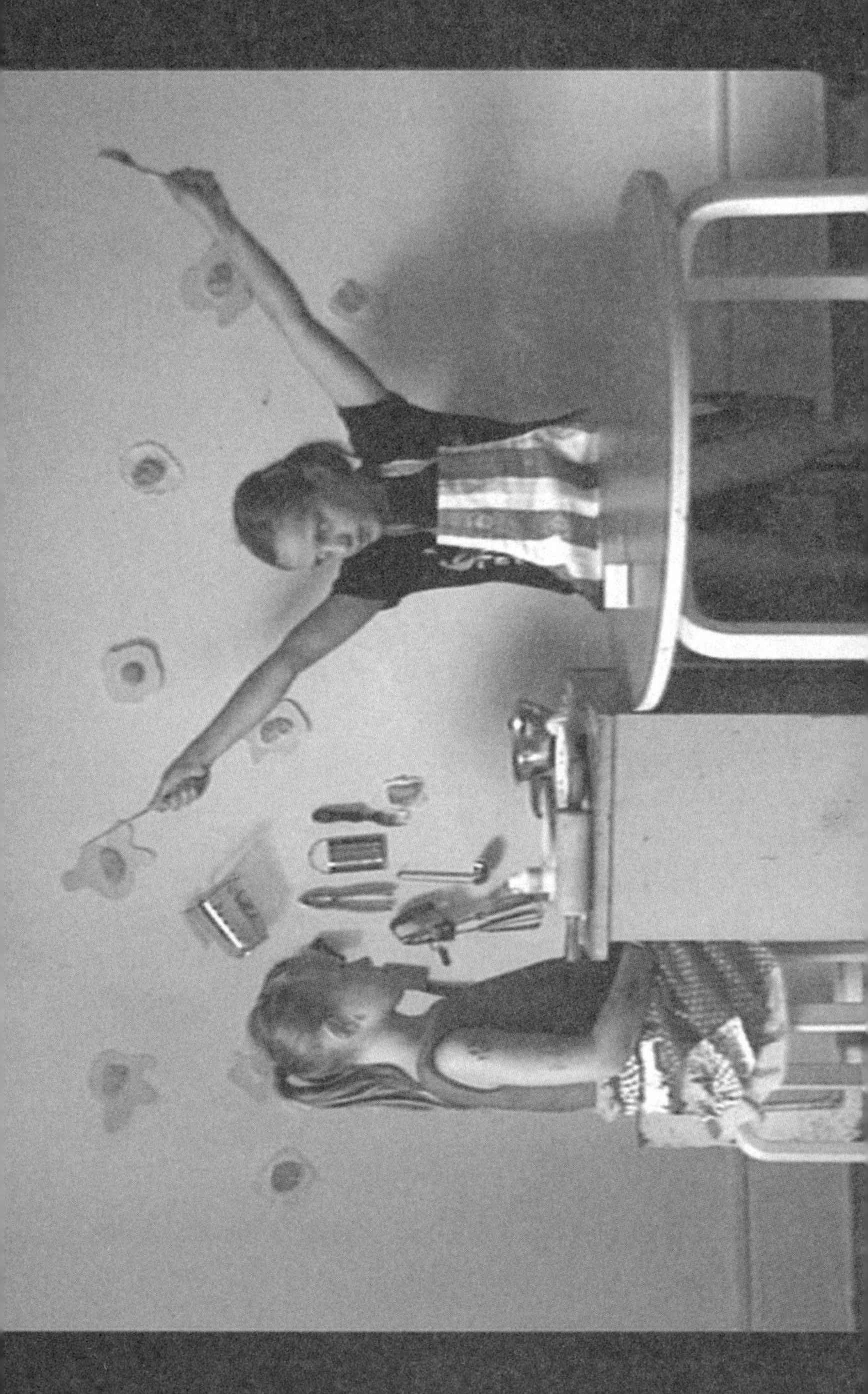

LUCIE: Z.

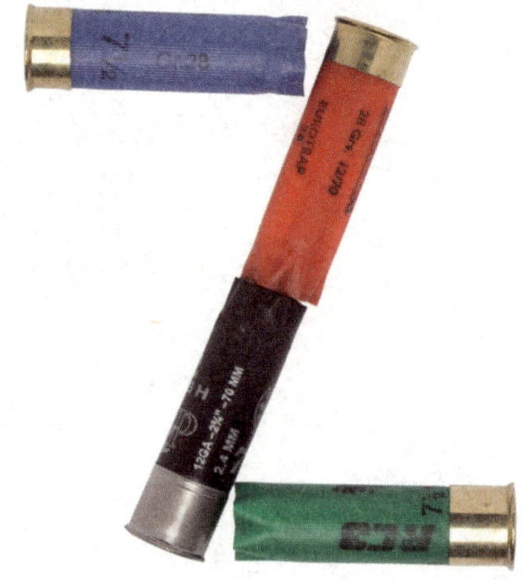

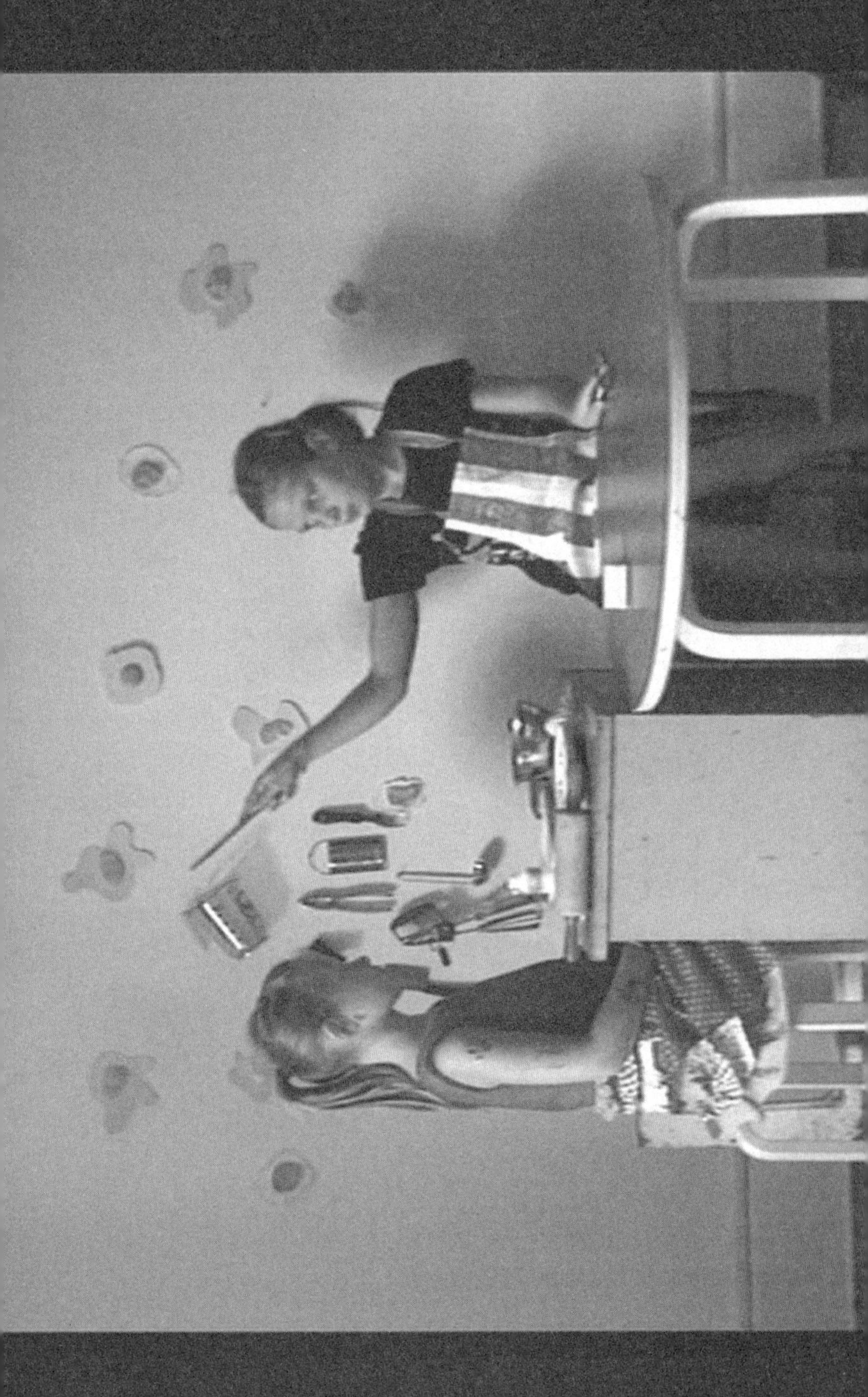

LUCIE: Art must be beautiful. Artist must be beautiful. Art must be beautiful. Art must be beautiful. Artist must be beautiful. Artist must be beautiful. Art must be beautiful. Artist must be beautiful.

Art Must Be Beautiful
from Marina Abramović, 1976

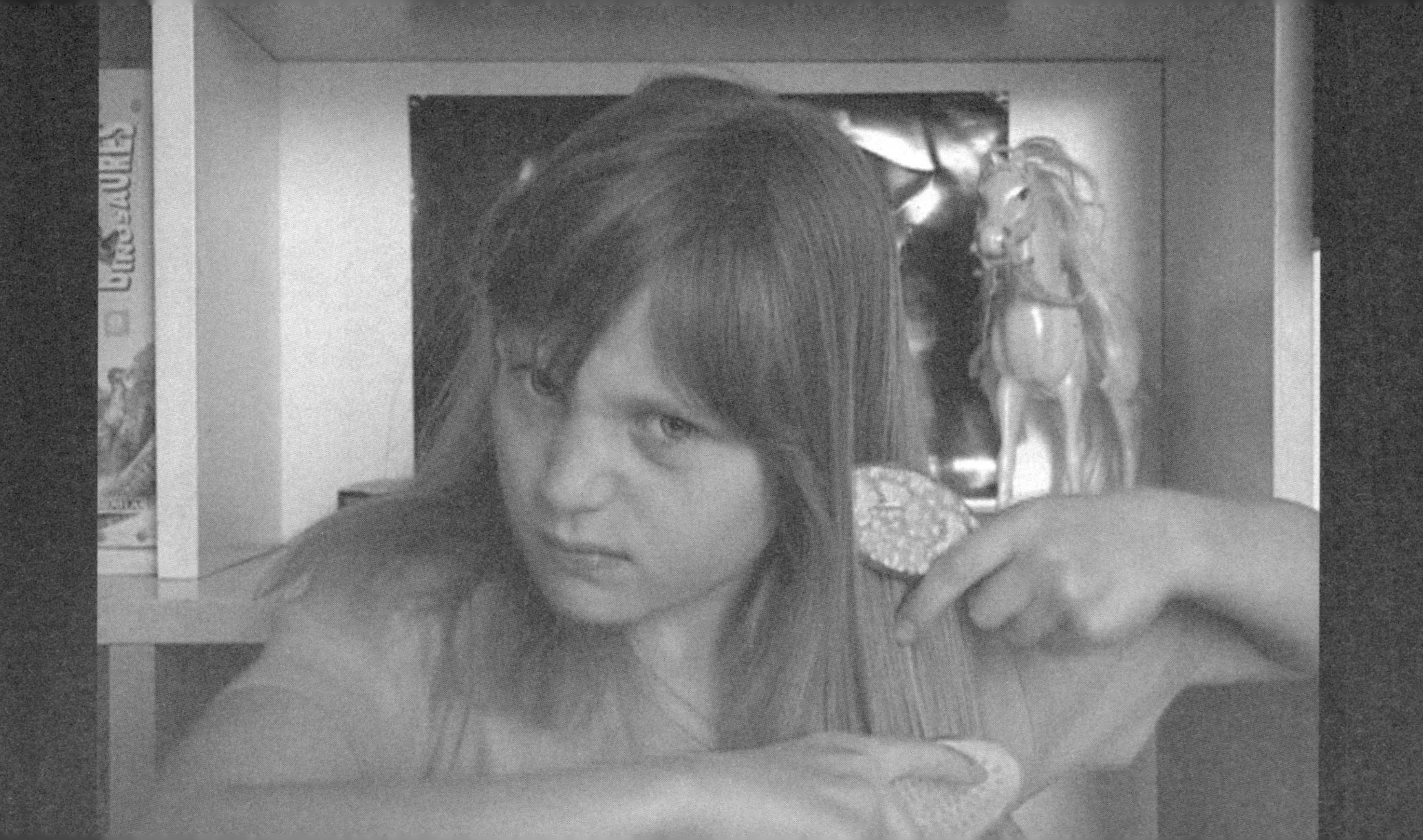
DINOSAURES

LUCIE: Great Art and Culture. The male artist attempts to solve his dilemma of not being able to live, of not being female, by constructing a highly artificial world in which the male is heroized, that is, displays female traits, and the female is reduced to highly limited, insipid subordinate roles, that is, to being male. The male artistic aim being, not to communicate. Open bracket. Having nothing inside he has nothing to say. Close bracket. But to disguise his animalism, he resorts to symbolism and obscurity. Open bracket. Deep stuff. Close bracket. The vast majority of people, particularly the educated ones, lack faith in their own judgement, and are humble, respectful of authority. Open bracket. "Daddy knows best" is translated into adult language as "Critic knows best," "Writer knows best," "Ph.D. knows best." Close bracket. Are easily conned into believing that obscurity, evasiveness, incomprehensibility, indirectness, ambiguity and boredom are marks of depth and brilliance. Great Art proves that men are superior to women, that men are women, being labelled Great Art, almost all of which, as the anti-feminists are fond of reminding us, was created by men. We know that Great Art is great because male authorities have told us so, and can't claim otherwise, as only those with exquisite sensitivities far superior to ours can perceive and appreciate the greatness. The proof of superior sensitivity being that they appreciated the slop, that they appreciated.

S.C.U.M.
from Carole Roussopoulos
& Delphin Seyring, 1976

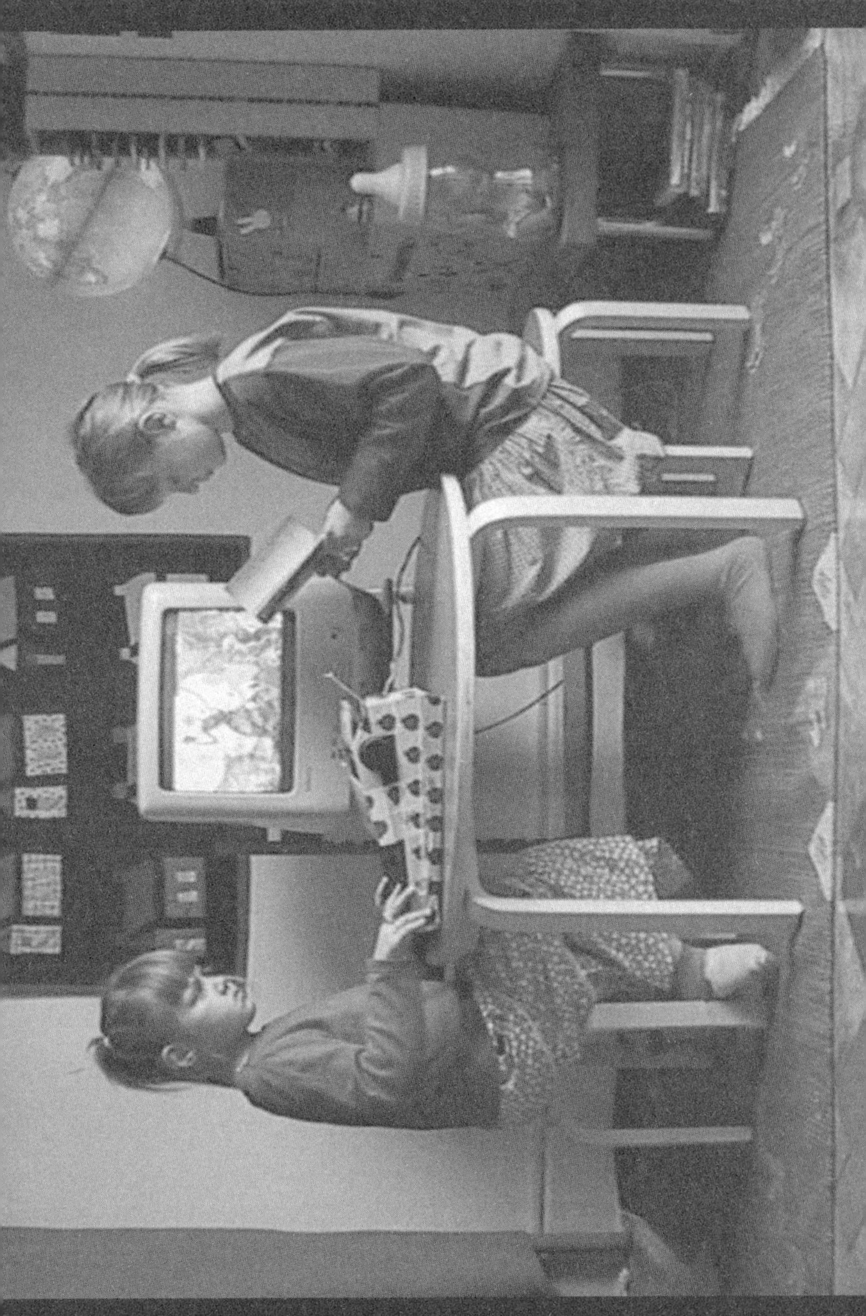

LUCIE: If I put my hands behind my head, my arms form two triangles. If I lean forward, the back of my head is visible. Stella is chewing gum, she is wearing a red dress with white polka dots. The mouse behind her has a bow tie made out of the same material. I am wearing a skirt, a black t-shirt top, upon which is written: "I don't know if it's art, but I know I like it." Which means: "I don't know if it's art, but I know I like it."

Performer Audience Mirror
from Dan Graham, 1975

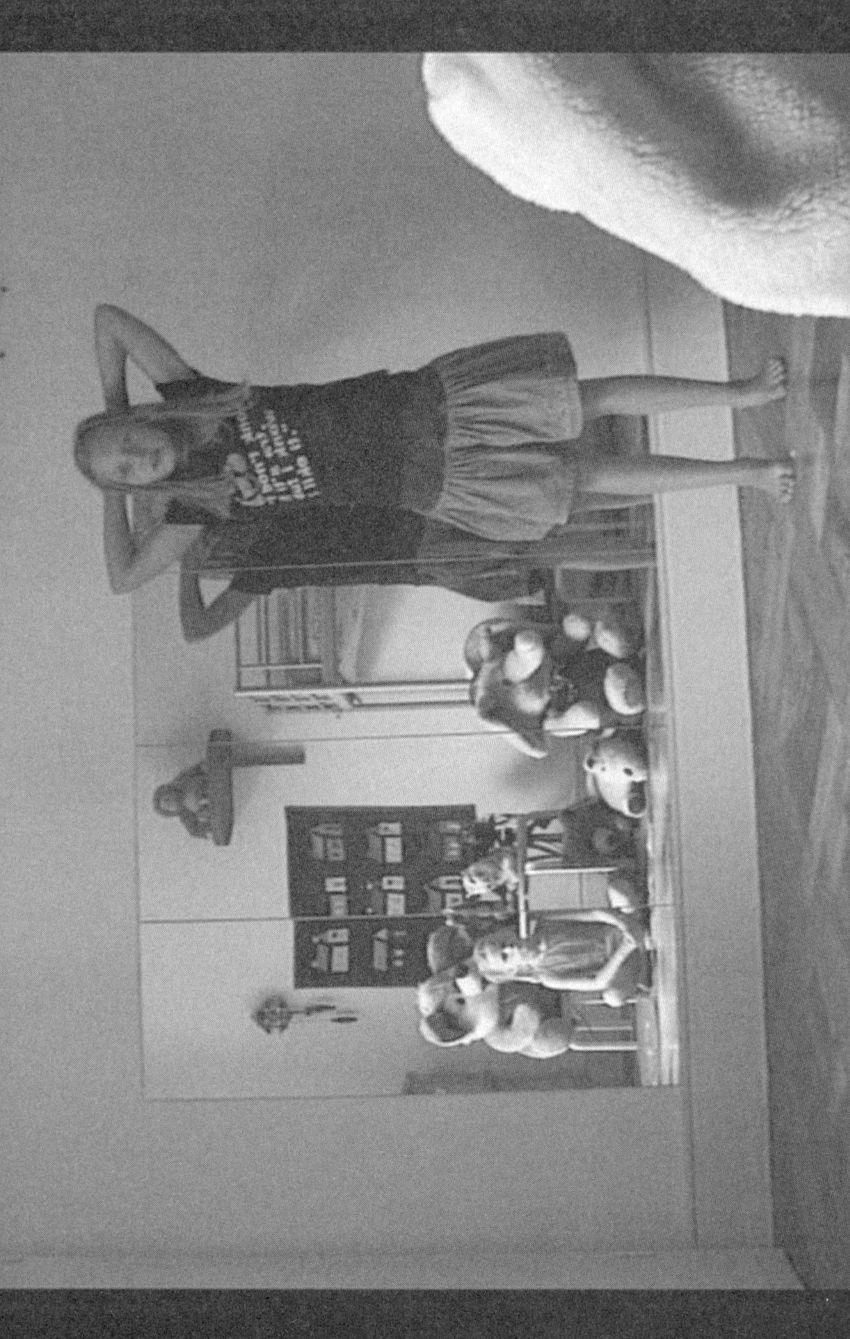

Relation in Time
from Marina Abramović
and Ulay, 1977

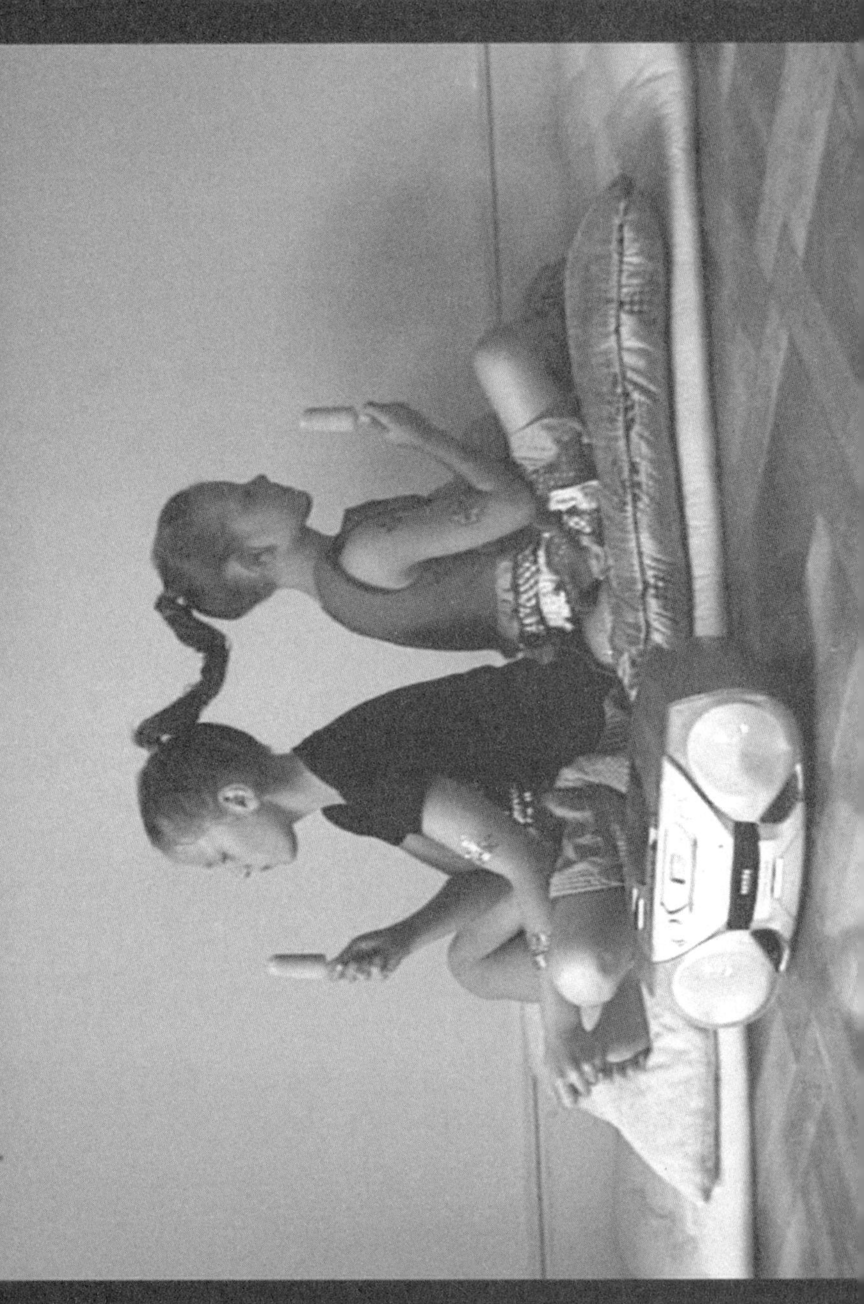

Program for a Proletarian Children's Theatre

2006
7', color, sound, DV
Language: French, English subtitles
Format of distribution 16/9

Textual reference:
Walter Benjamin, "Programm eines proletarischen Kindertheaters" [1928] in *Über Kinder, Jugend und Erziehung. Mit Abbildungen von Kinderbüchern und Spielzeug aus der Sammlung Benjamin*, Edition Suhrkamp, Berlin: 1969, pp. 79–85

LUCIE: Every proletarian movement finds itself confronting many different forces for which it is unprepared. The most powerful of these, as well as the most dangerous, is the younger generation. We are calling for, and shall not cease to call for, instruments for the class-conscious education of proletarian children.

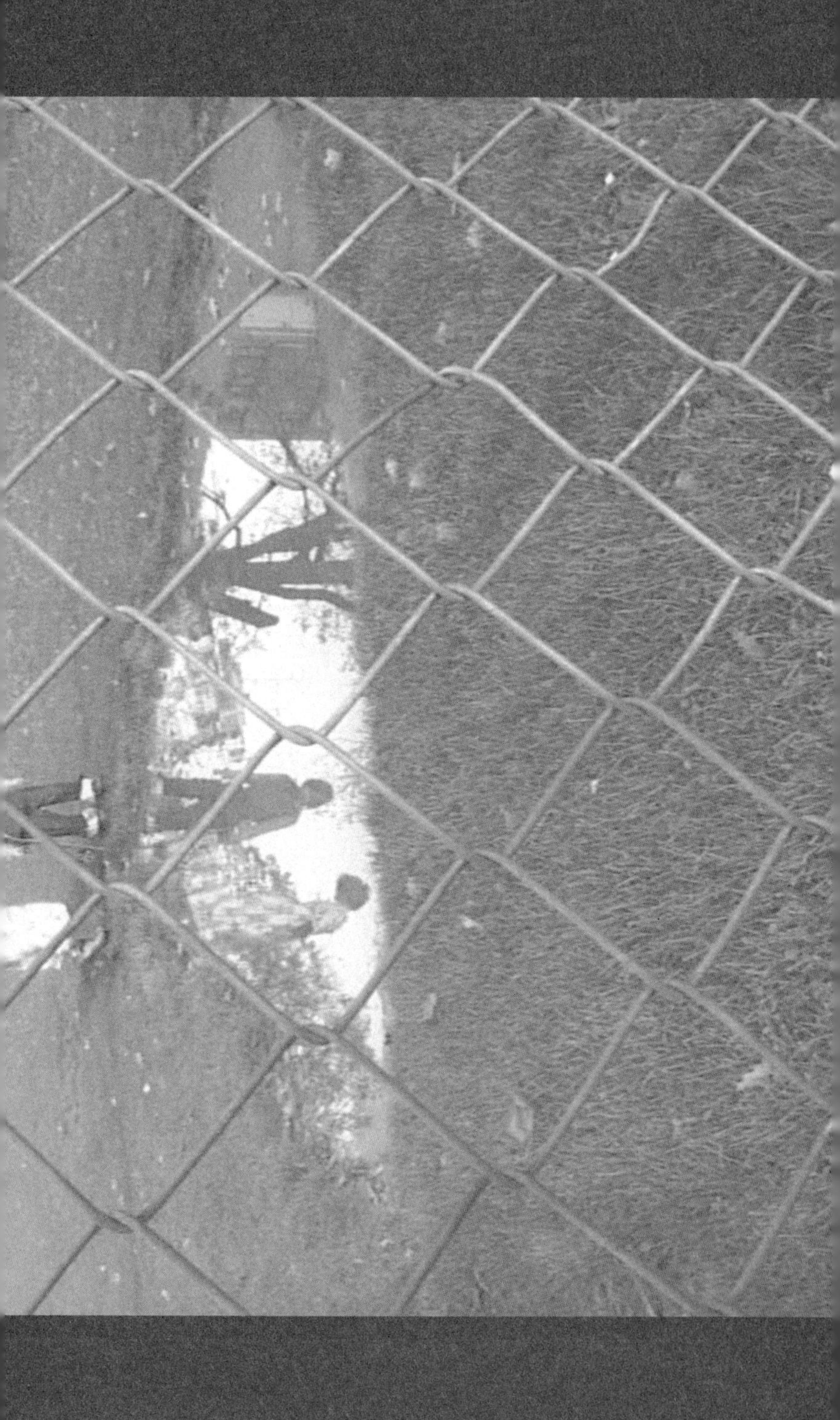

LUCIE: Proletarian education needs first and foremost a framework, an objective space within which education can be located. The bourgeoisie, in contrast, requires an idea toward which education leads.

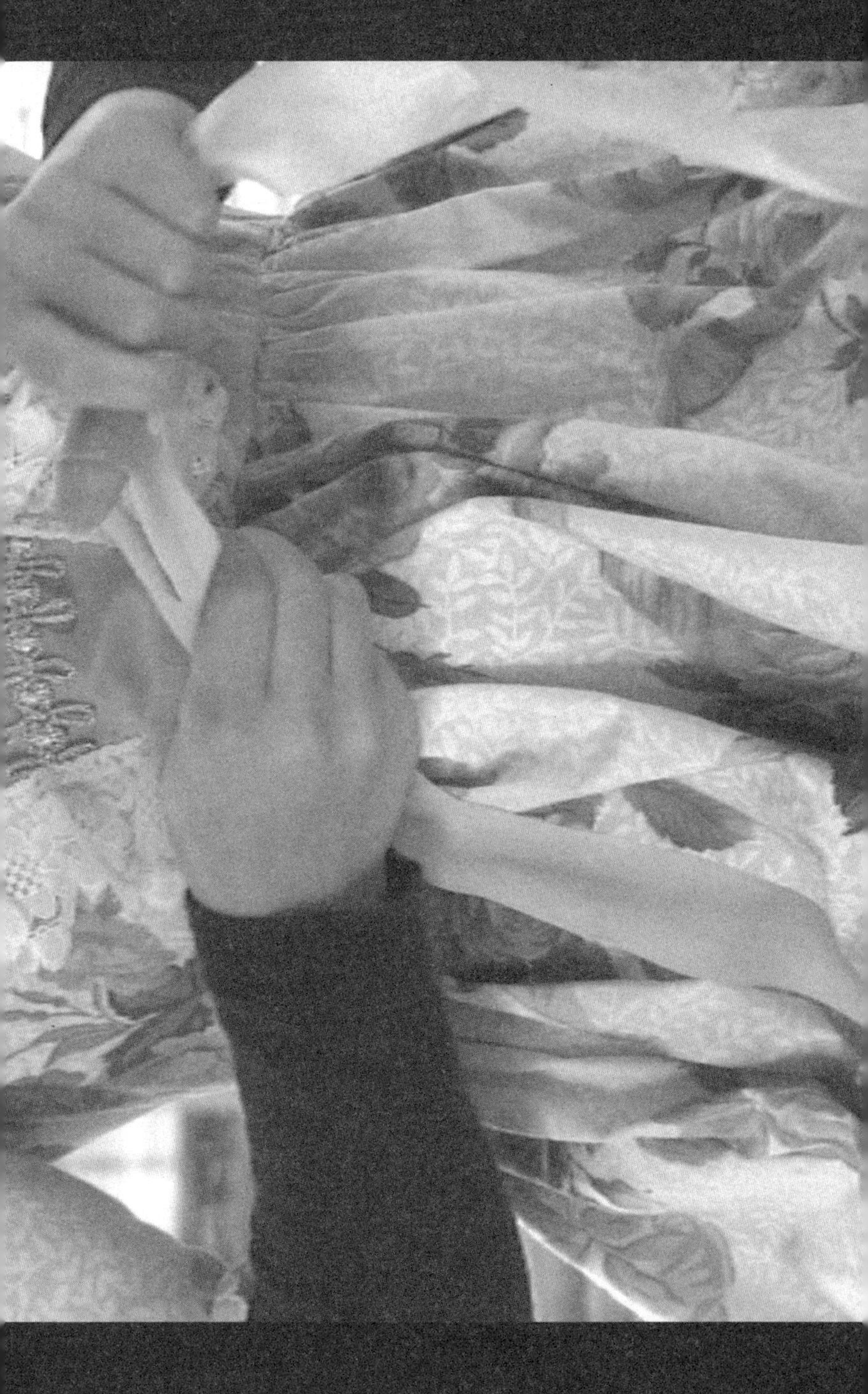

LUCIE: The education of a child requires that his entire life has to be engaged. Proletarian education requires that the child has to be educated within a clearly defined space. This is the positive dialectic of the problem. It is only in the theatre that the whole of life can appear as a defined space, framed in all its plenitude; and this is why proletarian children's theatre is the dialectical site of education.

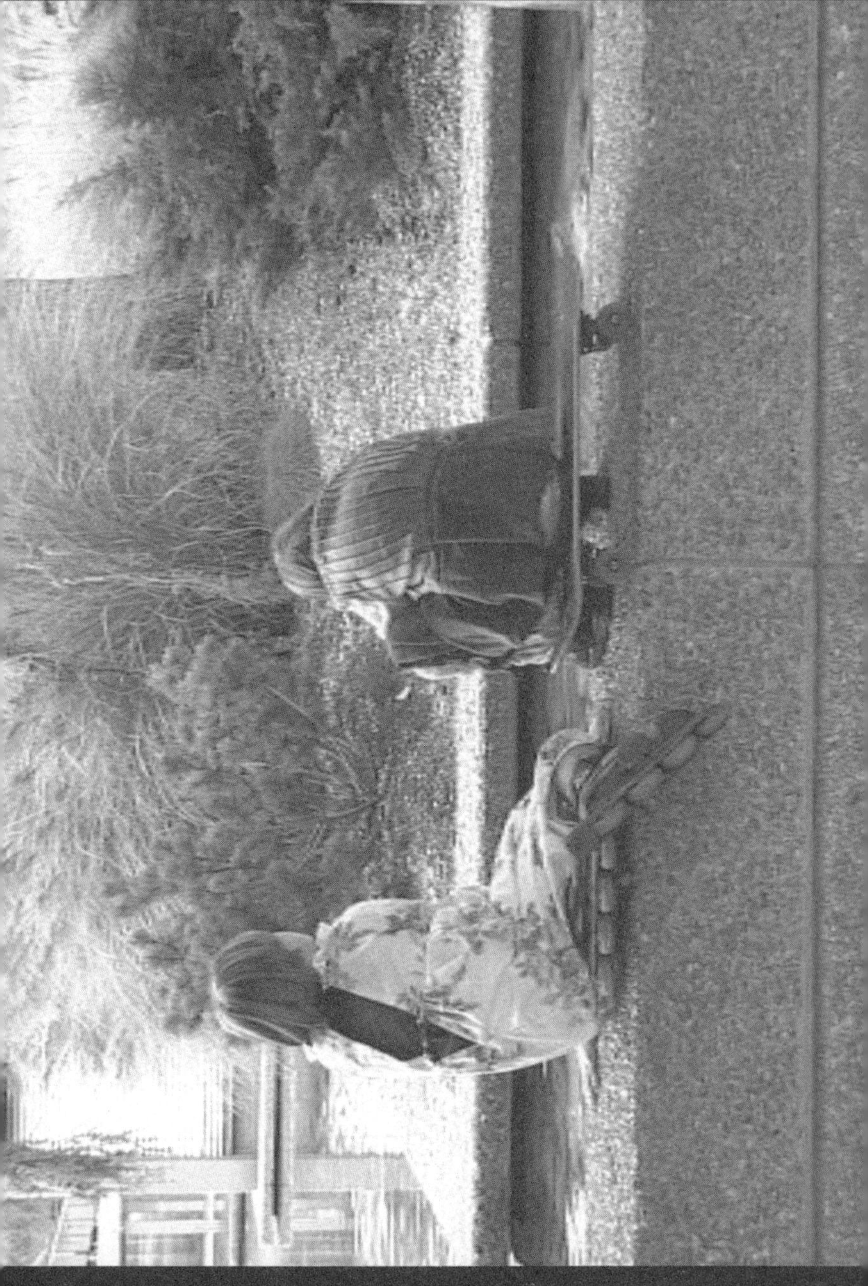

LUCIE: Economically, the theatre of the modern bourgeoisie is determined by the profit motive; sociologically, both in front of the curtain and backstage, it is primarily an instrument of sensation. The proletarian children's theatre is quite different.

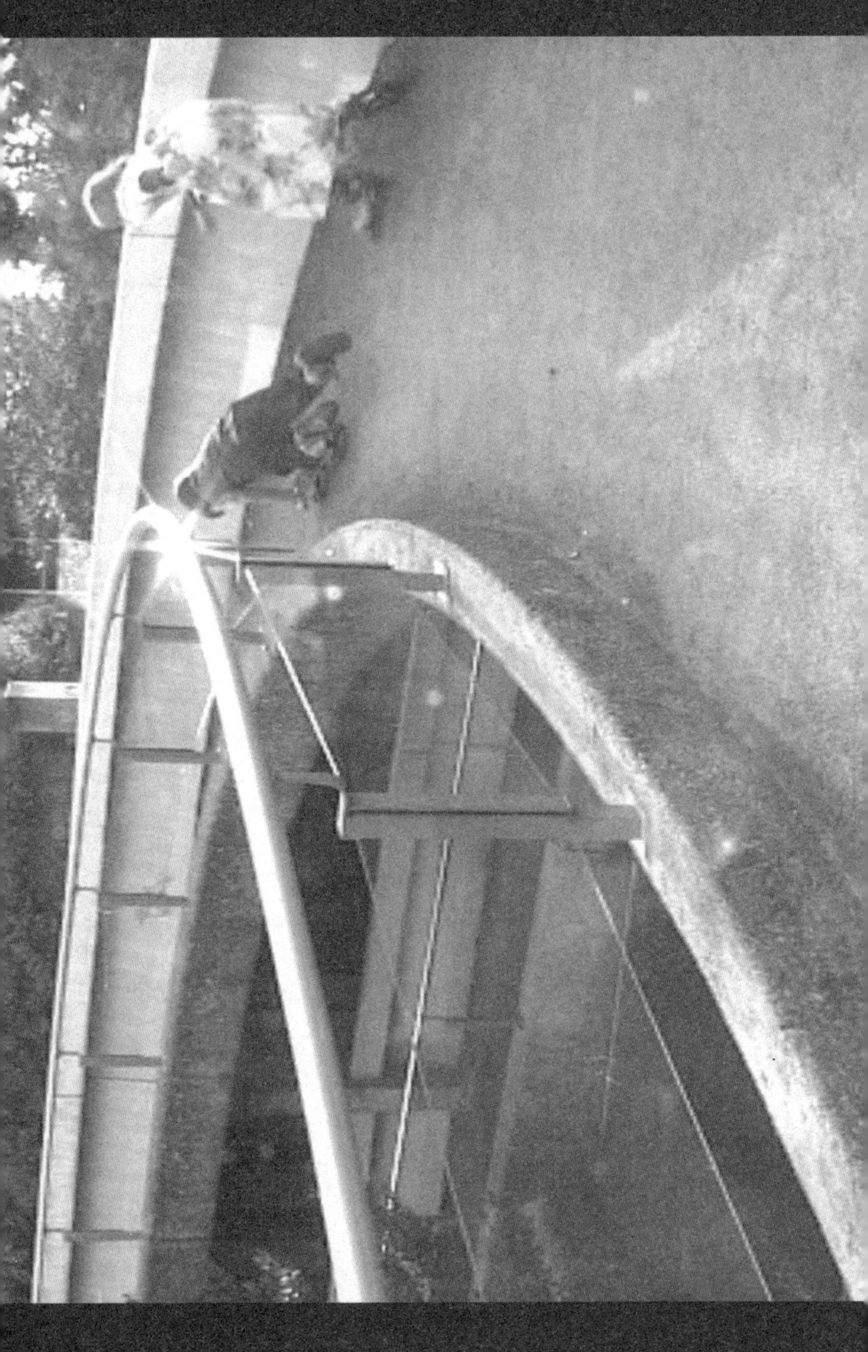

LUCIE: In the view of the bourgeoisie, nothing presents a greater danger to children than the theatre. What we find expressed is the fear that the theatre will unleash in children the most powerful energies of the future.

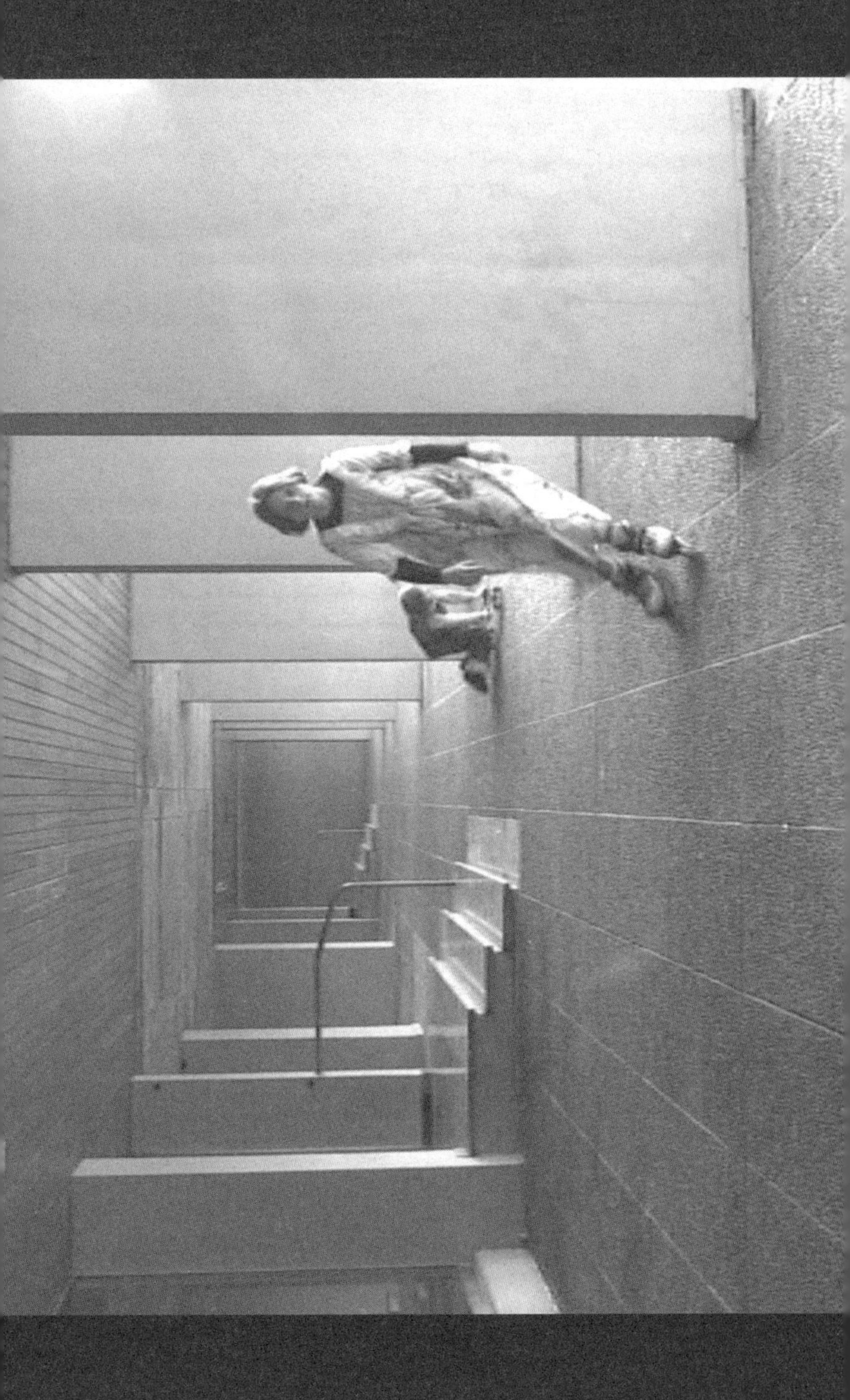

LUCIE: And this fear causes bourgeois education theory to anathematize the theatre.

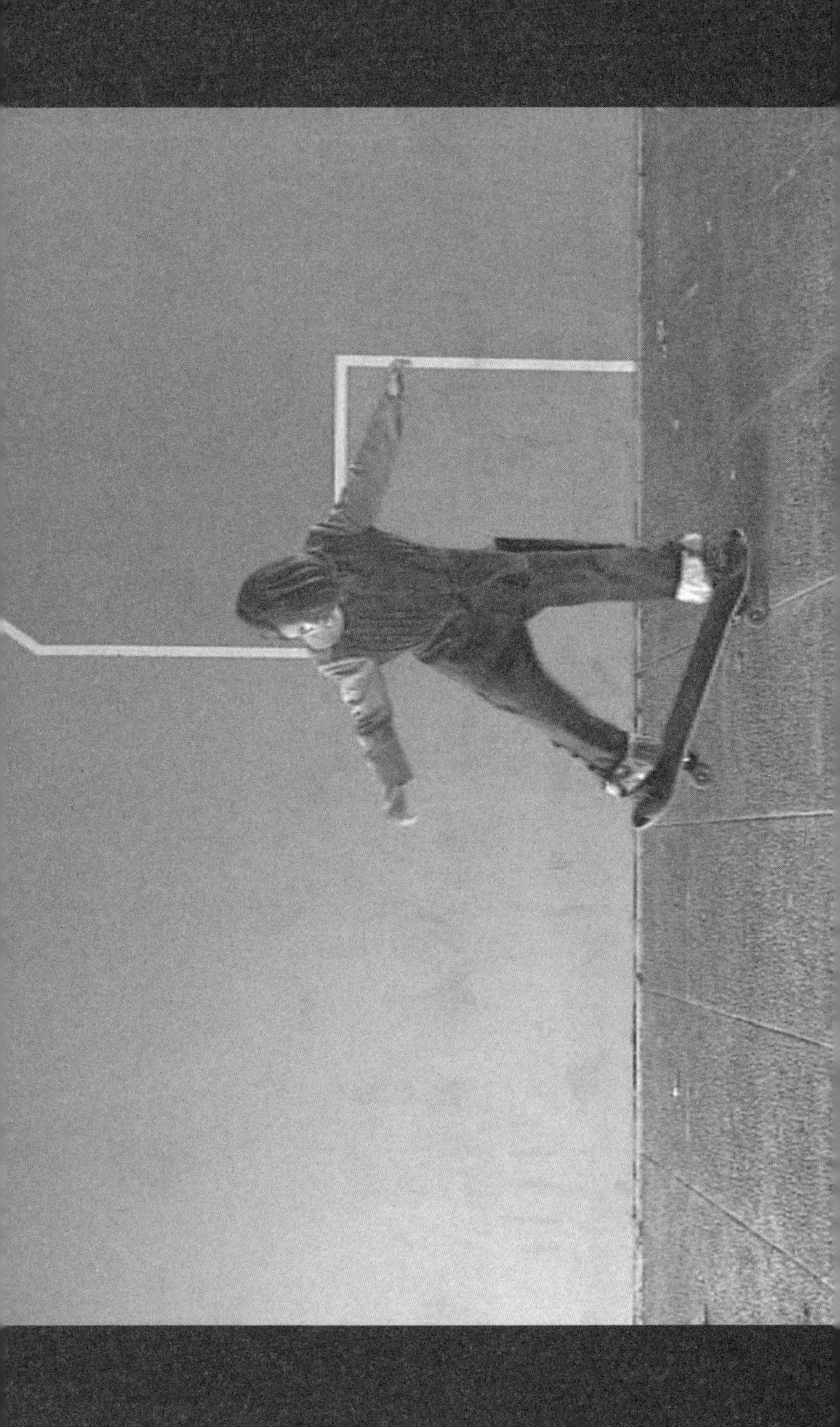

LUCIE: We may easily imagine how it would react once the fire came too close—the fire in which, for children, reality and play coincide and are fused so that acted sufferings can merge with real sufferings, acted beatings can shade into real beatings.

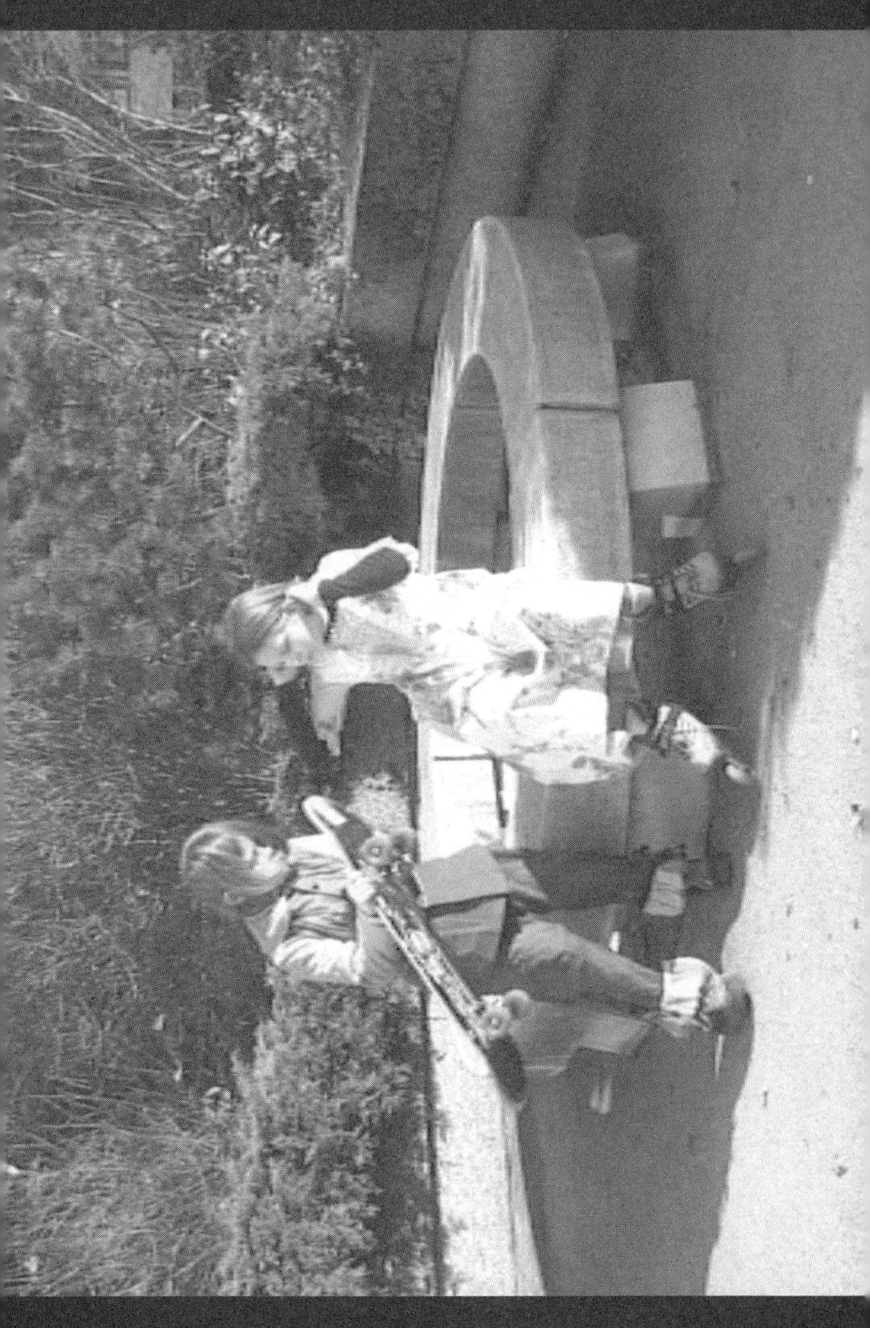

Little Pedagogical Treatise

2008
7', color, sound, DV
Language: French, English subtitles
Format of distribution 16/9

Textual reference:
Pier Paolo Pasolini, “Mes propositions sur l’école et la télévision” [1975] in *Lettres luthériennes. Petit traité pédagogique*, Les éditions Points, Paris: 2008, pp. 205–212

LUCIE: Regarding compulsory education and television, at first glance we have to say that my two modest propositions clearly aim at temporary abolition. To be precise, I'd say: waiting for better days, meaning a new development.

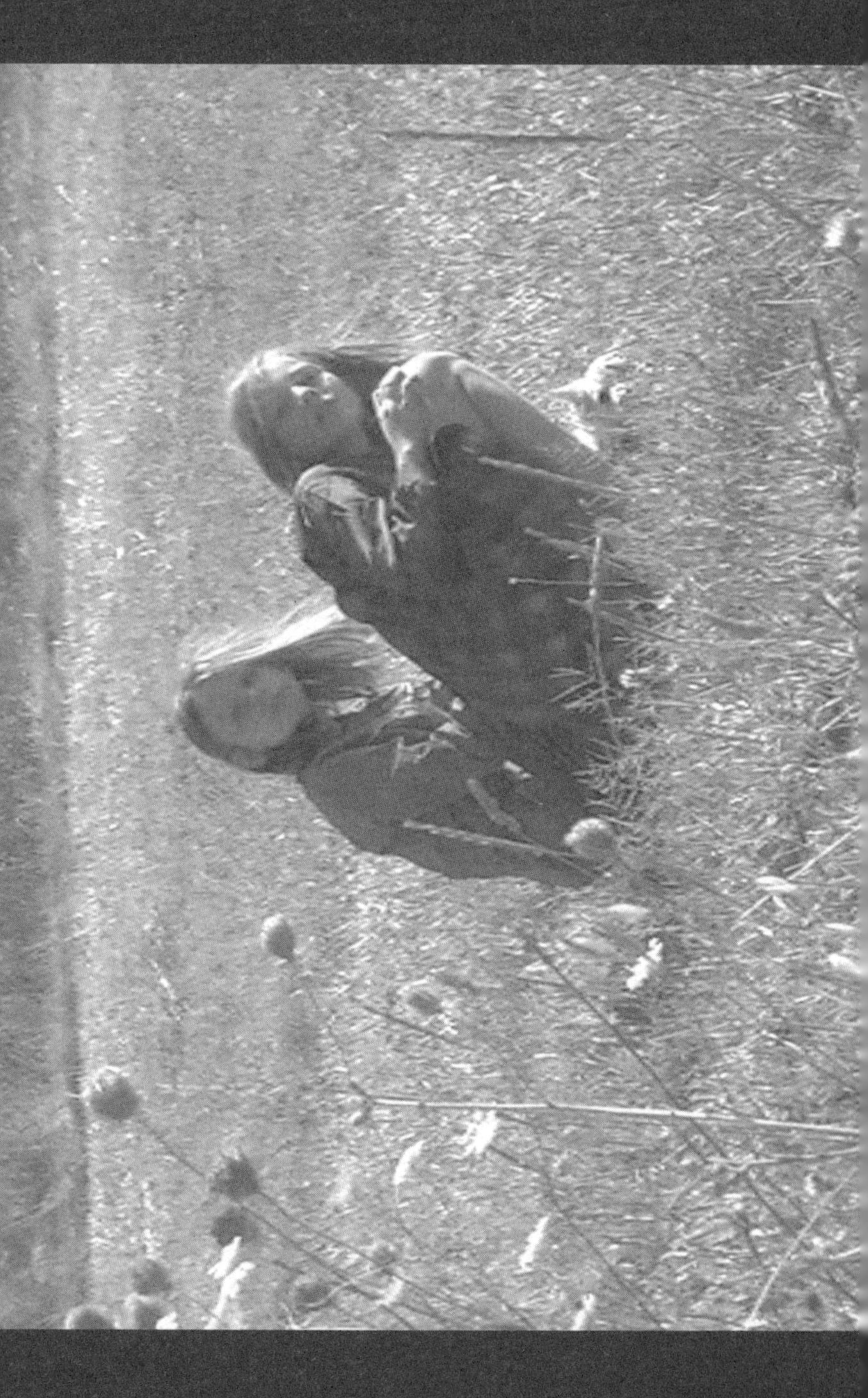

LUCIE: That is the core of the issue.

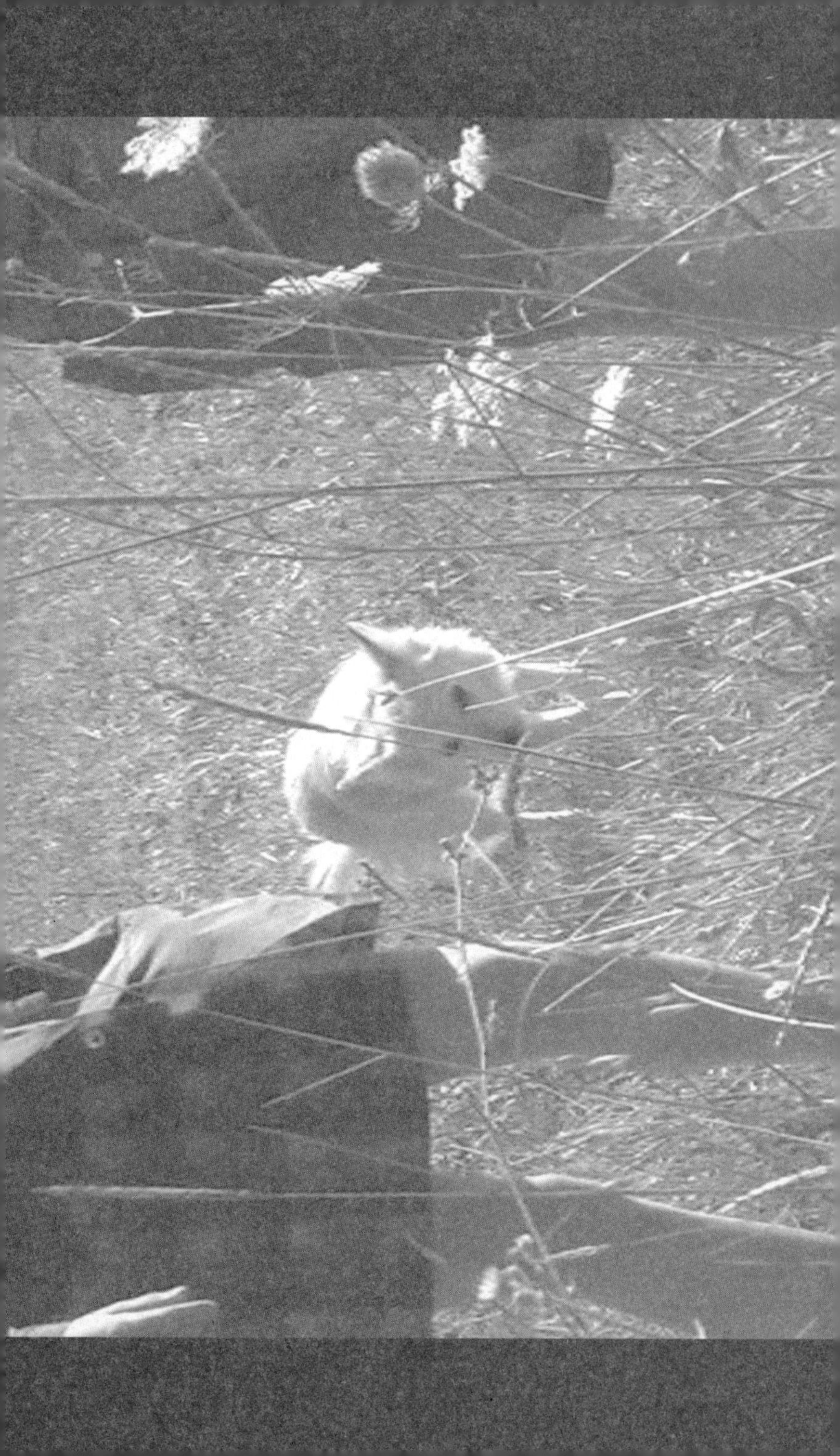

LUCIE: In other words. I demand the intervention of the Italian Communist Party, the best left-wing forces, whose interest in radical reform of the school system and television should be obvious.

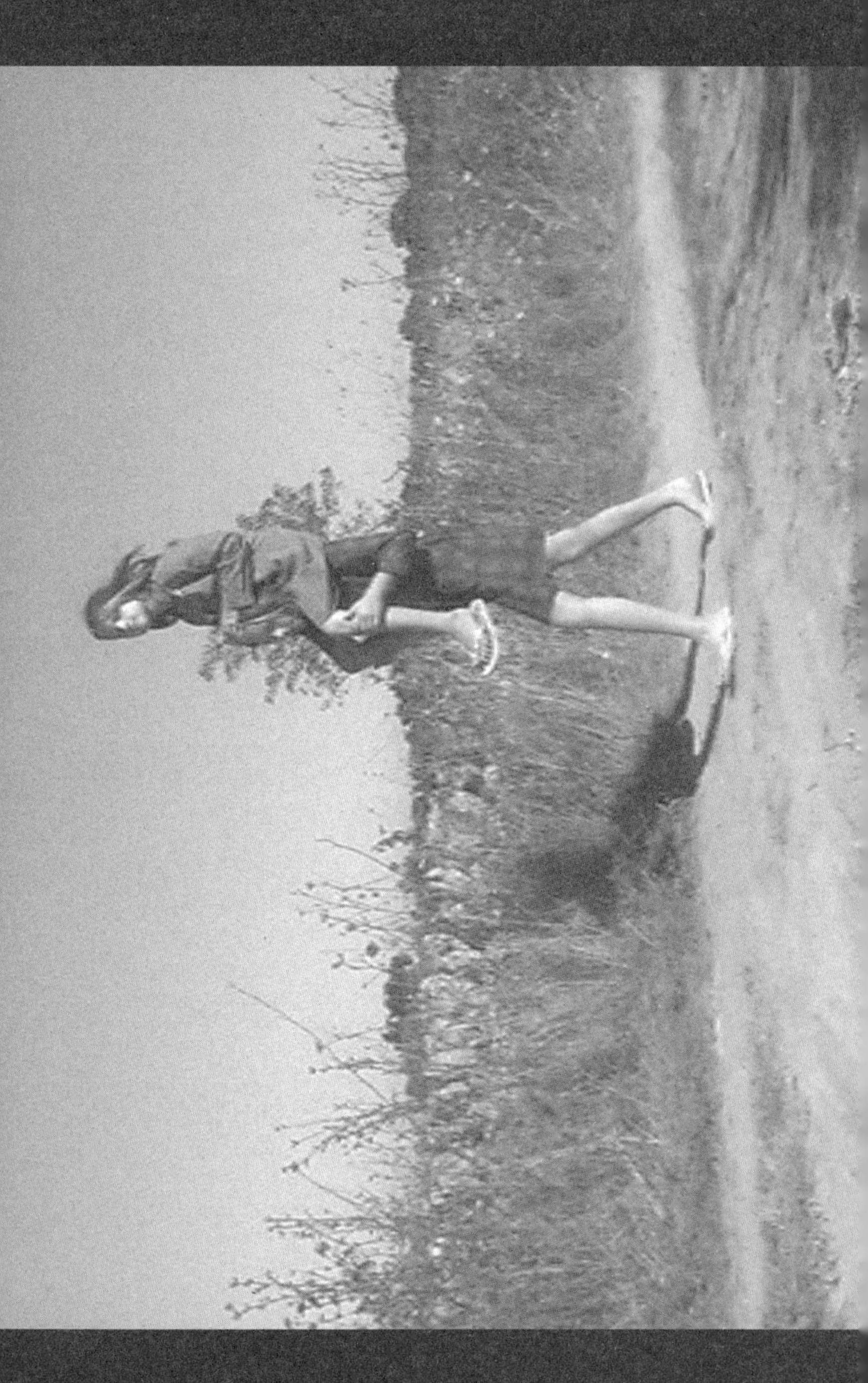

STELLA: Waiting for such radical reform it would be best to abolish schools and televison. I realize this is utopic, nonetheless I am firmly convinced about it.

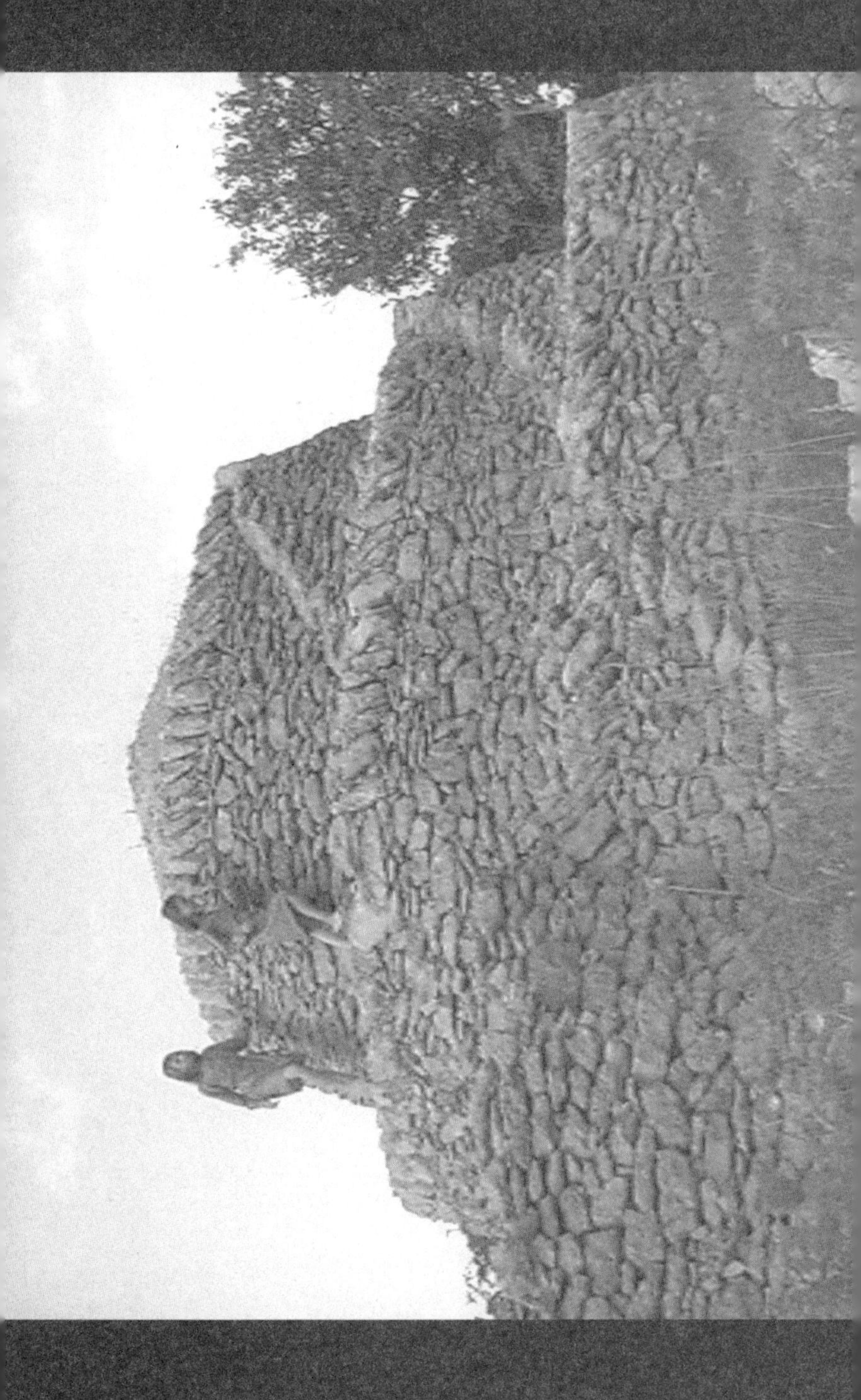

LUCIE: Every day that passes is fatal for both students and viewers.

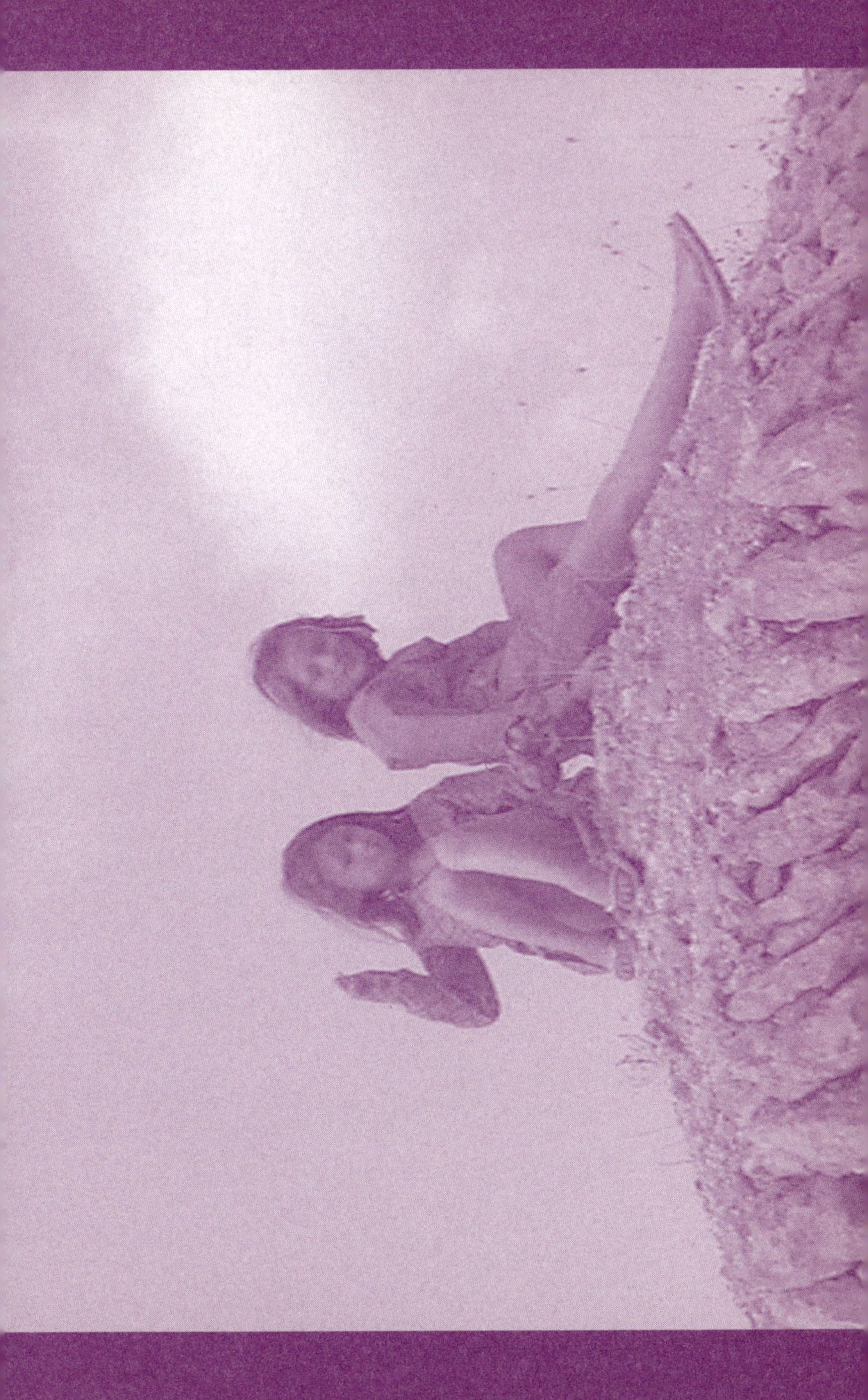

STELLA: Not long ago, during a seminar in Lecce in which I improvised a debate with teachers, I described what I believe compulsory school should be.

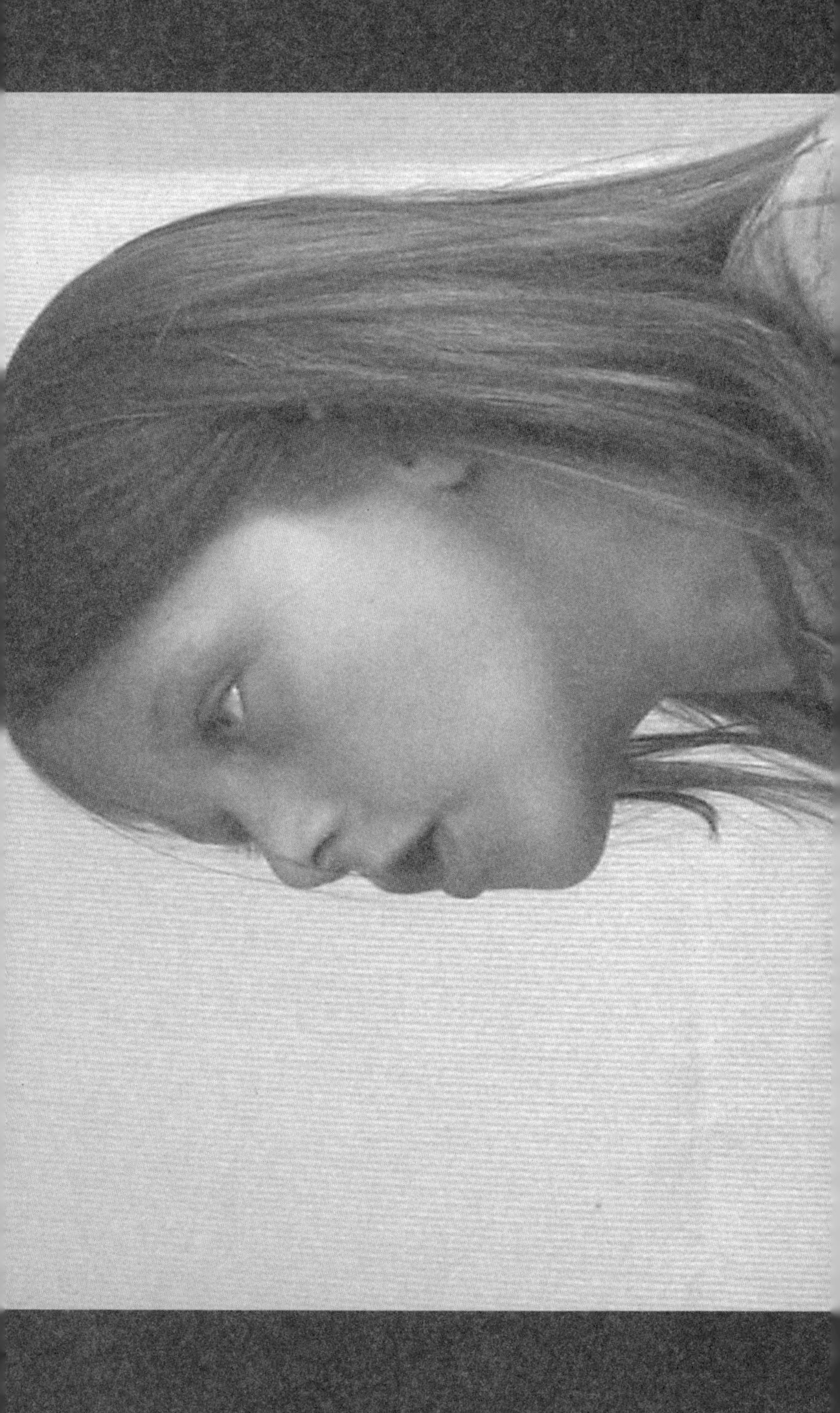

LUCIE: New disciplines have to be added.

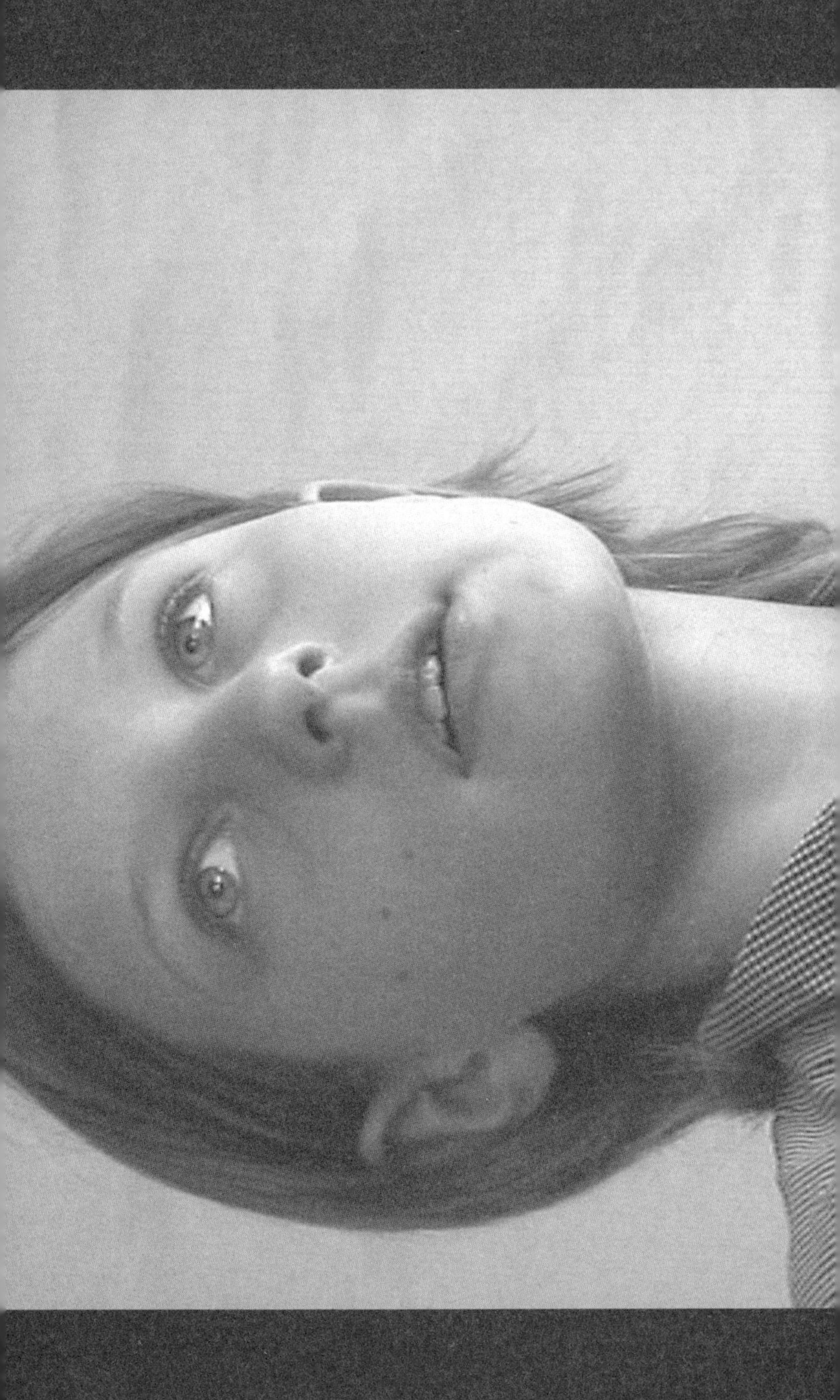

STELLA: Like driver's education.

LUCIE: Paired with awareness of street codes,

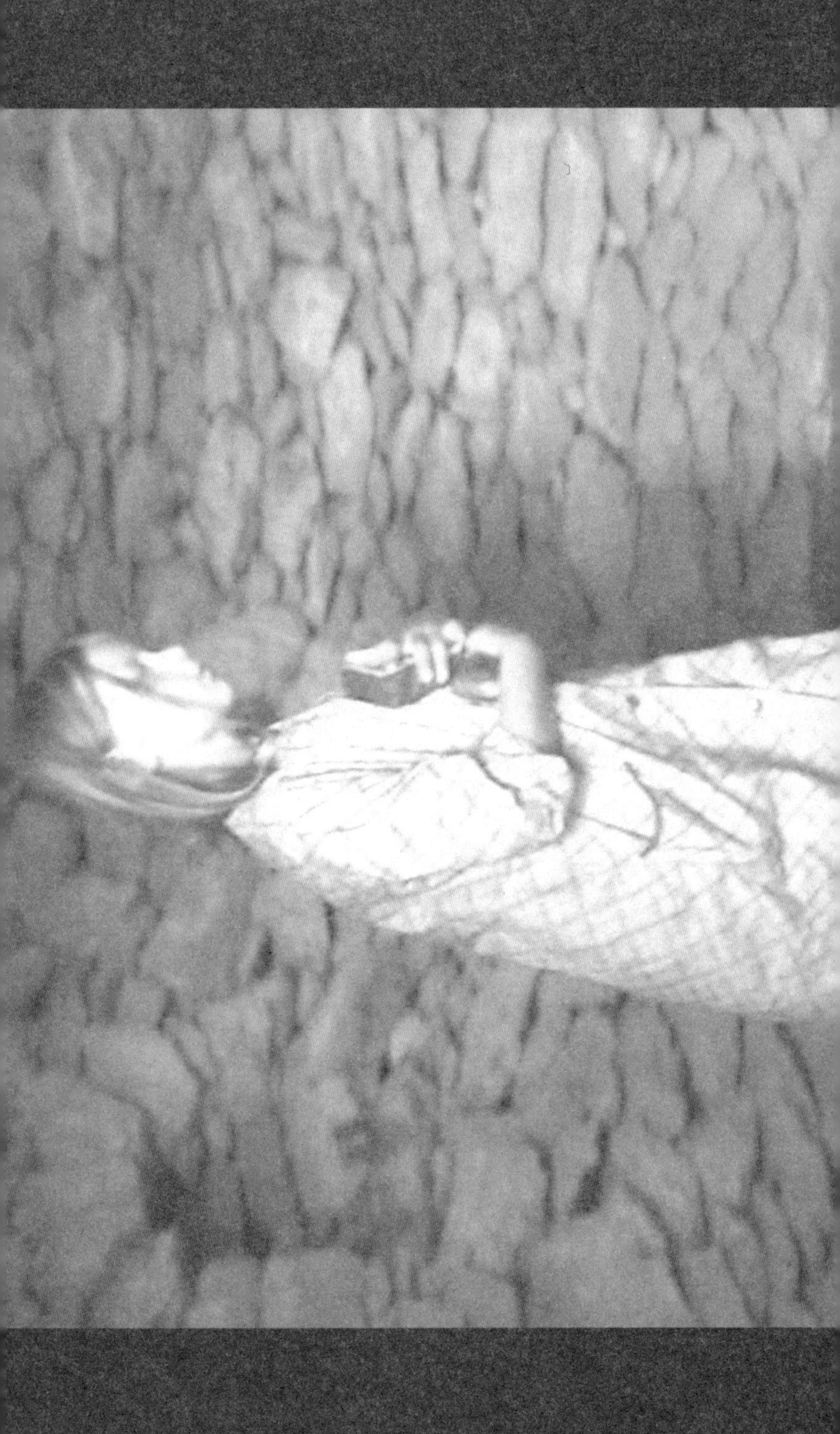

STELLA: urbanism,
LUCIE: ecology,
STELLA: hygiene,
LUCIE: sex education,

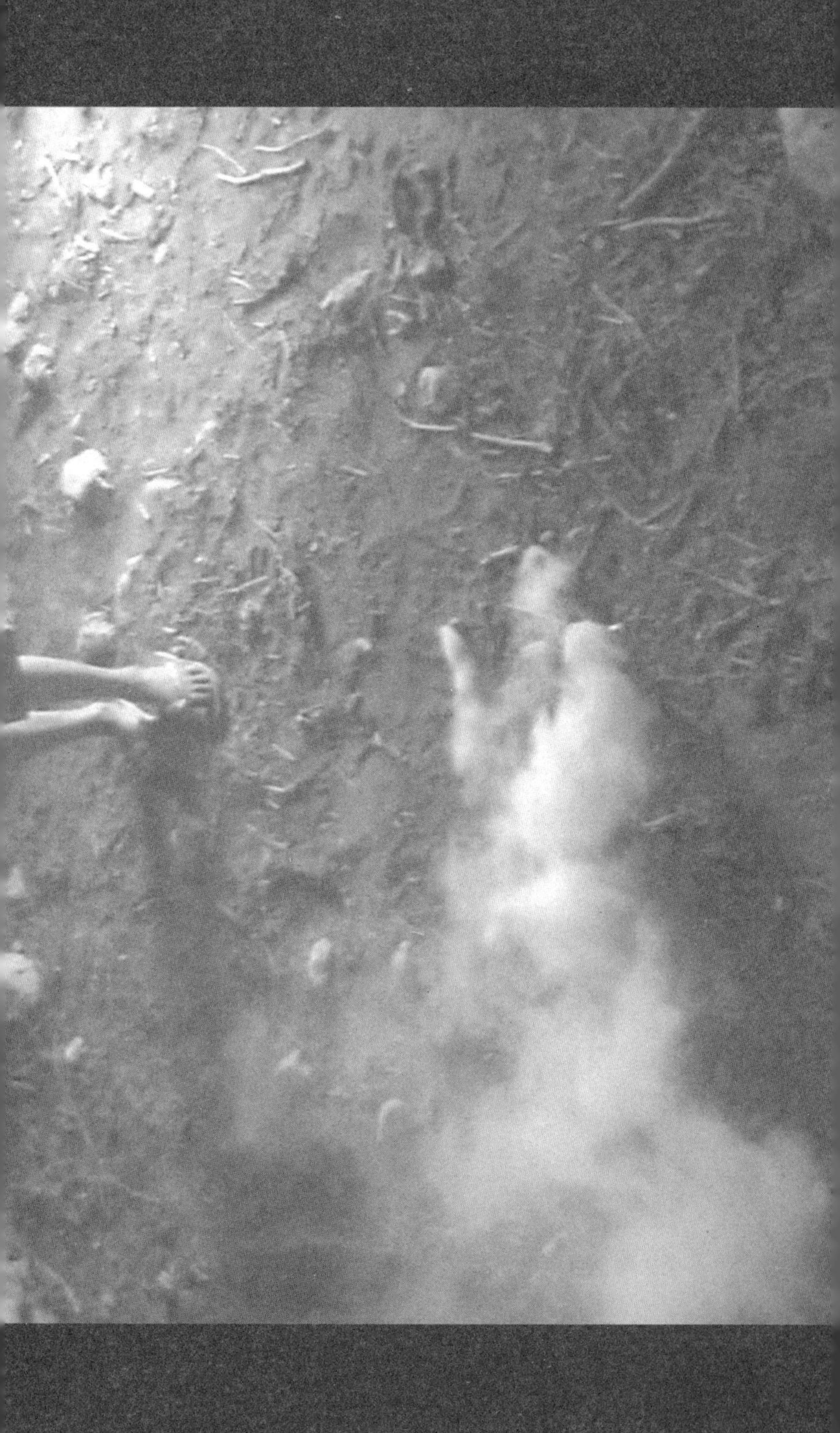

STELLA: and especially I would add a lot of reading, a lot of free reading.

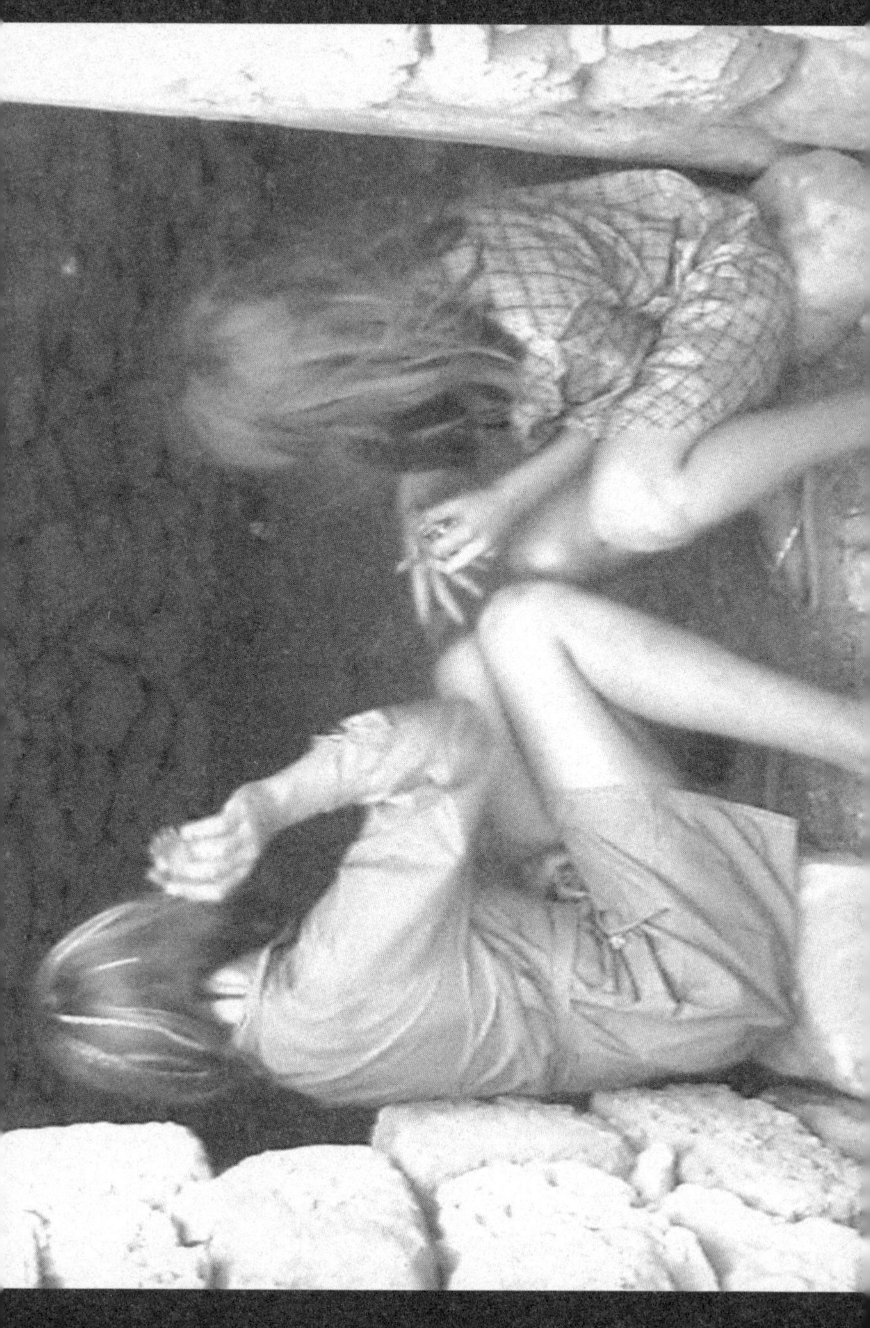

LUCIE: Freely commented.

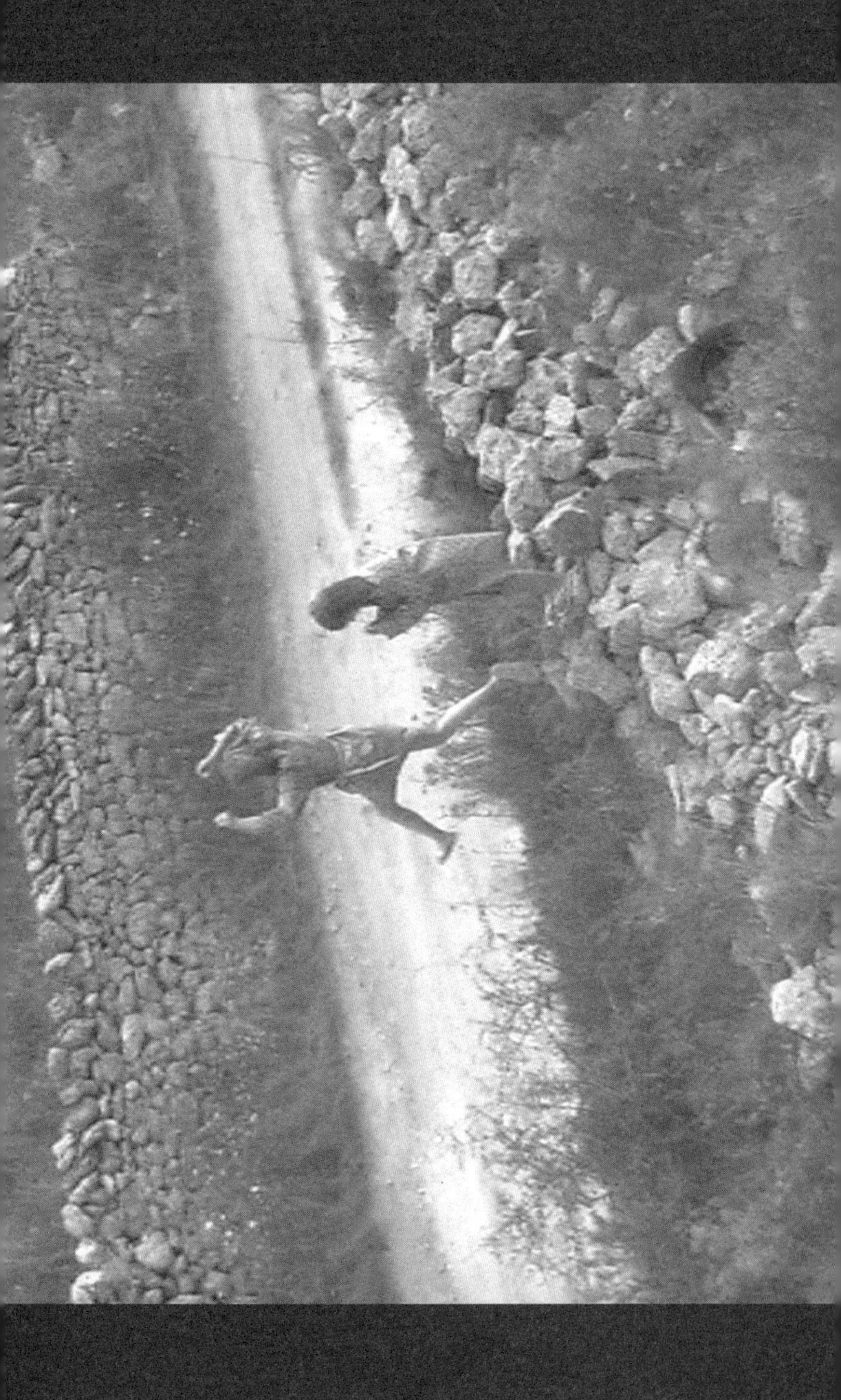

Taranta

2009
13' 40", color, sound, HD
Language: French, English subtitles
Format of distribution 16/9

Textual references:
Gilles Deleuze et Félix Guattari, “1730-Devenir intense, devenir animal, devenir imperceptible” in *Capitalisme et Schizophrénie 2: Mille Plateux*, Les Éditions de Minuit, Paris: 1980, p. 284
Salvatore Quasimodo, Notes on *Tarantula (La Taranta)* by Gianfranco Mingozzi, documentary, 18', Italy: 1962

ANGELA: I would like to tell you a story that happened in my family. It begins with distant ancestors, and continues with my grandmother, Nonna Lucia, and my father, Salvatore. It's about the bite of a spider called the Tarantula.

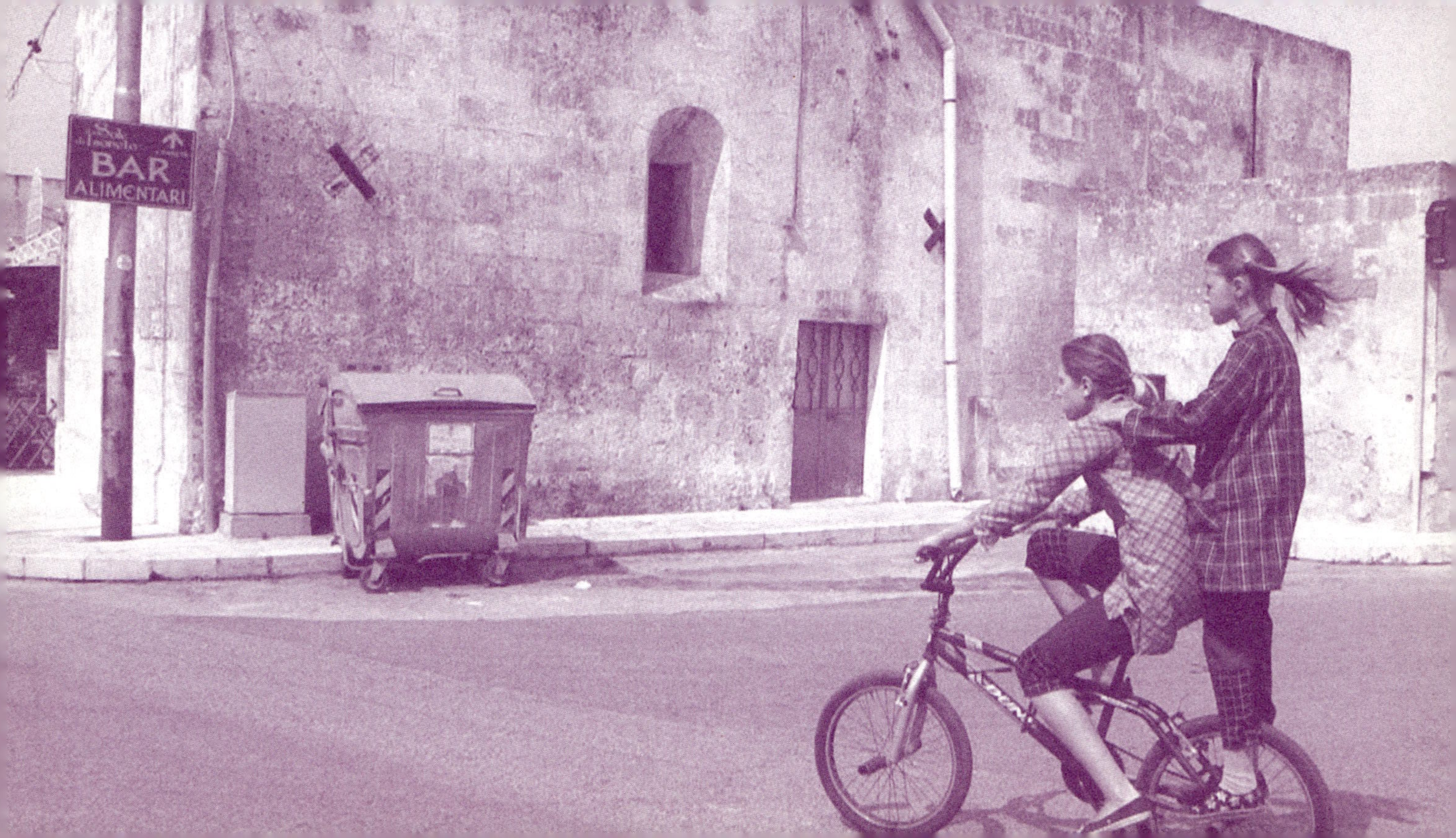
BAR
ALIMENTARI

ANGELA: Many people have avoided being bitten by the Tarantula. Nonna Lucia and her son Salvatore were bitten though. Maybe their descendents, me, you, others. I want to tell you this story now, right now, because I don't know how much longer I will be able to do so. At the same time, I would like to give you the key to understanding a culture, that of the dance called the Tarantella.

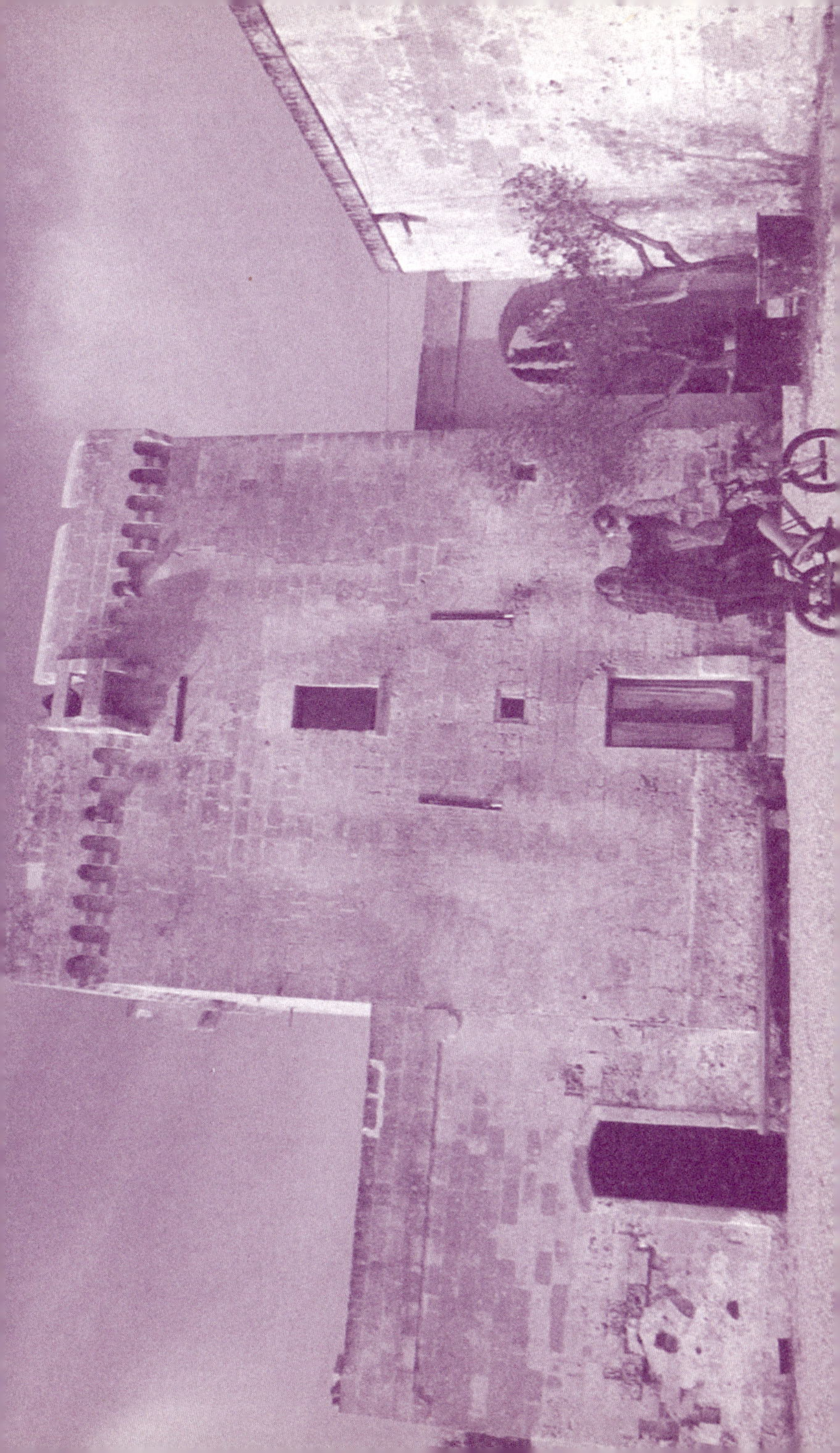

ANGELA: It's a tragic tale, like a Greek tragedy, in which future generations carry the destiny of their ancestors, without possibility of escape, living their lives with the weight of this destiny.

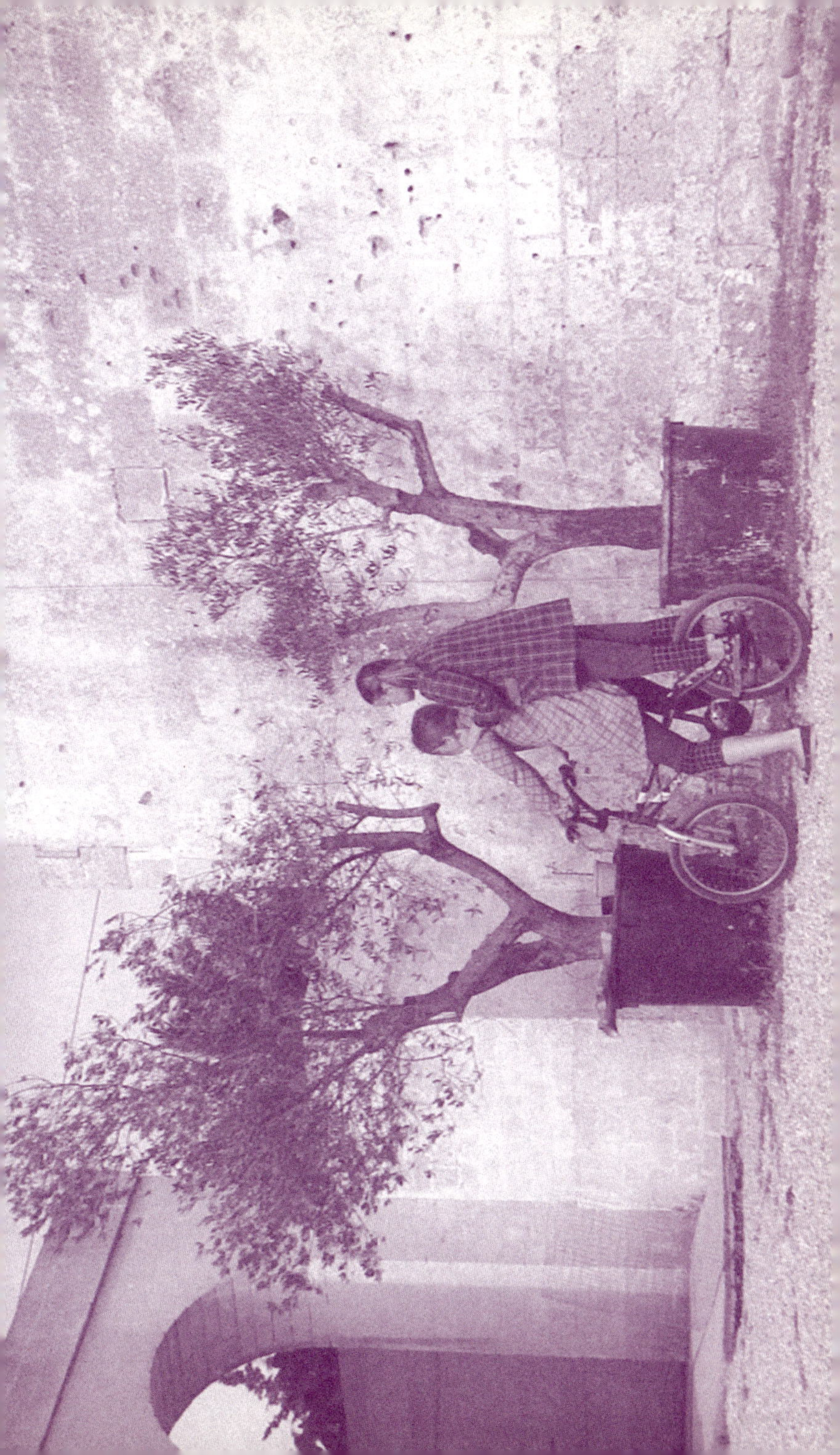

ANGELA: From that point, though, it becomes a futurist myth, in which modern heroines struggle to carry the burden of the story.

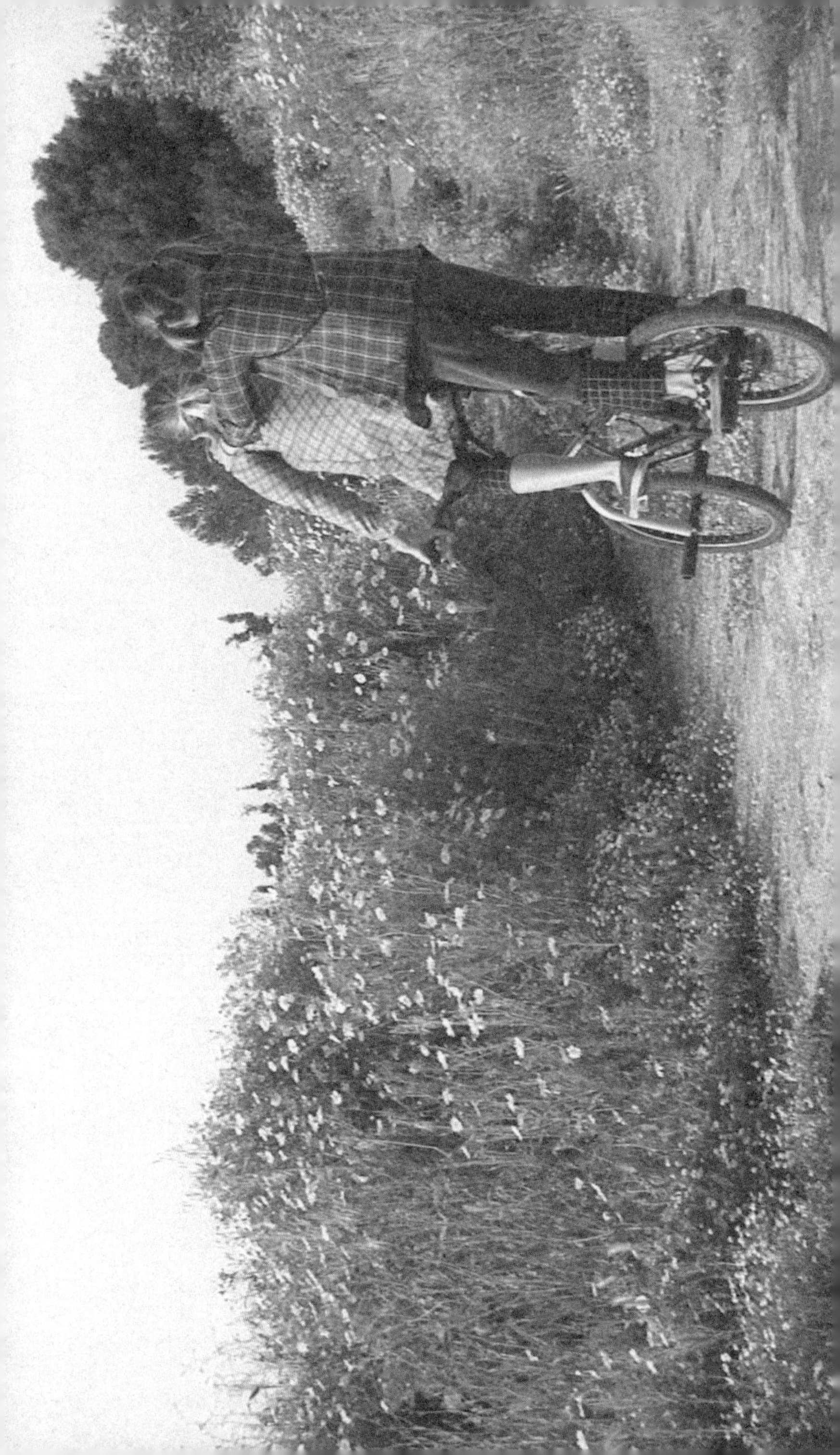

STELLA: They are all alike—it's a family.

LUCIE: A pack!

STELLA: A pack of female wolves!

LUCIE: This pack contains a special animal.

STELLA: But how can we tell which is the strange one?

LUCIE: Something has to happen, and then we will know which it is that has special powers.

STELLA: Look! That's Her…

LUCIE: She shows herself to us, and we show ourselves to Her.

LUCIE: By showing ourselves to Her, we erase all difference between us.

STELLA: We have become spiders, will we ever become human again?

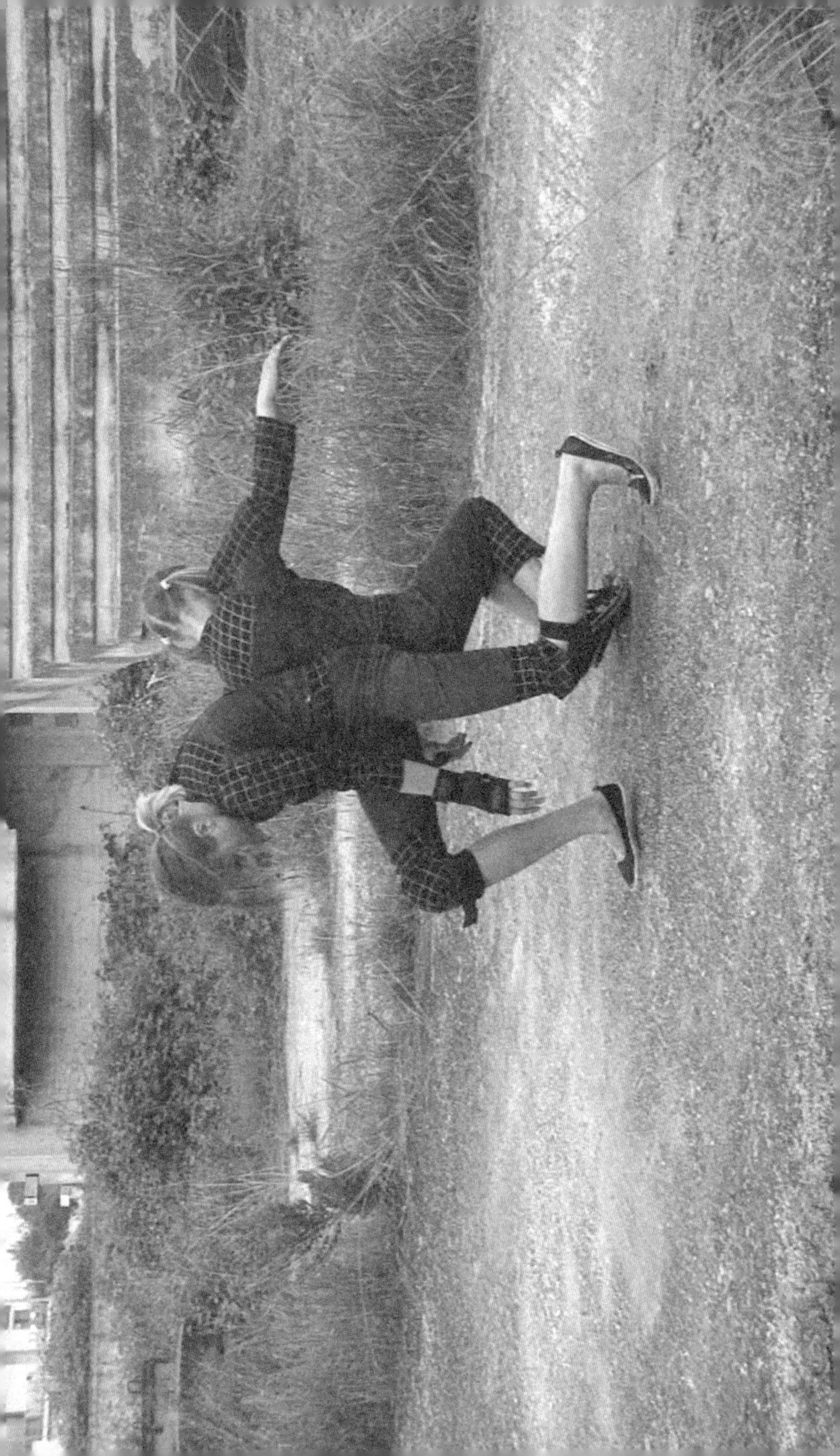

LUCIE: No, you are spider!

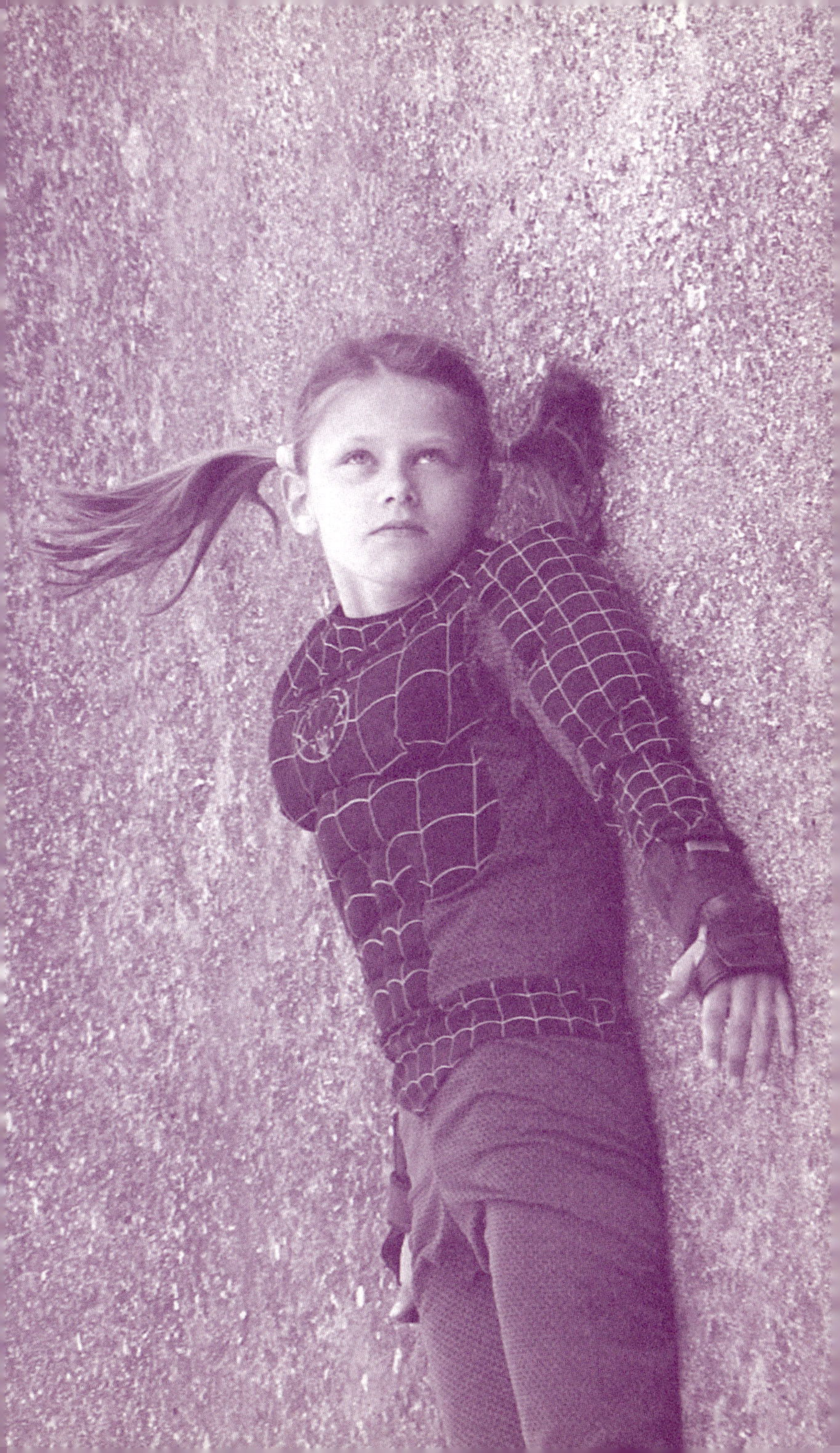

Concettina

2010
10', color, sound, HD
Language: Italian, English subtitles
Format of distribution 16/9

Textual reference:
Pier Paolo Pasolini, “Gennariello” [1975] in *Lettere luterane*, Edizioni Garzanti, Milano: 2009, pp. 27–76

STELLA: First of all, you are and must be very cute. Perhaps not in the conventional sense. You might be tiny and frail, you might already have in your face the marks that will inevitably make you look like a mask.

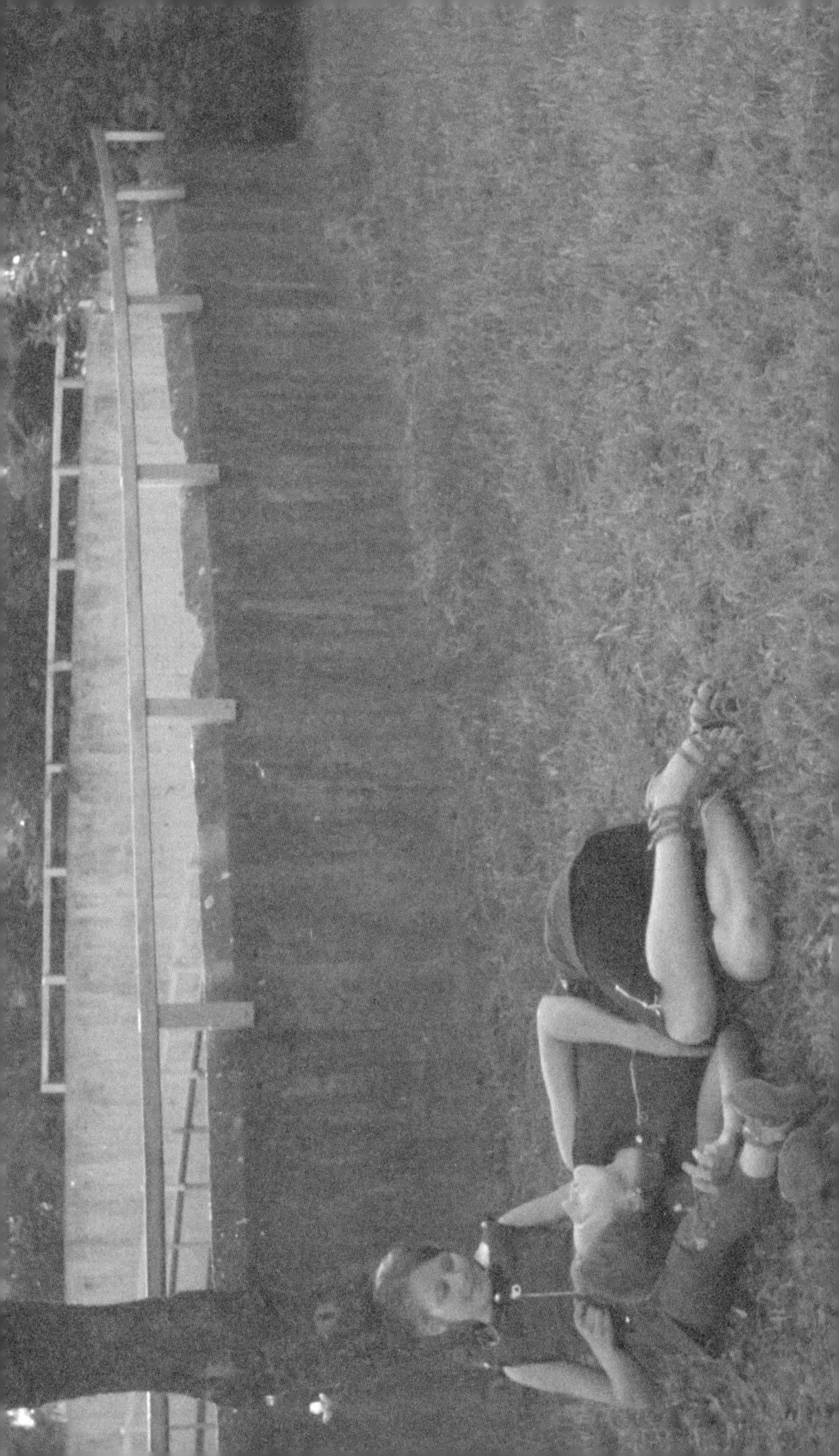

STELLA: Mind you, if you were ugly, really ugly, it would be the same. As long as you were funny and normally intelligent and caring as you are. In that case, you only need to have happy eyes: just as if, instead of being a Gennariello, you were a Concettina.

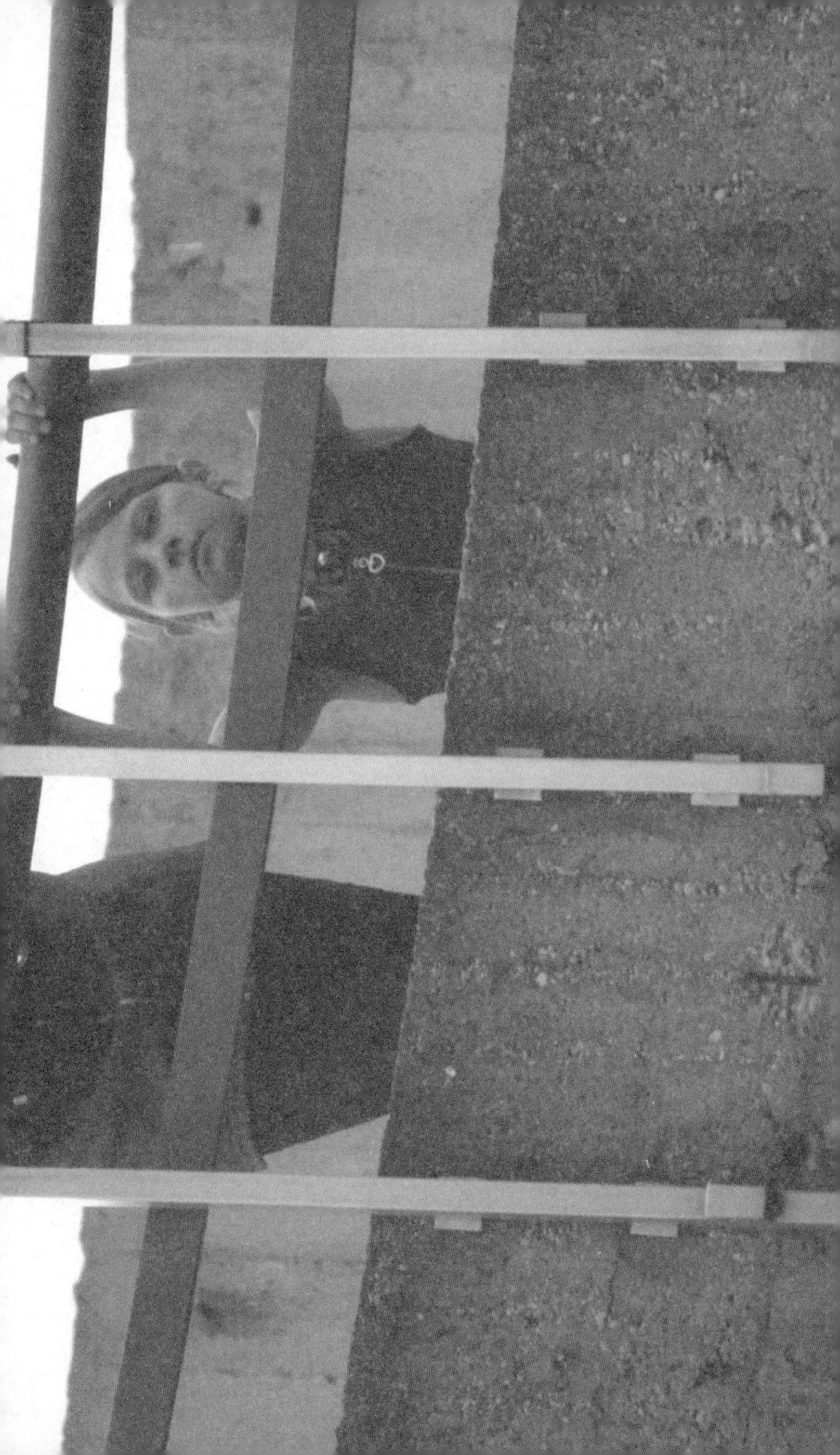

STELLA: A questionable and controversial female writer and director, an unorthodox communist that makes money through cinema, a rogue woman, something like D'Annunzio.

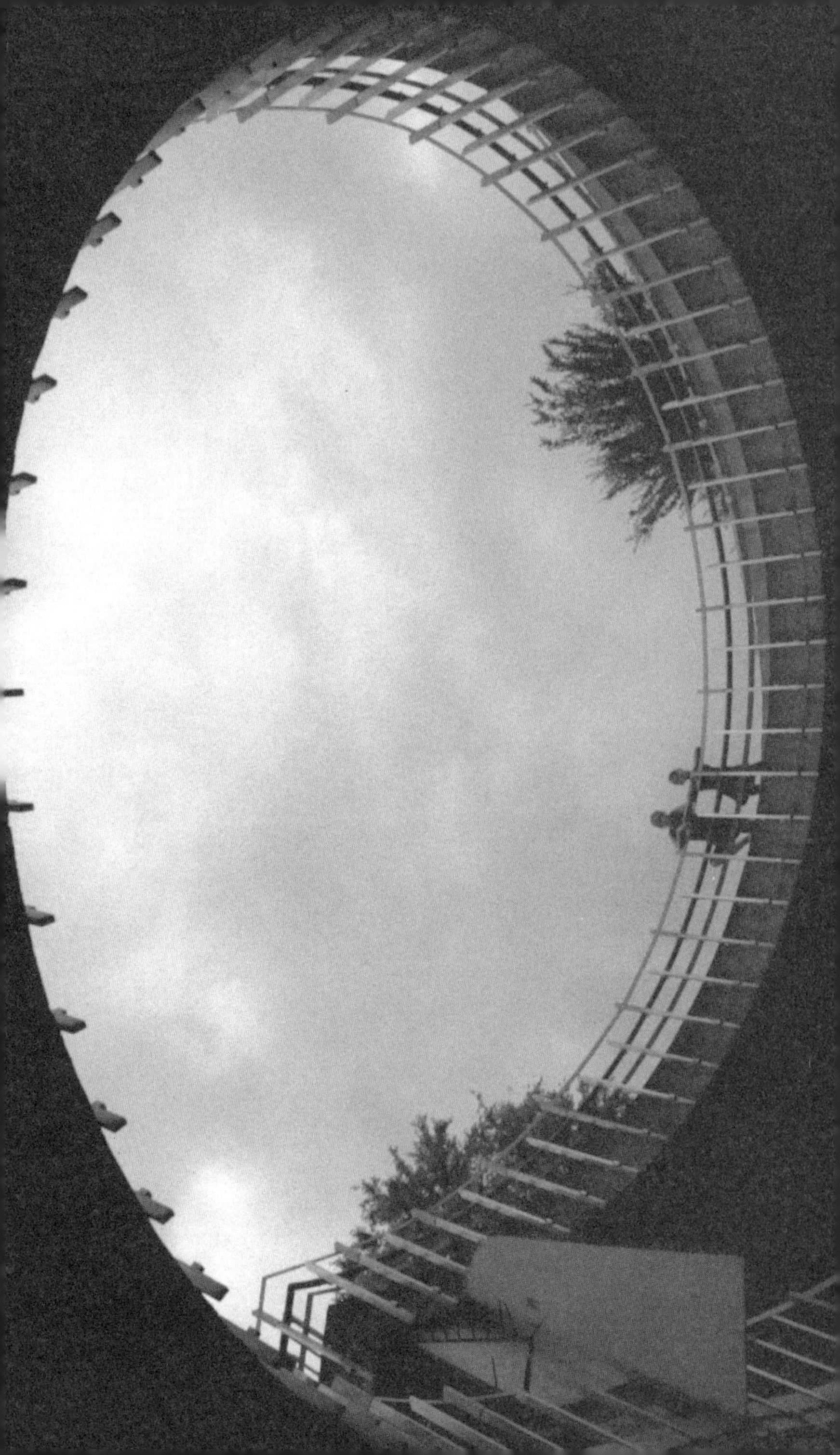

LUCIE: In my opinion, what, superficially, do these people have in common? A terrible, unstoppable anxiety to conform.

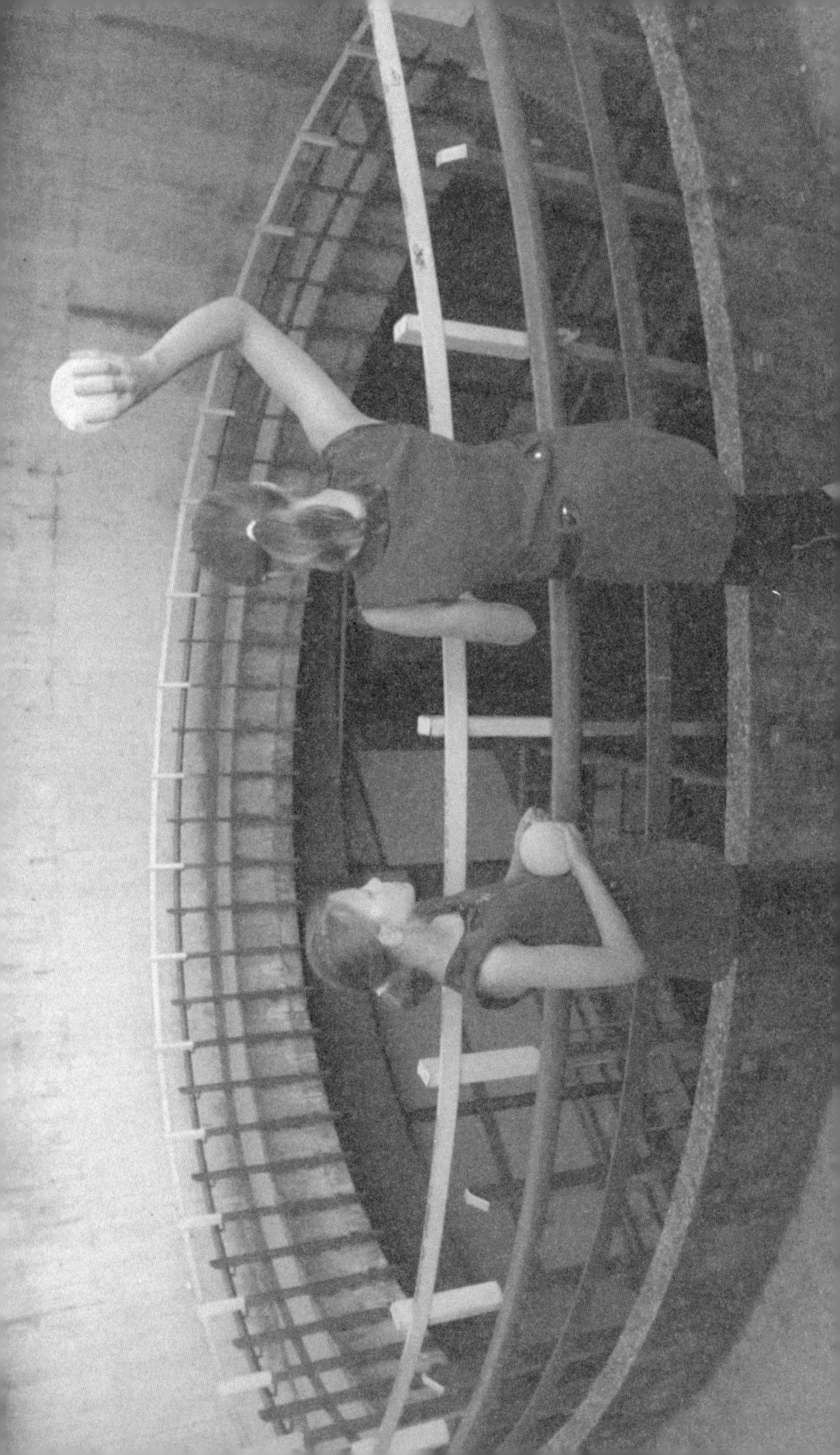

STELLA: The persuasion to follow a hedonistic conception of life and thus to be good consumerists.

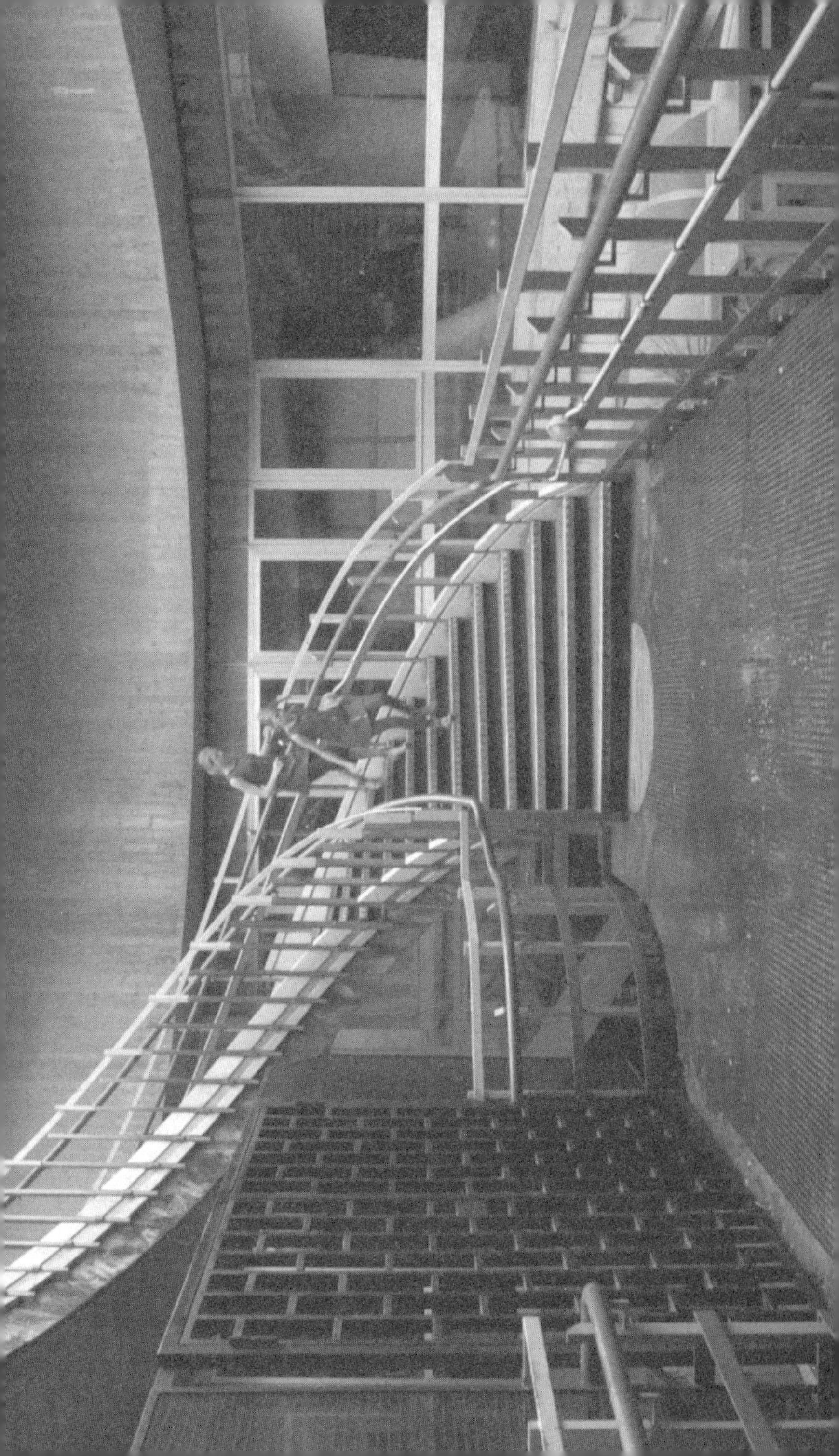

STELLA: Nothing forces you to observe things like making a movie.

LUCIE: The writer's look of a rural or urban landscape may exclude all sorts of things, focusing only on the exciting and important ones.

STELLA: The director's look, of the same landscape, instead must be aware, almost listing them, of all things therein.

LUCIE: While for a writer things are destined to become words, therefore symbols, in a filmmaker's work things remain things.

STELLA: Verbal signs are therefore symbolic and conventional, while in film signs are things themselves, in their materiality and their reality.

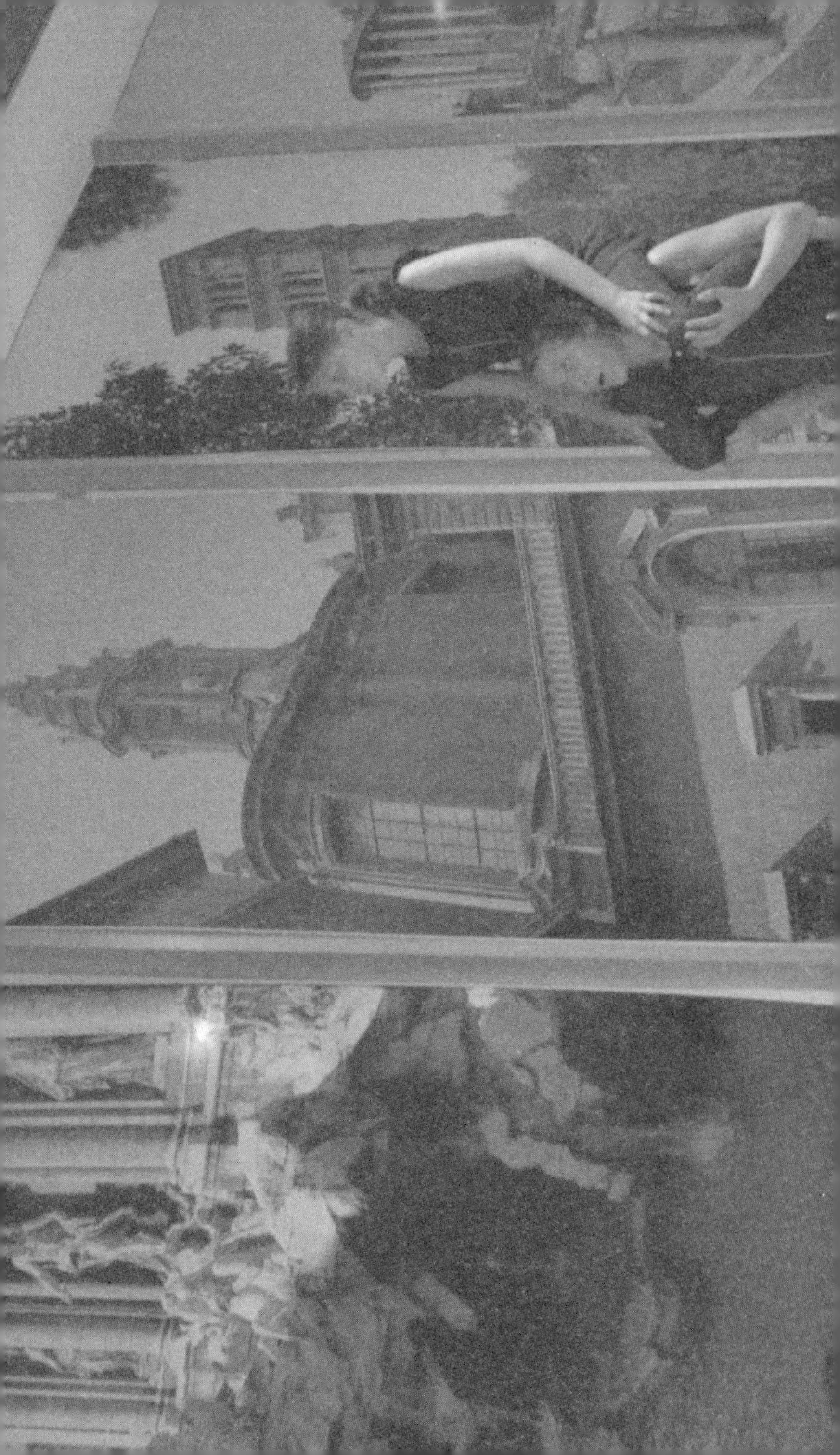

STELLA: Nowadays the first duty of intellectuals would be to teach people not to listen to the linguistic monstrosities of those in power, to scream at every word they say, with disgust and condemnation.

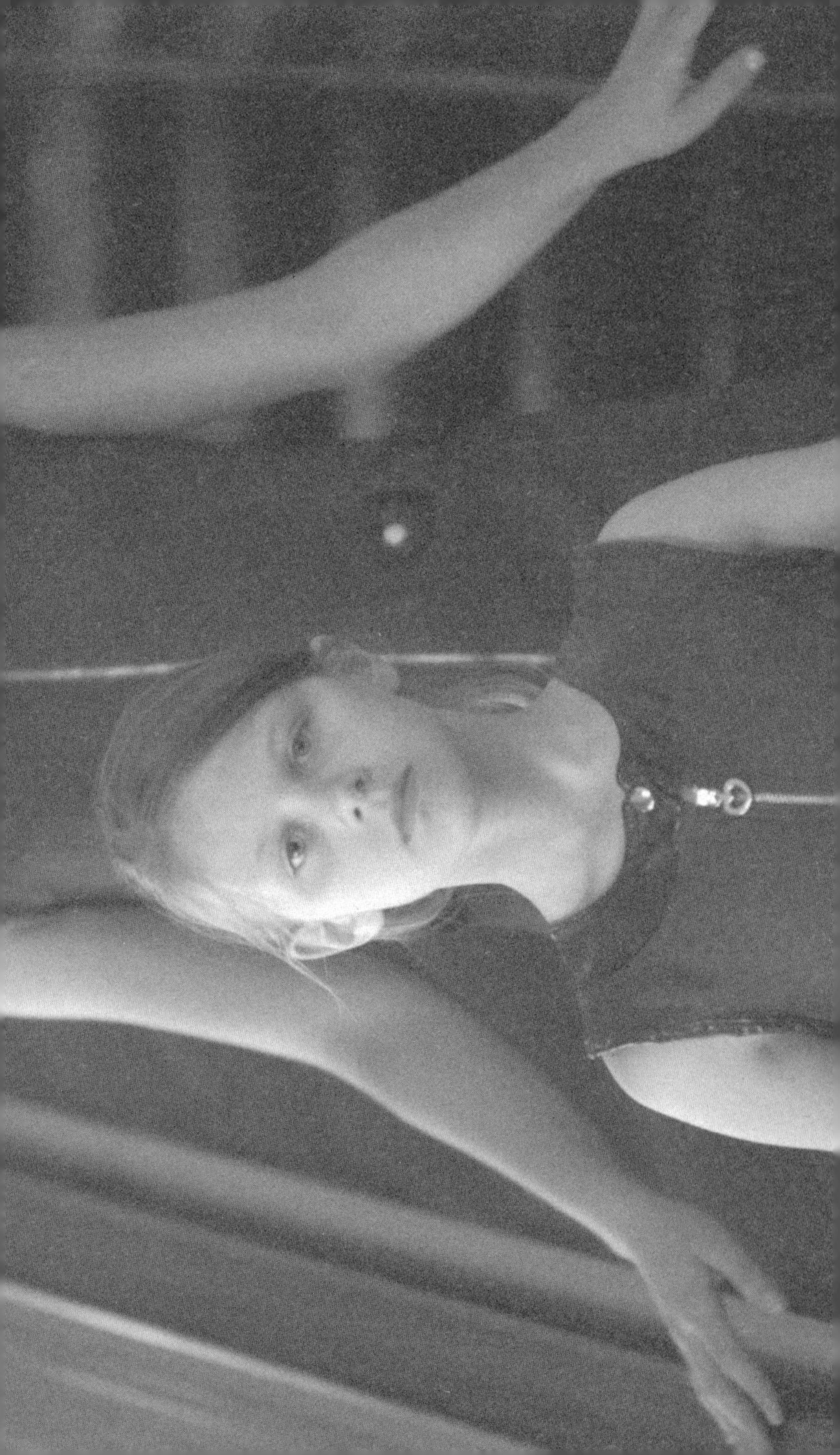

LUCIE: I don't know one single example or case of real tolerance. To tolerate someone is the same as condemning them. Tolerance is actually a form of more sophisticated condemnation.

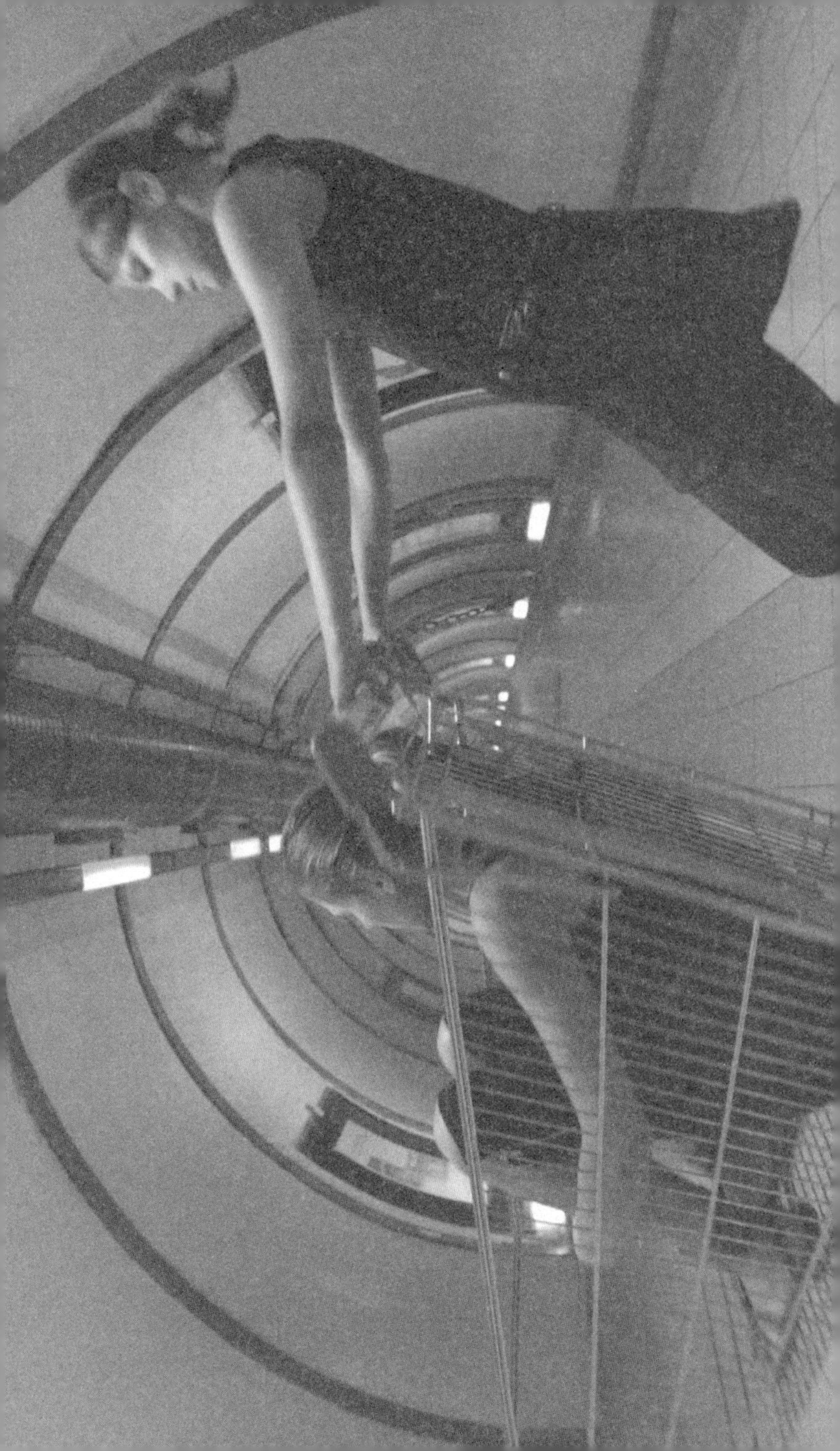

STELLA: School is the cultural organization that completely uneducated you, and makes you look like a poor idiot to me, humiliated, even degraded, unable to understand, trapped in a vice of mental weakness, which, besides, puts you in distress.

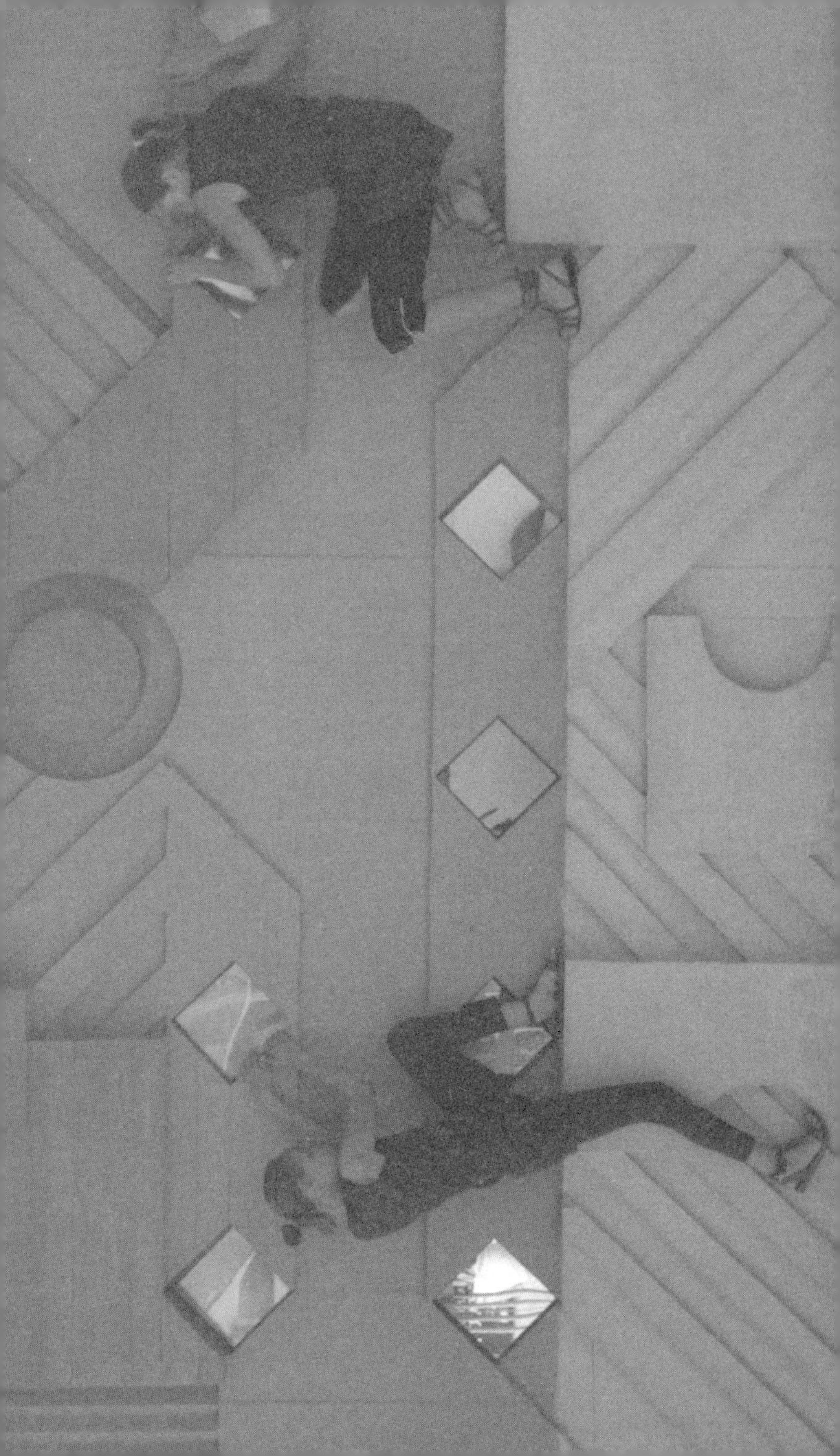

LUCIE: So instead of dedicating this pedagogical essay for a girl to Rousseau's monstrous shadow, we will dedicate it to the disdainful shadow of De Sade.

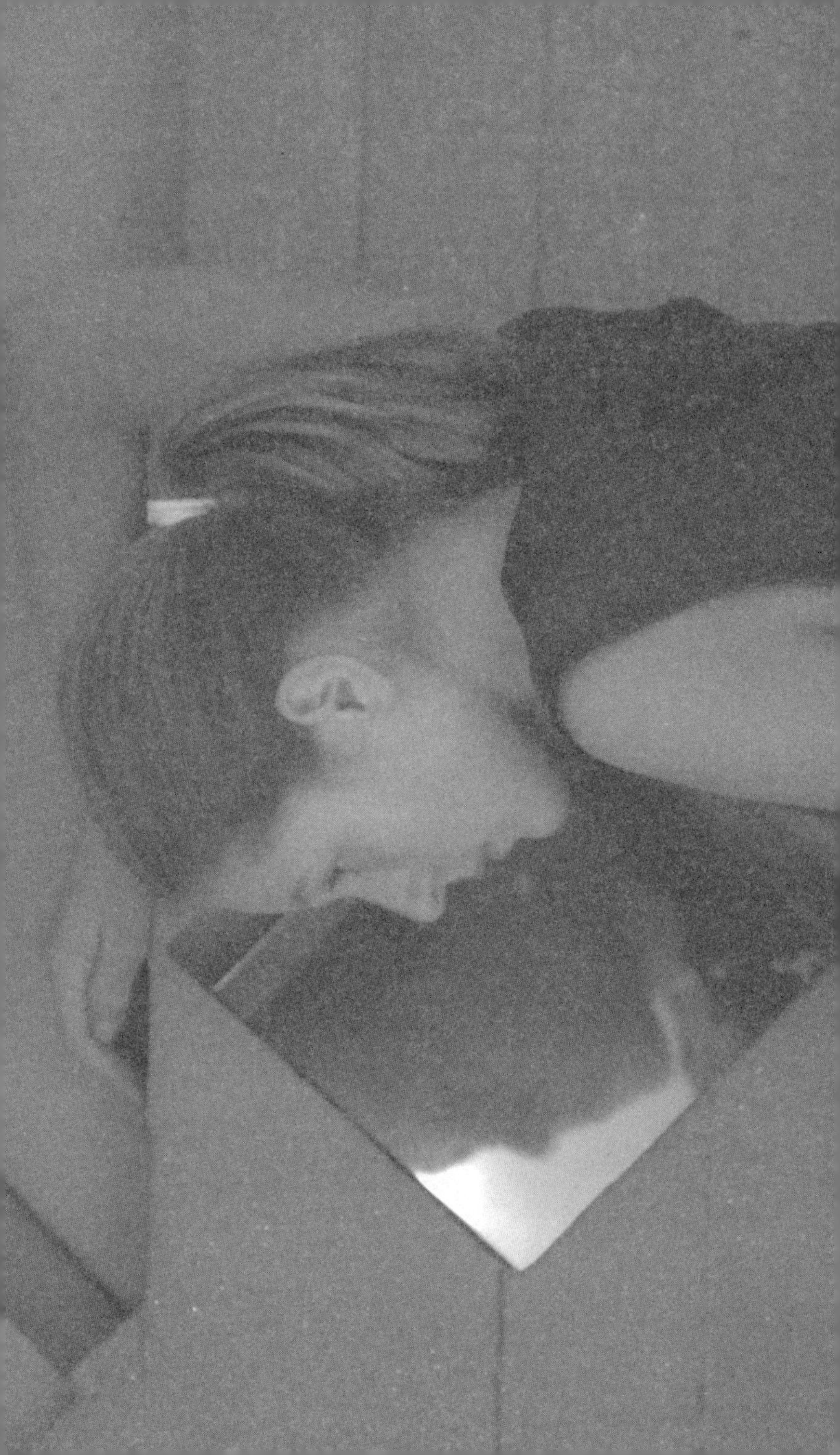

LUCIE: The first image of my life is a white, transparent tent hanging almost still from a window overlooking a pretty sad and dark alley. This tent terrifies and anguishes me: it is not something threatening or disturbing, but something cosmic.

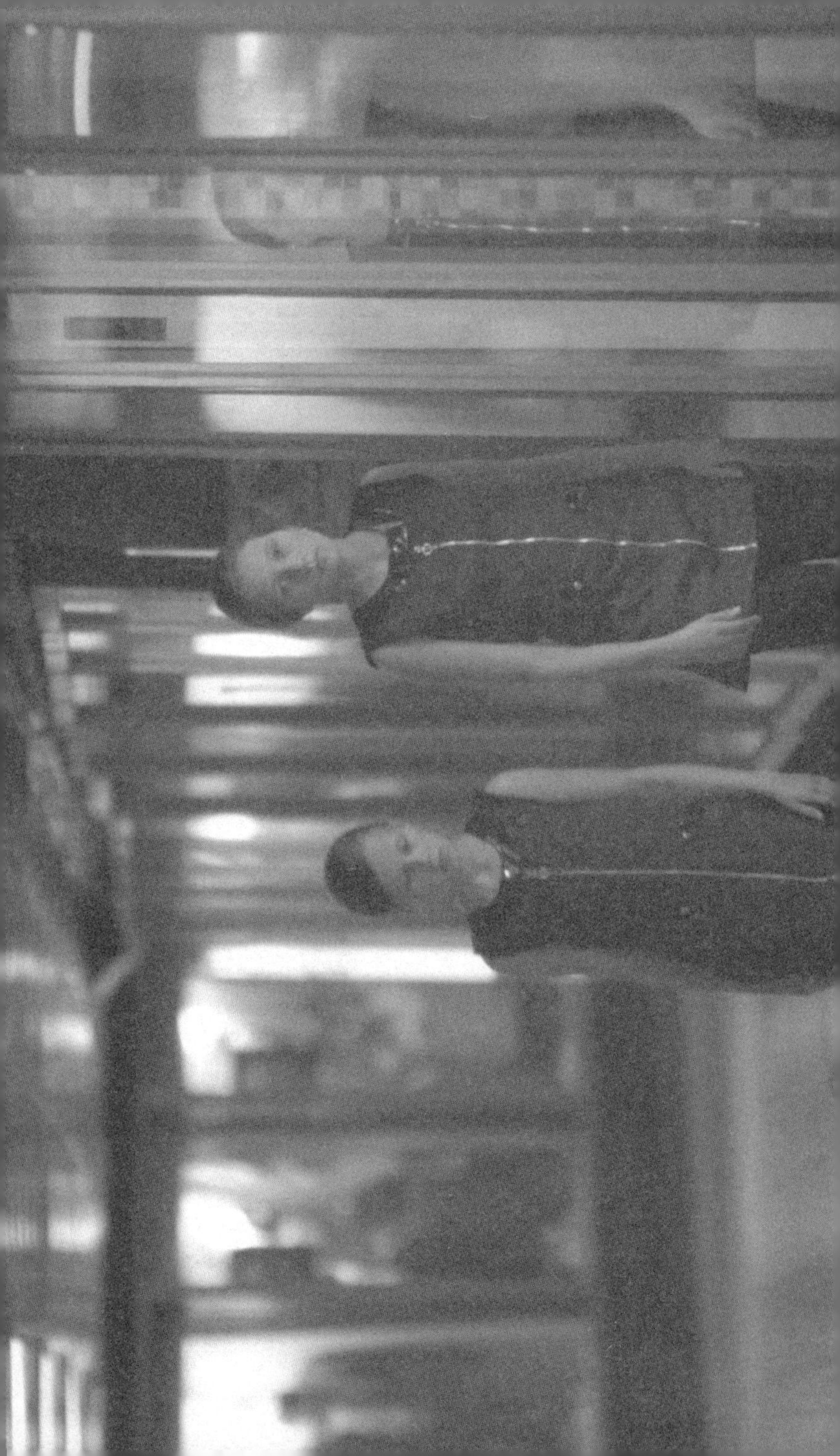

LUCIE: The education given to a girl through objects, things, physical reality, in other words through the material phenomena of her social status, makes that girl what she physically is, and what she will be for her whole life. To be educated is her own flesh as a representation of her spirit.

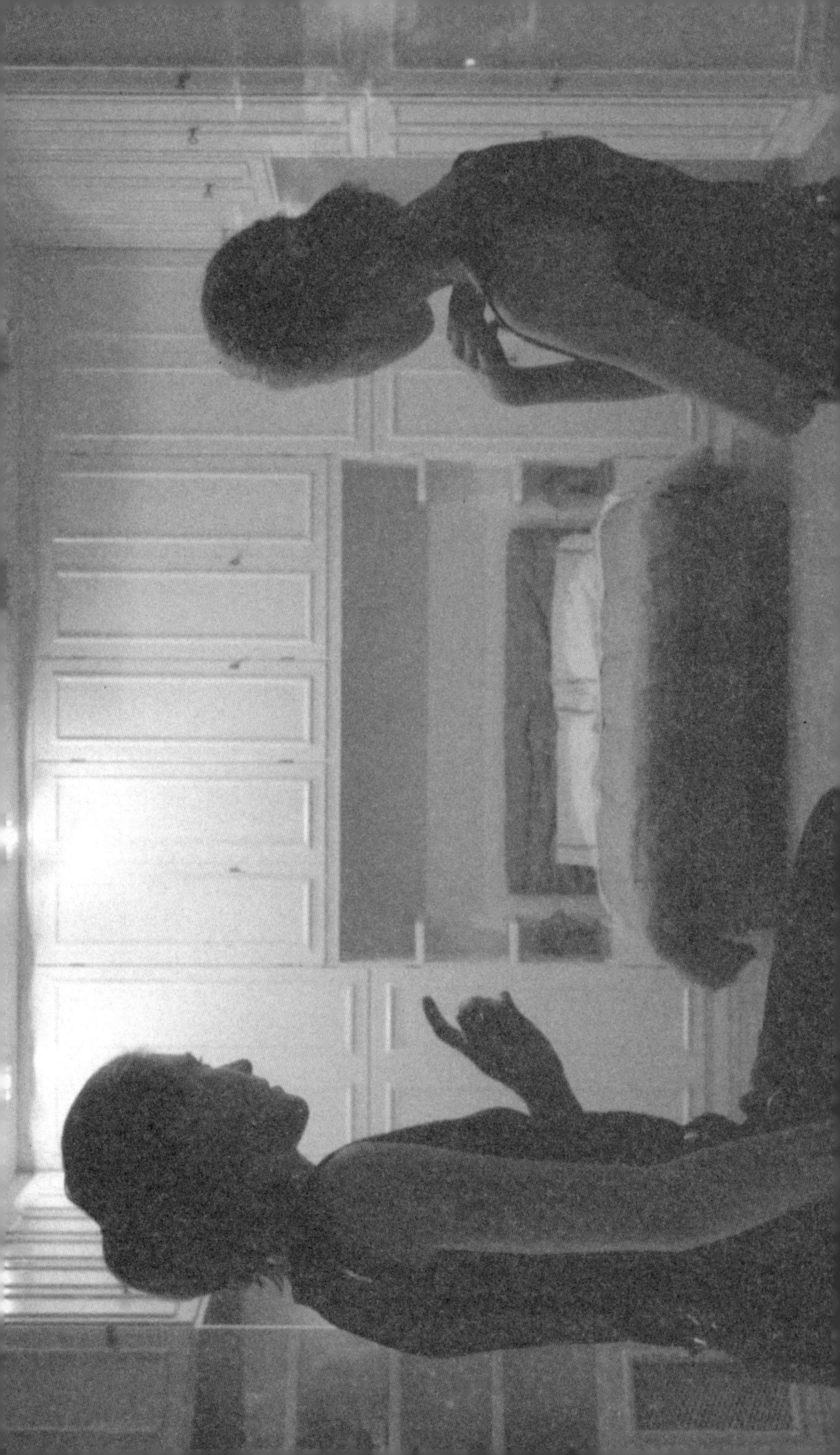

STELLA: I will first describe those girls that can approximately be called "Obedient." Their first feature is the unconscious feeling that their arrival into the world was particularly undesired, they feel dependent and unwanted. This increases enormously their anxiety for normality, their total and unconditional acceptance of the masses, their will not to look different nor even slightly distinct.

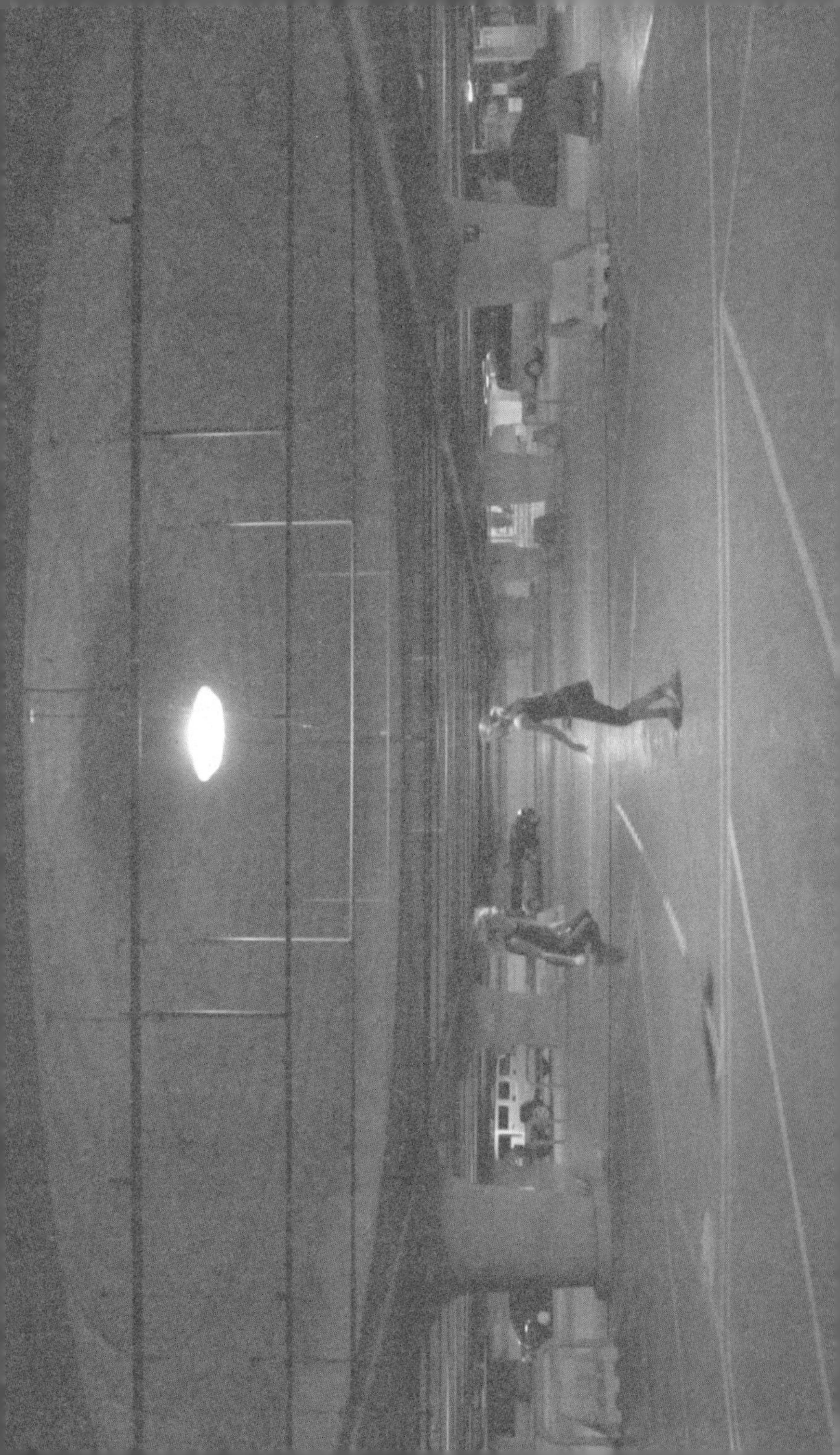

LUCIE: Thus what they first teach you is to live conformism aggressively.

STELLA: They teach you renunciation. Renunciation: absolute routine, everyday, surrender. Do not be afraid to be ridiculous, don't give up anything. Being good is the first commandment of consumer power, in the mental and behavioural universe in which I was born. Good at being happy. The hedonism of a consumer. The result is that happiness is completely false, while immediate unhappiness spreads more and more. Then I will describe the girls that can be approximately called "disobedient," that is, the few surviving real extremists, the misfits, the deviant, and finally, extremely rare, the "educated."

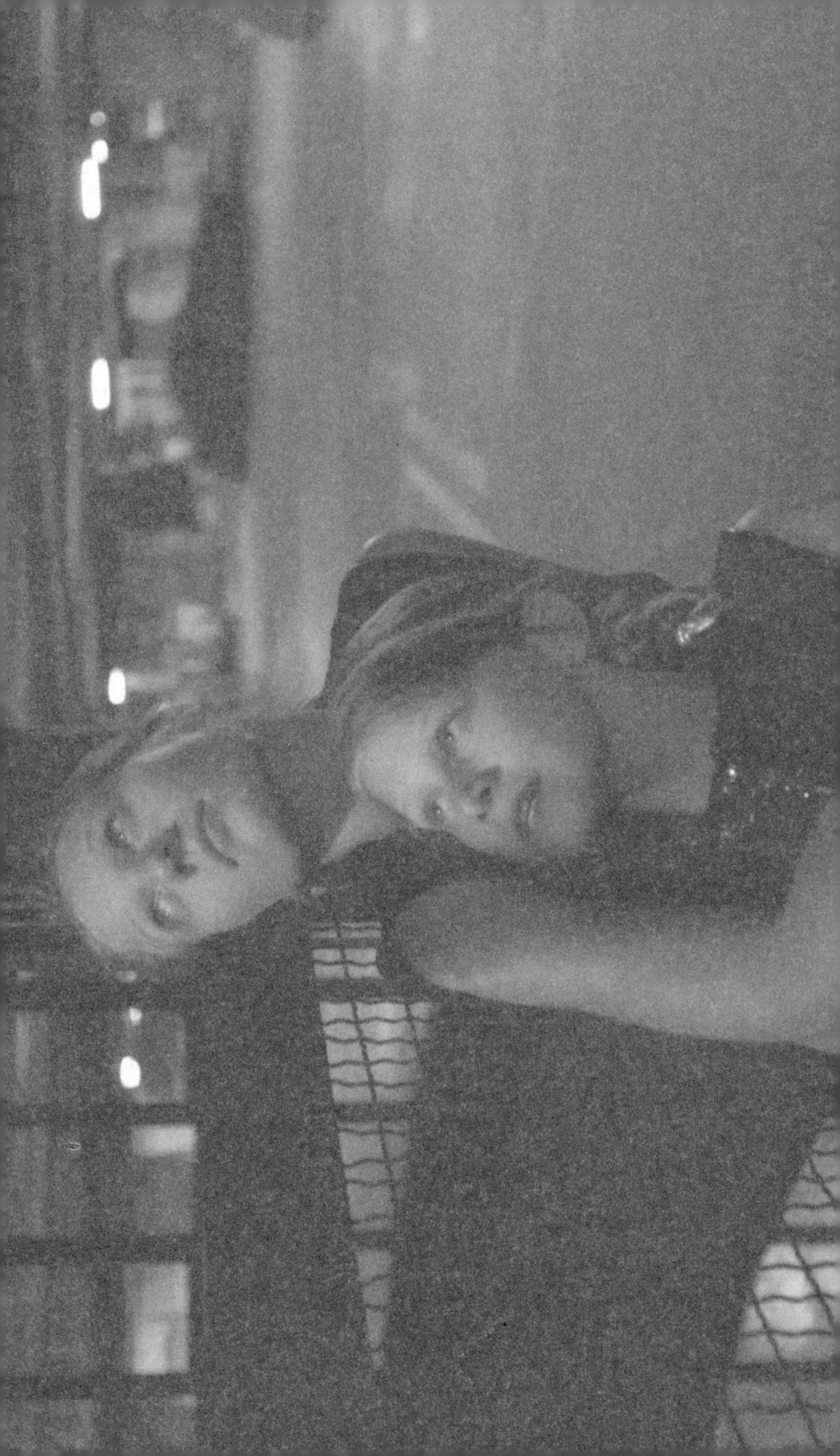

The Crisis in Education

2011
6' 50", color, sound, HD
Language: French, English subtitles
Format of distribution 16/9

Textual reference:
Hannah Arendt, "La crise de l'éducation" in *La crise de la culture*, Collection folio essais, Paris: 2008 [1961], pp. 223–252

LUCIE: A crisis in education would at any time give rise to serious concern even if it did not reflect, as in the present instance it does, a more general crisis and instability in modern society. For education belongs among the most elementary and necessary activities of human society, which never remains as it is but continuously renews itself through birth, through the arrival of new human beings.

STELLA: Human parents have not only summoned their children into life through conception and birth, they have simultaneously introduced them into a world. In education they assume responsibility for both the life and the development of the child and for the continuance of the world.

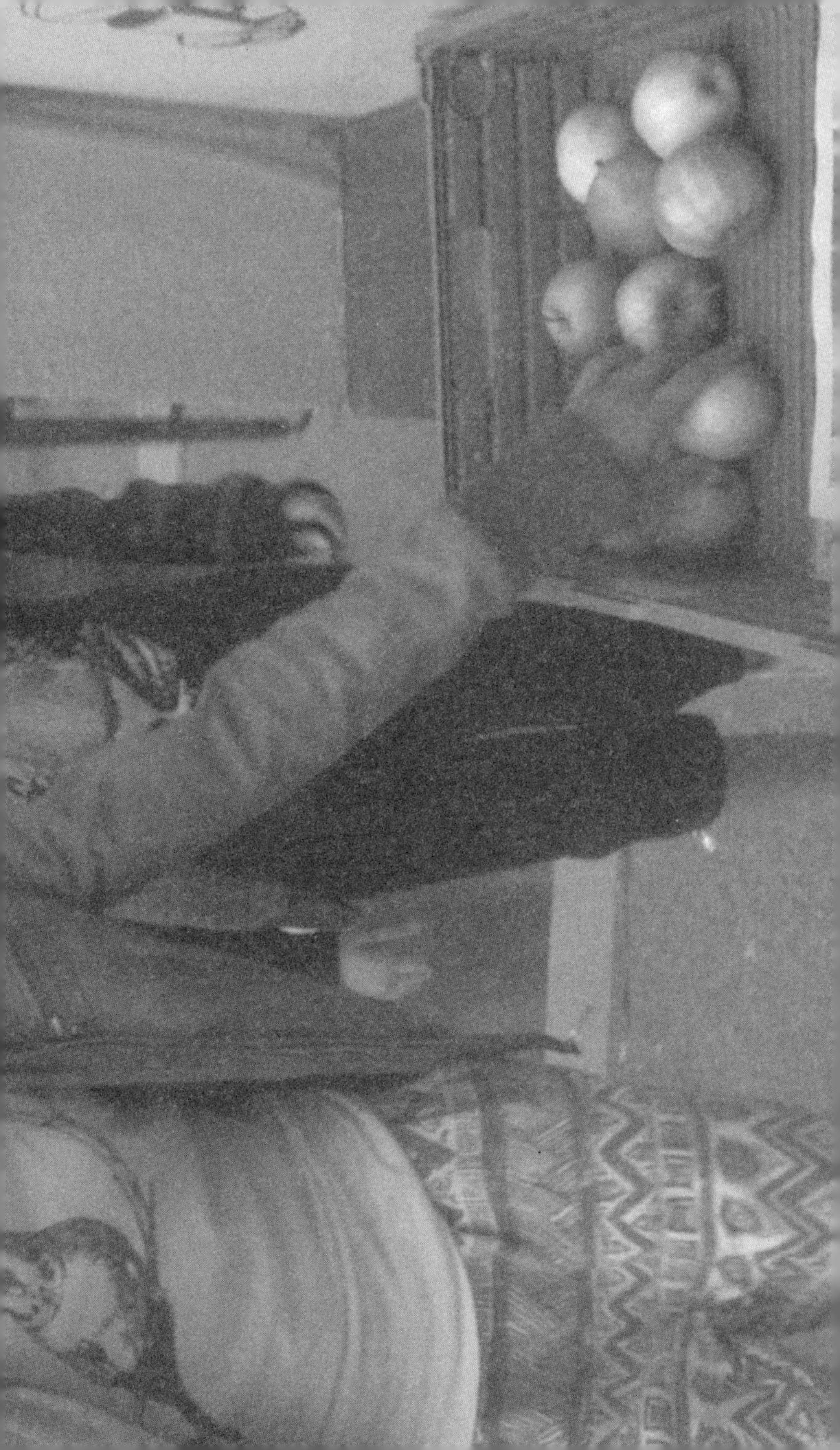

LUCIE: These two responsibilities do not by any means coincide; they may indeed come into conflict with each other. The responsibility for the development of the child turns in a certain sense against the world: the child requires special protection and care so that nothing destructive may happen to him from the world.

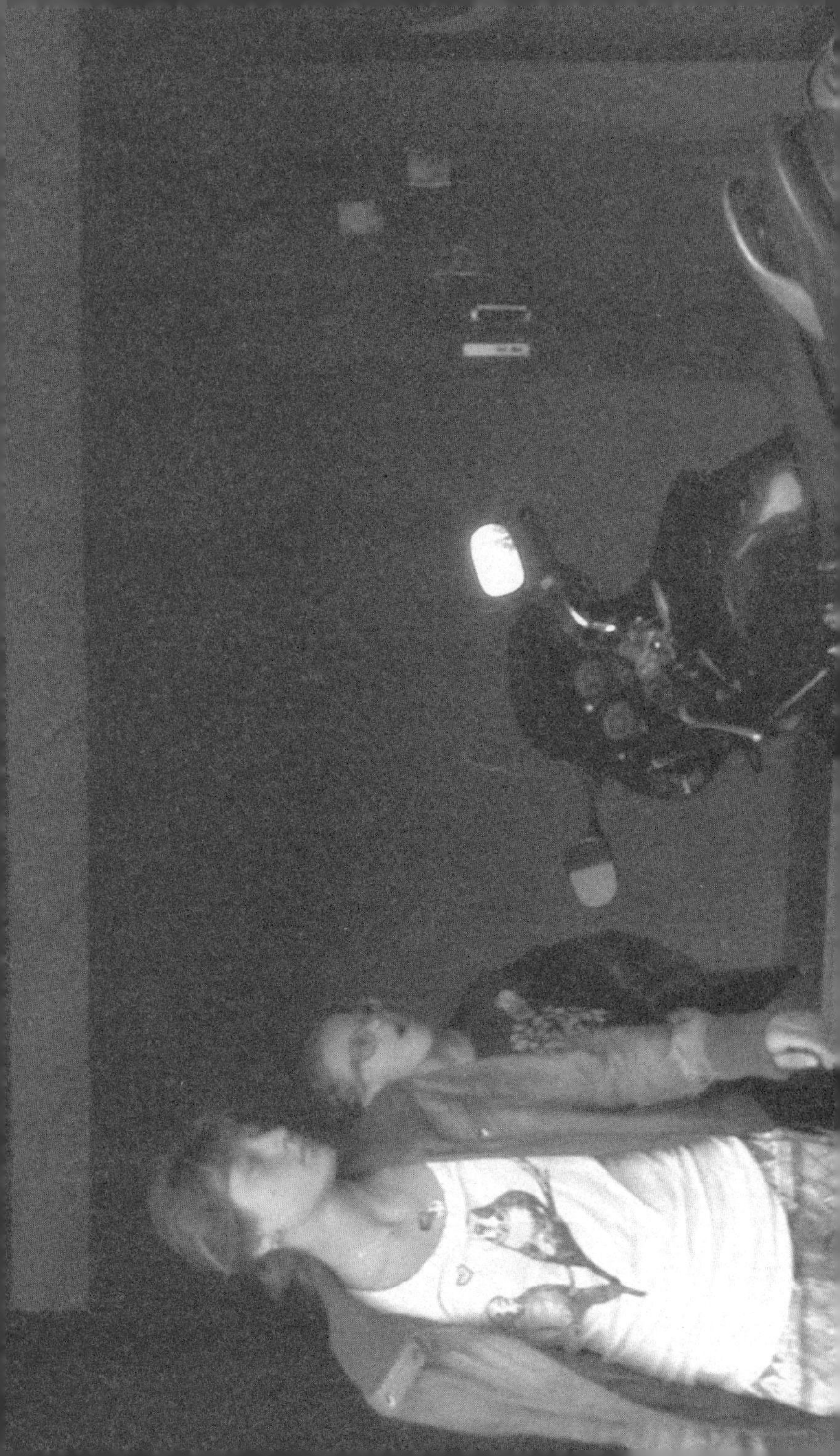

STELLA: But the world, too, needs protection to keep it from being overrun and destroyed by the onslaught of the new that bursts upon it with each new generation.

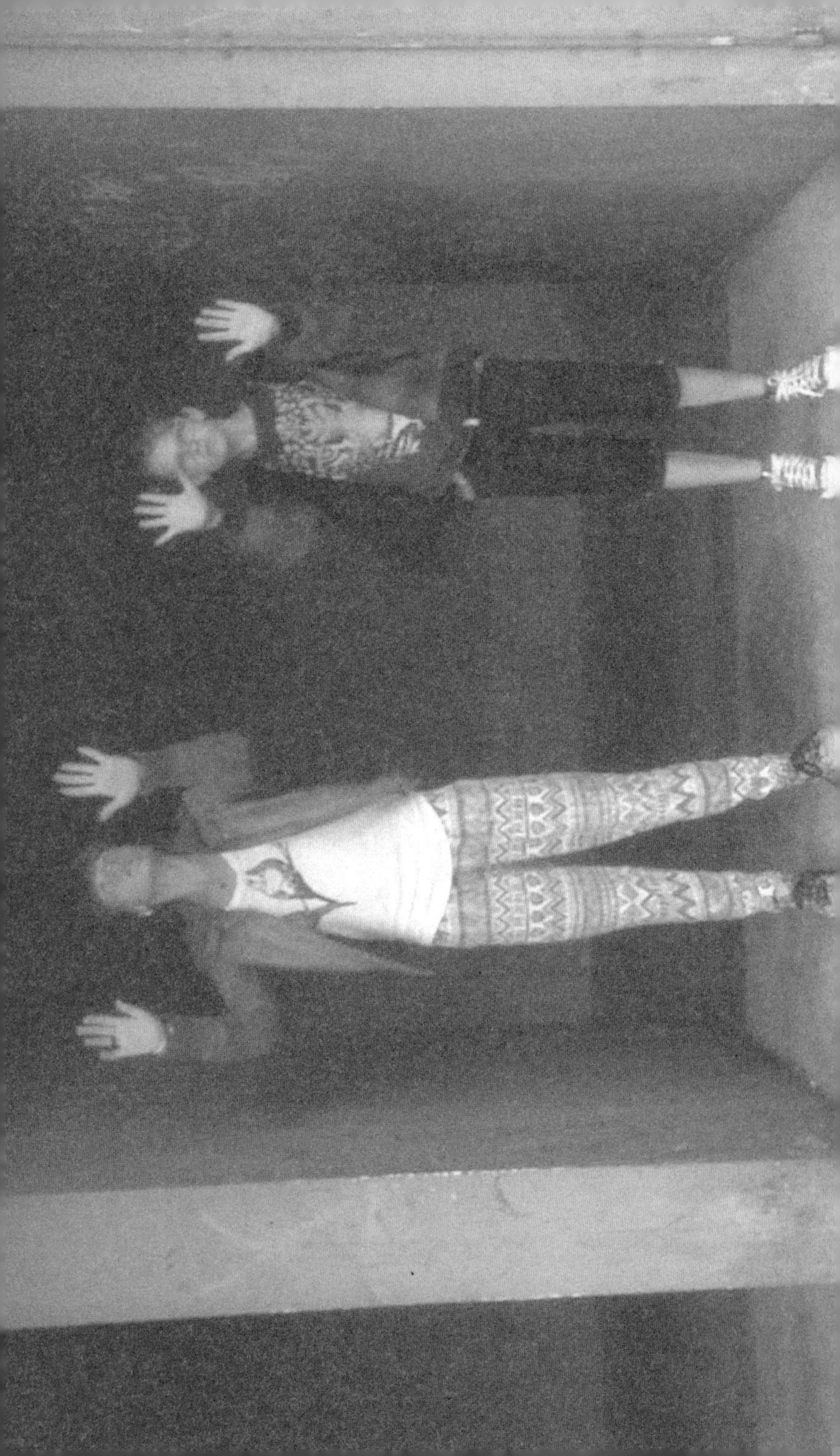

LUCIE: Therefore by being emancipated from the authority of adults the child has not been freed but has been subjected to a much more terrifying and truly tyrannical authority, the tyranny of the majority.

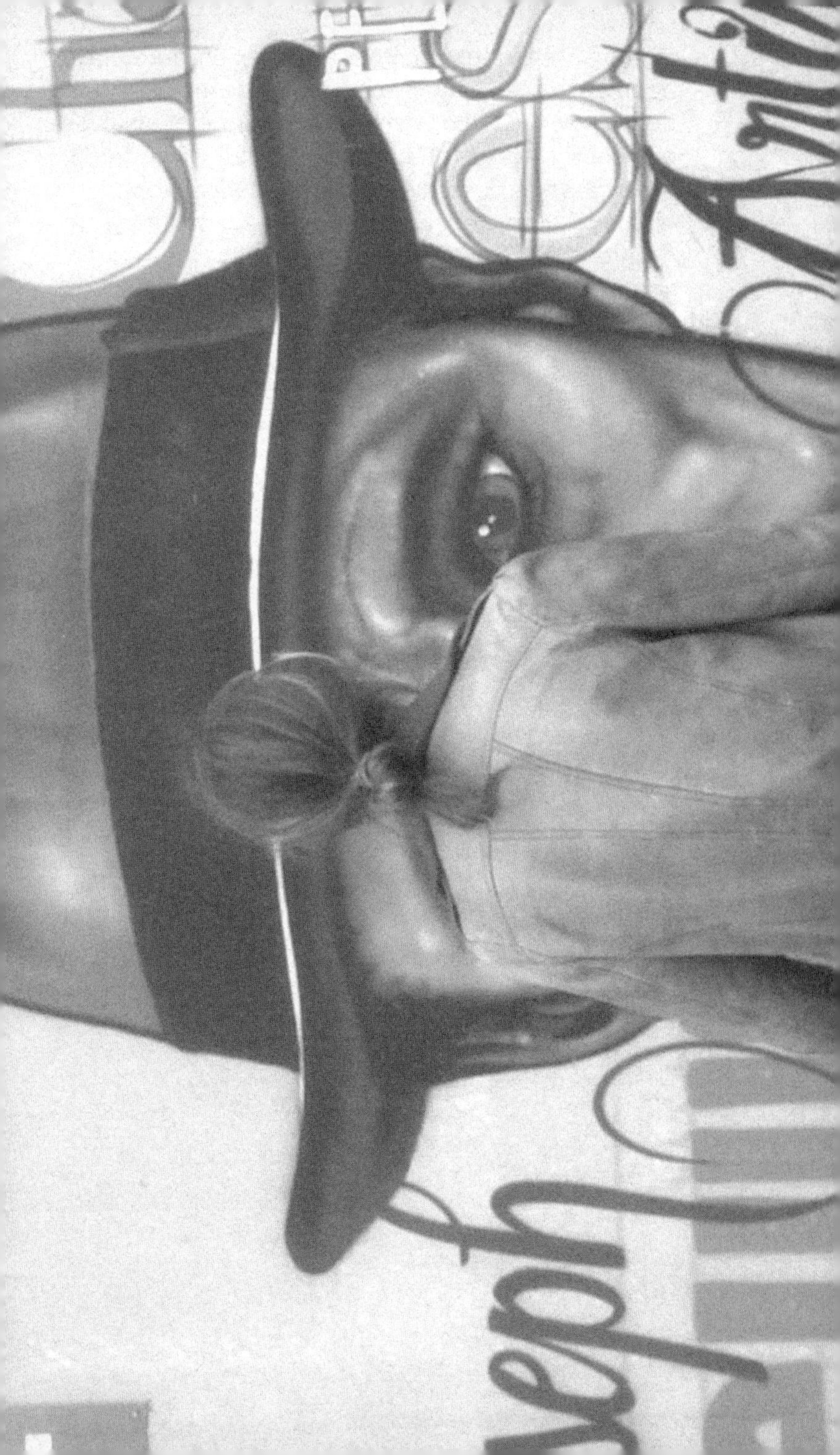

STELLA: In any case, the result is that the children have been so to speak banished from the world of grown-ups. They are either thrown back upon themselves or handed over to the tyranny of their own group, against which, because of its numerical superiority, they cannot rebel, with which because they are children, they cannot reason, and which they cannot flee to any other world because the world of adults is barred to them.

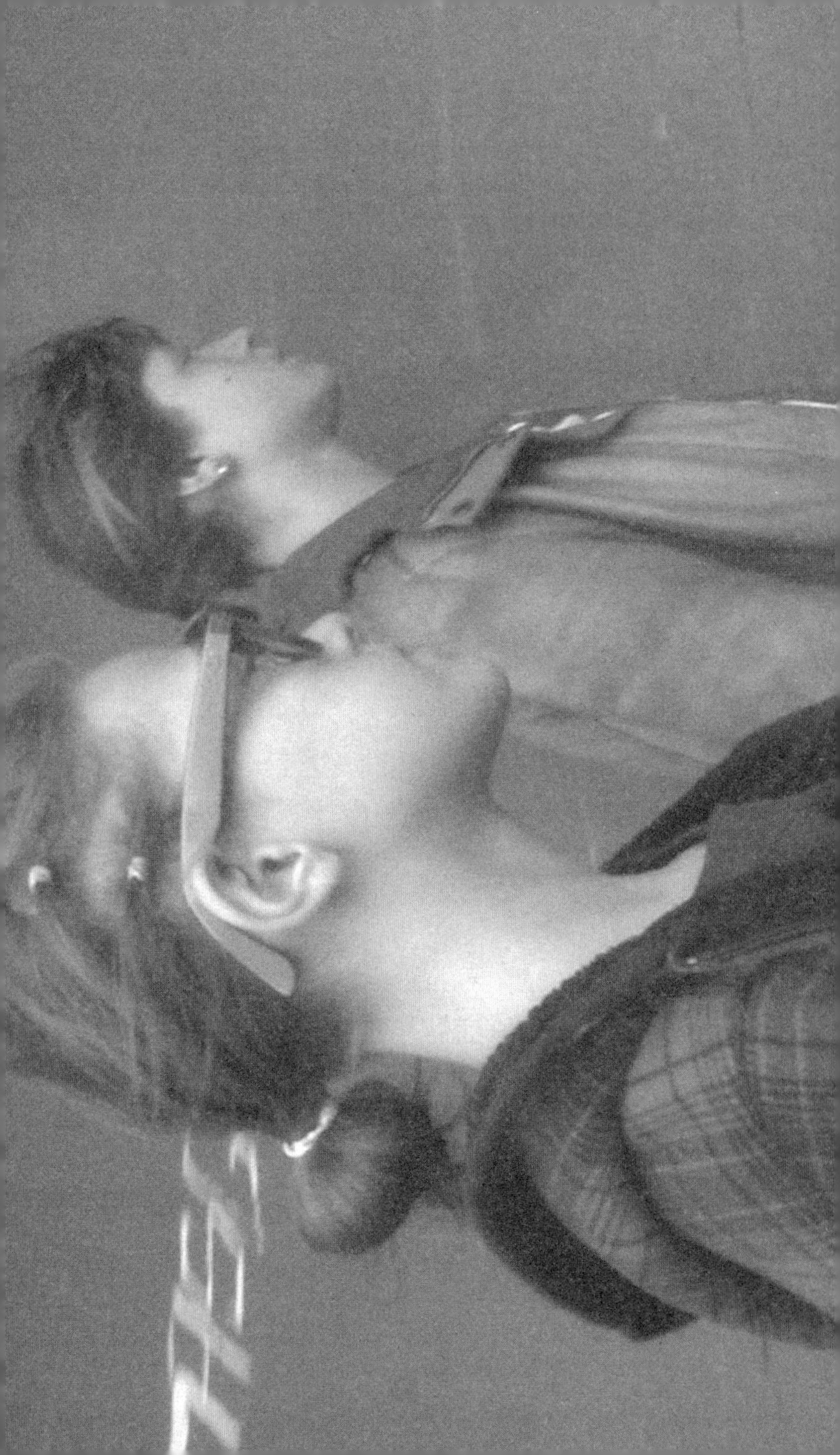

LUCIE: The reaction of the children to this pressure tends to be either conformism or juvenile delinquency, and is frequently a mixture of both.

STELLA: It seems to me that conservatism, in the sense of conservation, is of the essence of educational activity, whose task is always to cherish and protect the child against the world, the world against the child, the new against the old, the old against the new.

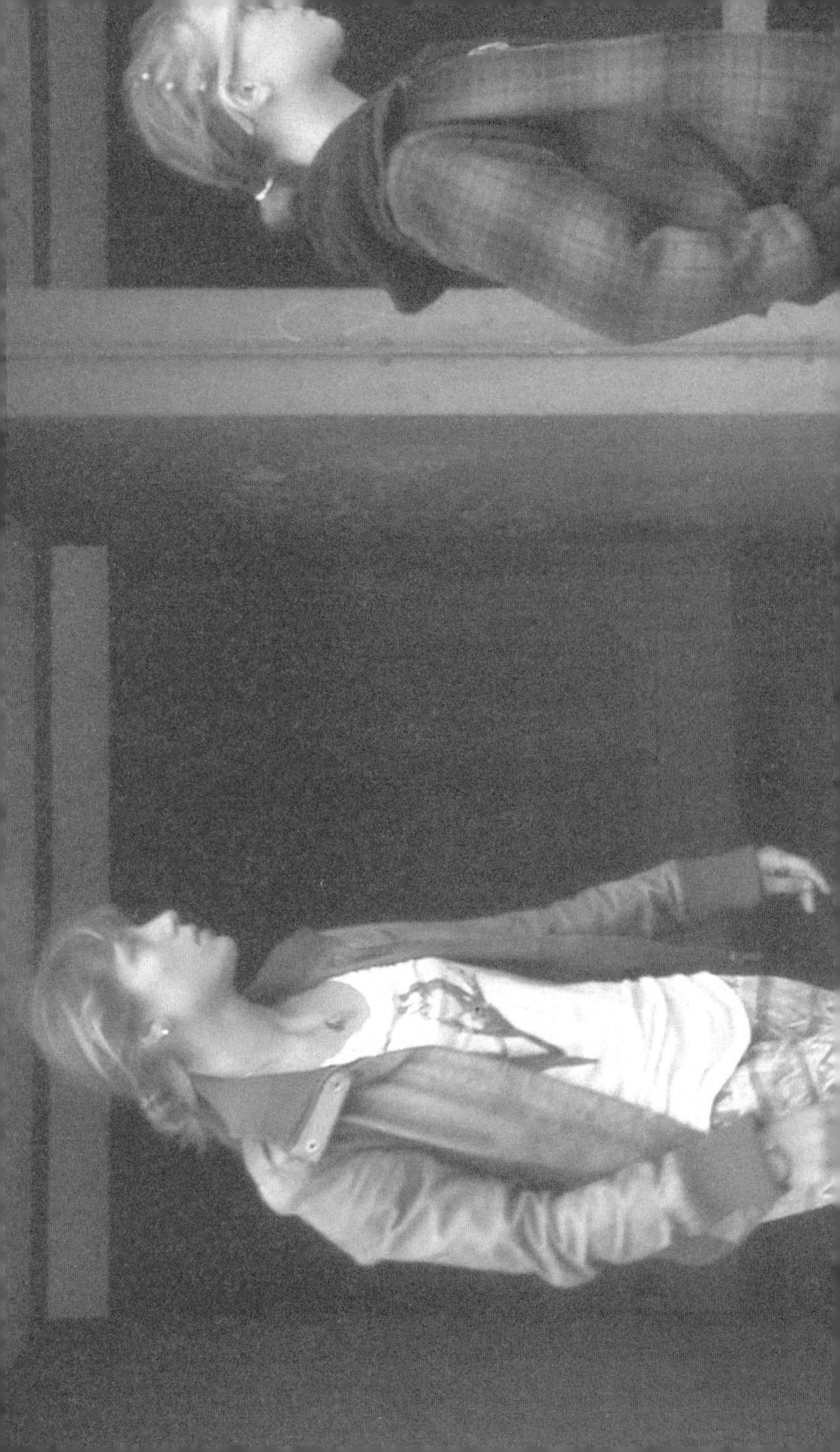

LUCIE: Basically we are always educating for a world that is or is becoming out of joint, for this is the basic human situation, in which the world is created by mortal hands to serve mortals for a limited time as home.

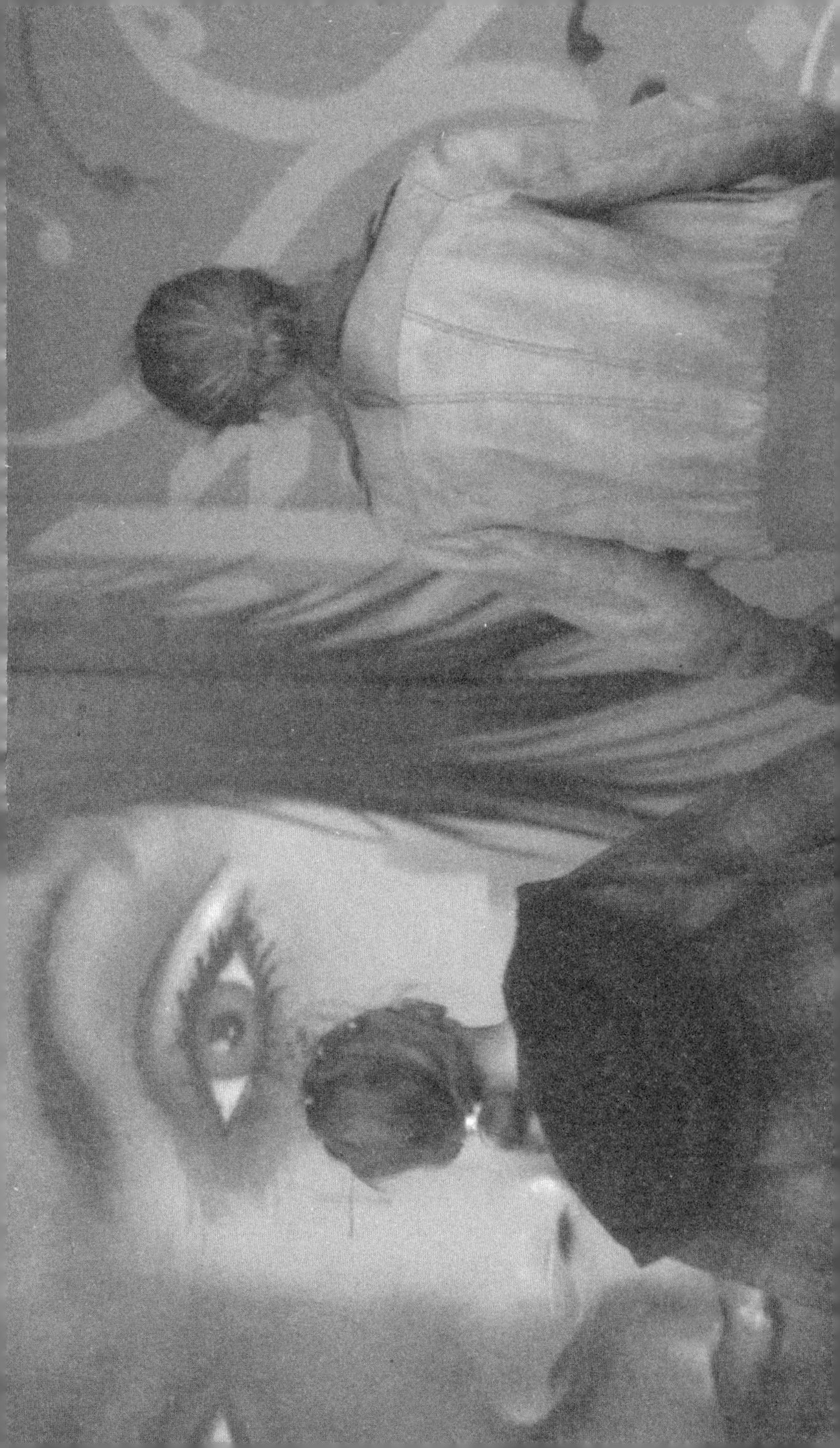

STELLA: Exactly for the sake of what is new and revolutionary in every child, education must be conservative; it must preserve this newness and introduce it as a new thing into an old world, which, however revolutionary its actions may be, is always, from the standpoint of the next generation, superannuated and close to destruction.

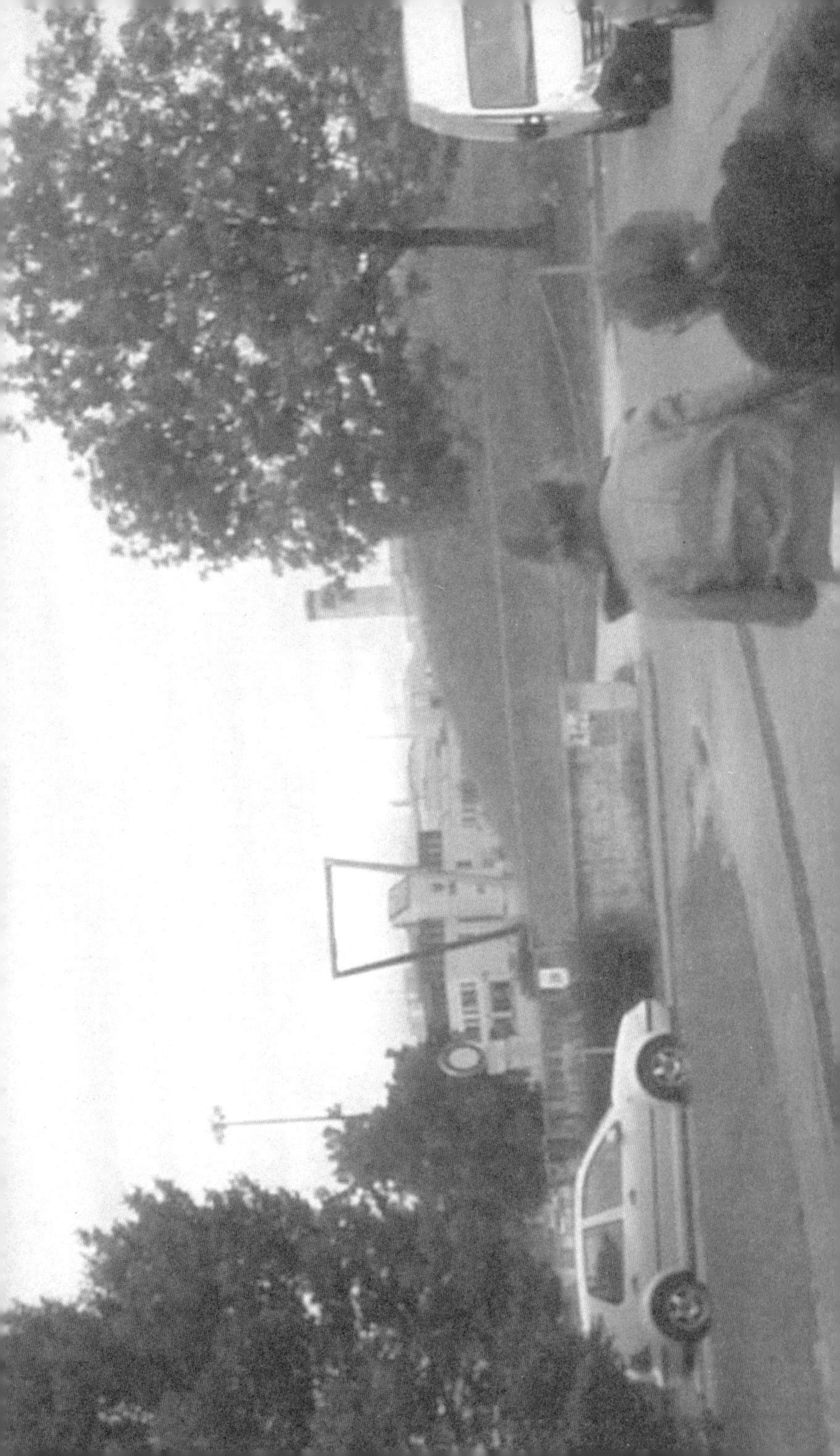

A crisis in education would at any time give rise to serious concern even if it did not reflect, as in the present instance it does, a more general crisis and instability in modern society. For education belongs among the most elementary and necessary activities of human society, which never remains as it is but continuously renews itself through birth, through the arrival of new human beings.

[illegible?] parents have not only summoned them into life through conception and birth, they have simultaneously introduced them into a world. In education they assume responsibility for both, the life and development of the child and for the continuance of the world.

Education for Autonomy

2015
11' 50", color, sound, HD
Language: French, English subtitles
Format of distribution 16/9

Textual reference:
Theodor W. Adorno, “Erziehung–wozu?” [1966] in *Erziehung zur Mündigkeit*, Edition Suhrkamp, Berlin: 1971, pp. 105–119

LUCIE: You know the story about the centipede who was asked which leg moved after which?

STELLA: Which paralysed her so much she could not take a single step?

LUCIE: Something similar is taking place in the field of education.

STELLA: It's true that once, education as a concept had a certain substance.

STELLA: Today it's more random.

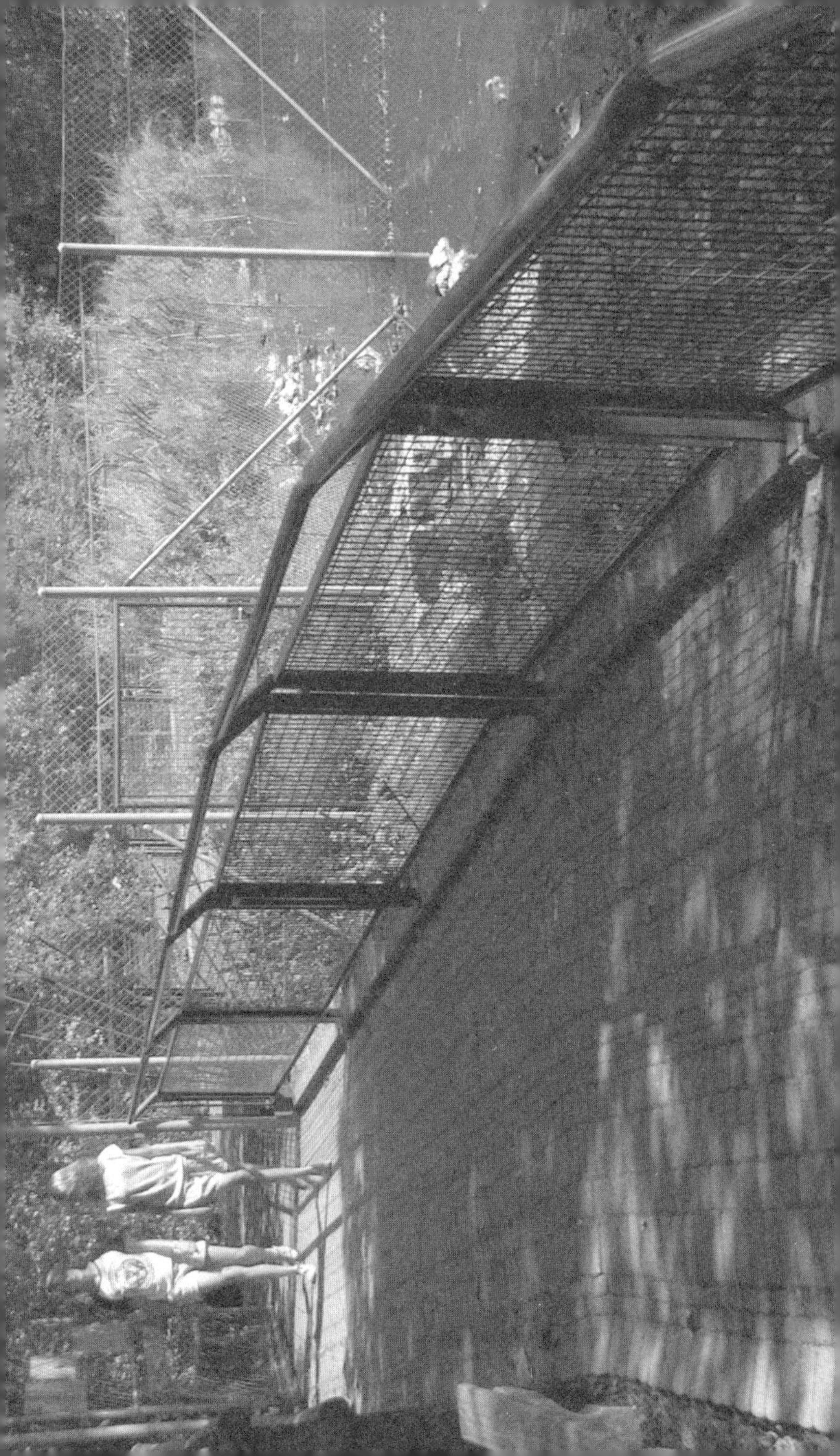

LUCIE: When the question is asked—"Education: for what purpose?"—once this "purpose" is lost, it can't be retrieved.

STELLA: It isn't possible to apply an objective to education from the outside.

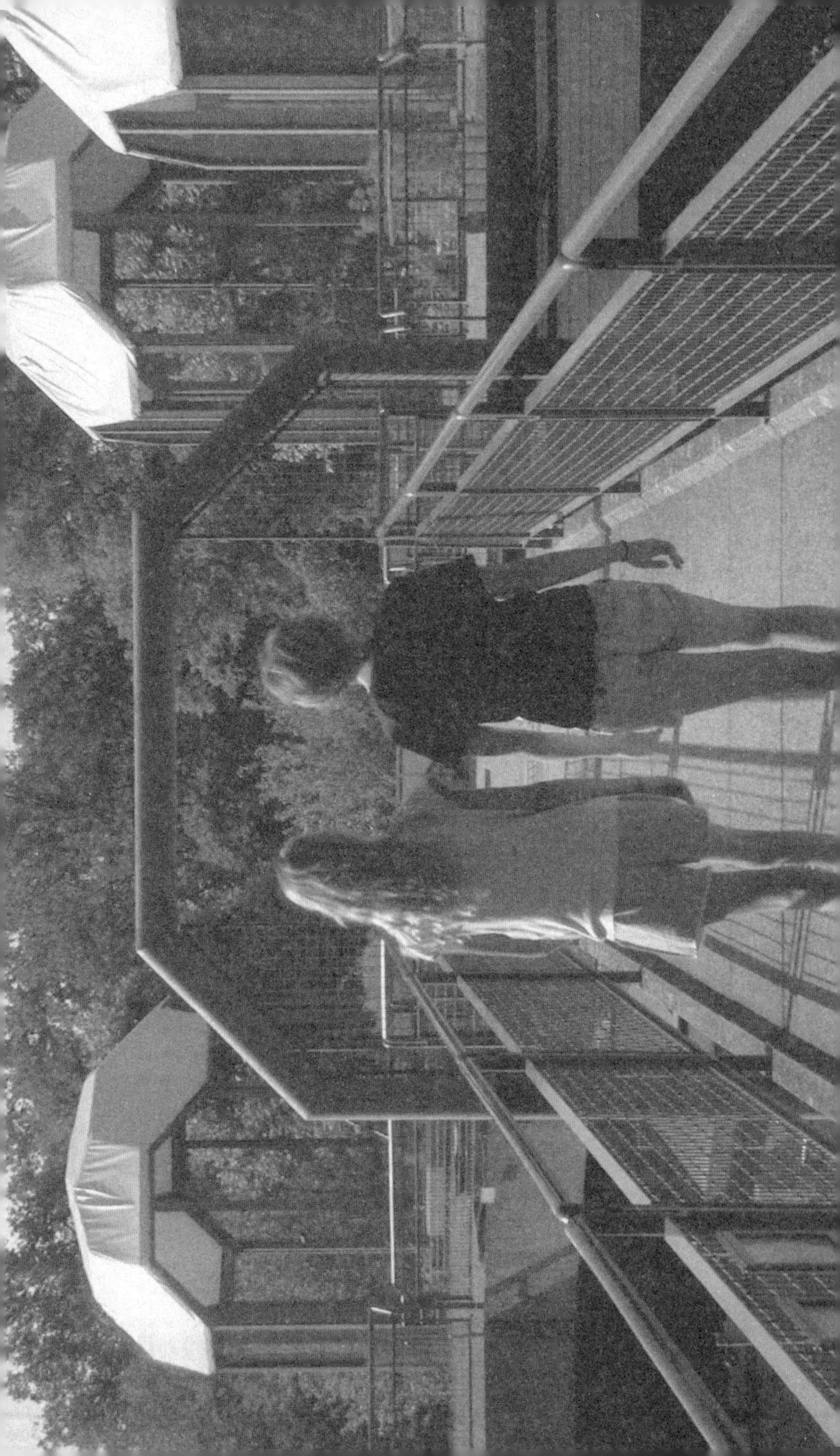

LUCIE: It's useless trying to discuss the previous state. The loss of innocence, so to speak. Obviously, it's lost for ever.

STELLA: Besides, the claim demanding the restoration of this state of innocence is clearly apparent when new models are invoked.

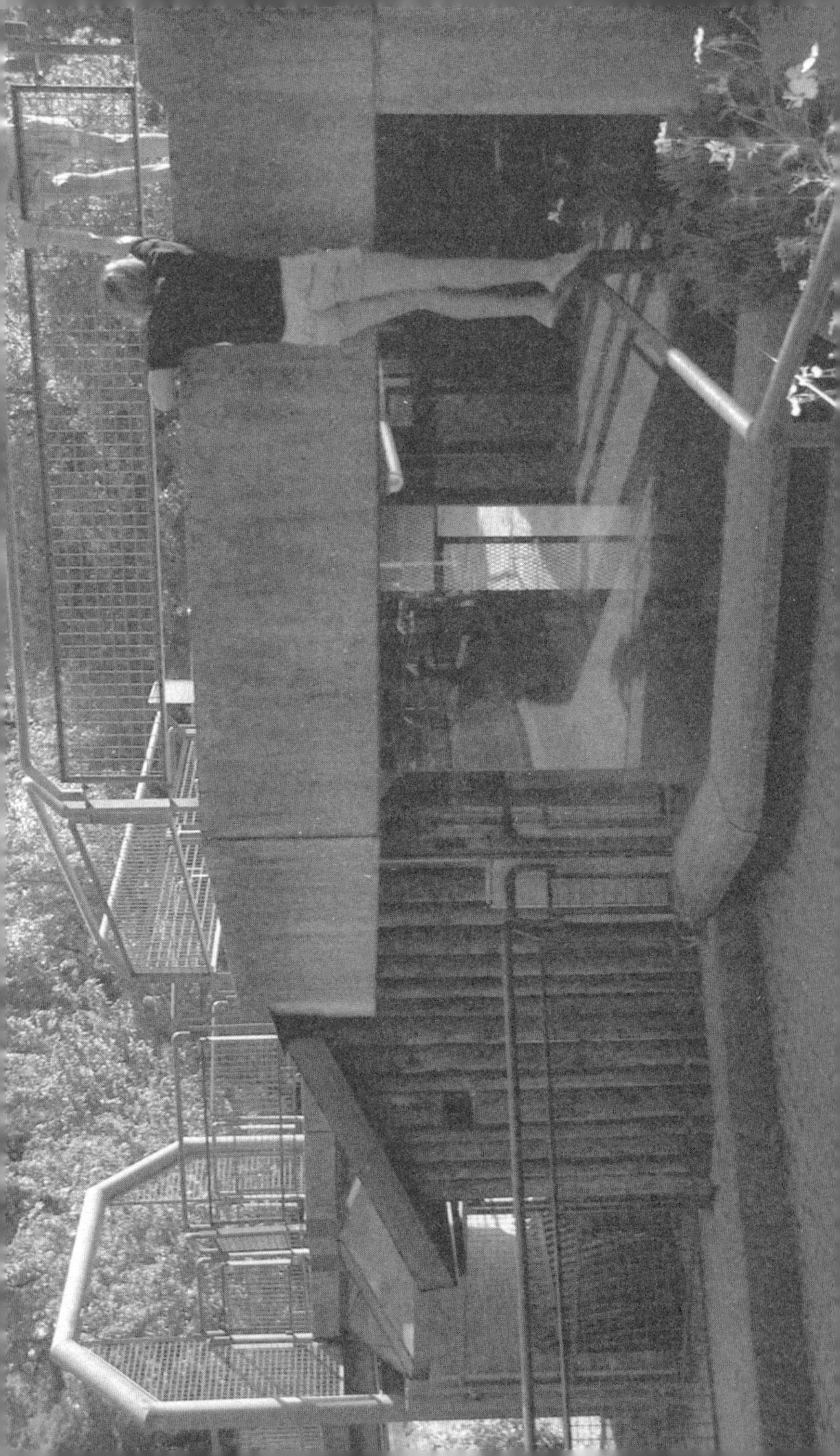

STELLA: This is where a decisive turning point is reached in modern teaching methods. These days, education should provide the means for knowing how to behave in the world, rather than transmitting some predetermined model.

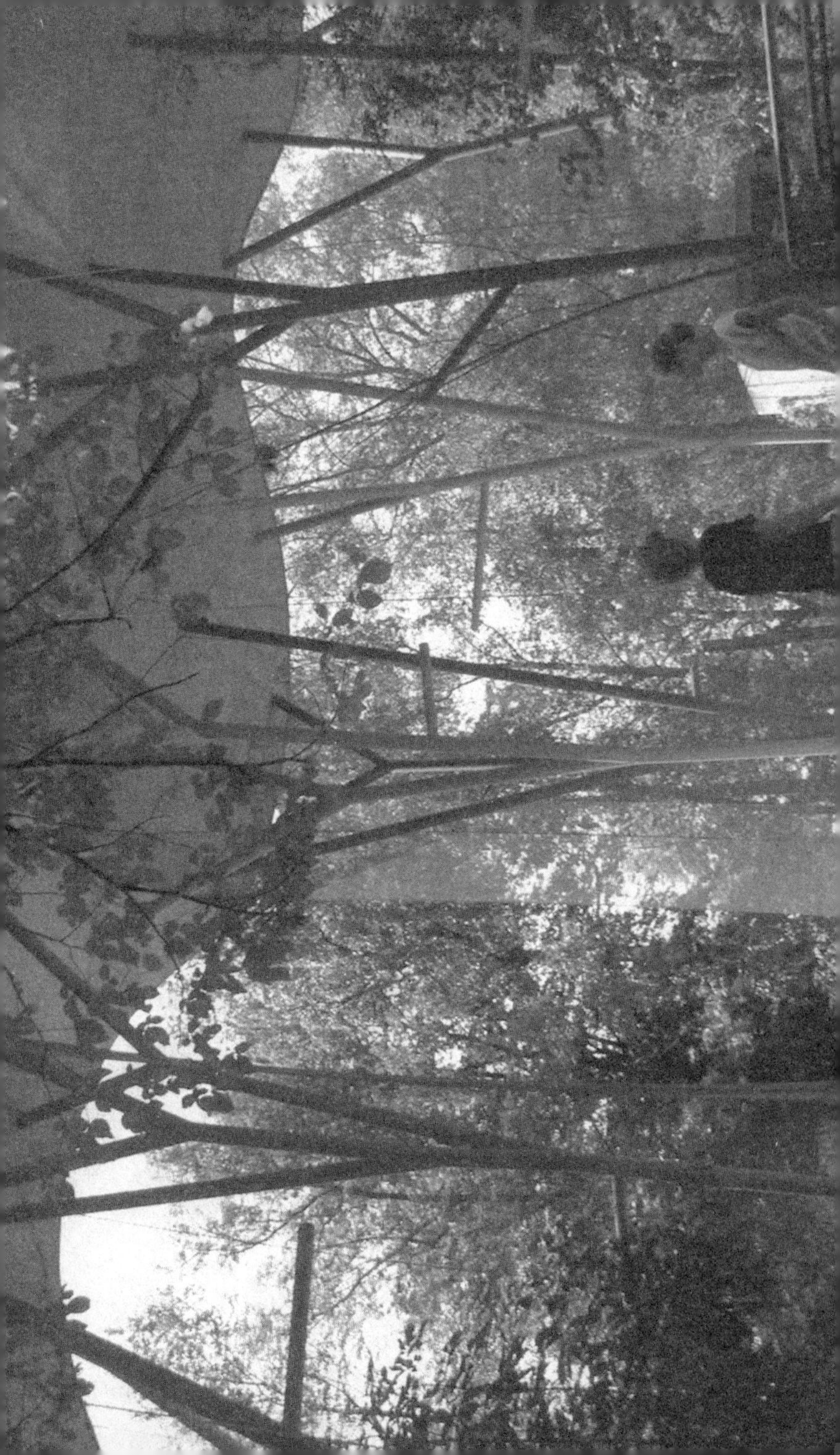

LUCIE: If you look at the transformation of social reality everything is speeding up all the time, and that requires flexibility on the part of the individual.

STELLA: As well as responsible and critical behaviour.

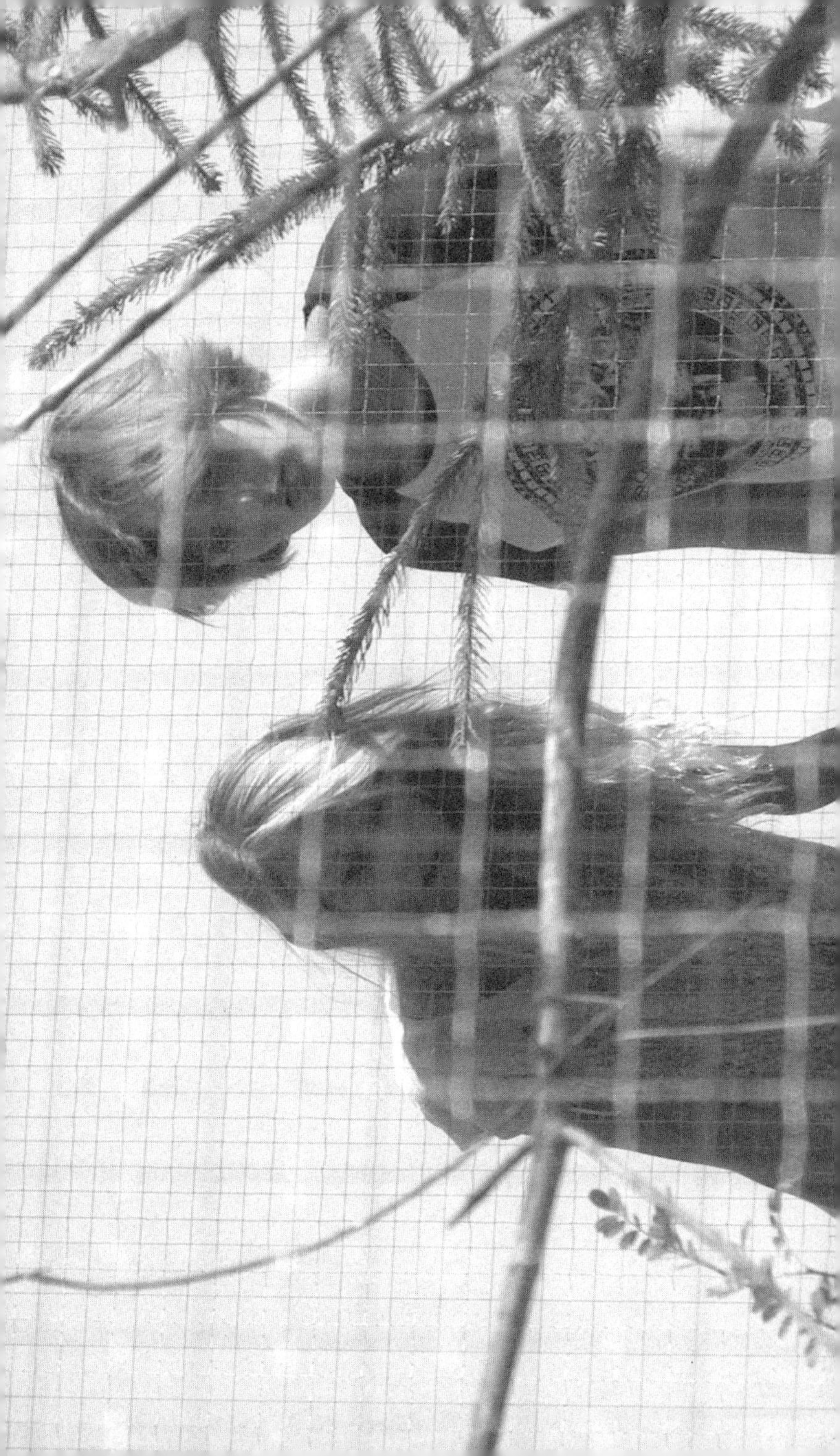

LUCIE: You wonder how anyone could feel they have the right to decide upon the finality of training for other people. This is contrary to the idea of an autonomous and responsible human being.

STELLA: Absolutely! We want humankind to become freed of its immaturity, for which it only has itself to blame.

LUCIE: For me, the purpose of education is to produce a genuine awareness. It does not involve any so-called "moulding" or shaping of a human being; we don't have the right to mould human beings from the outside.

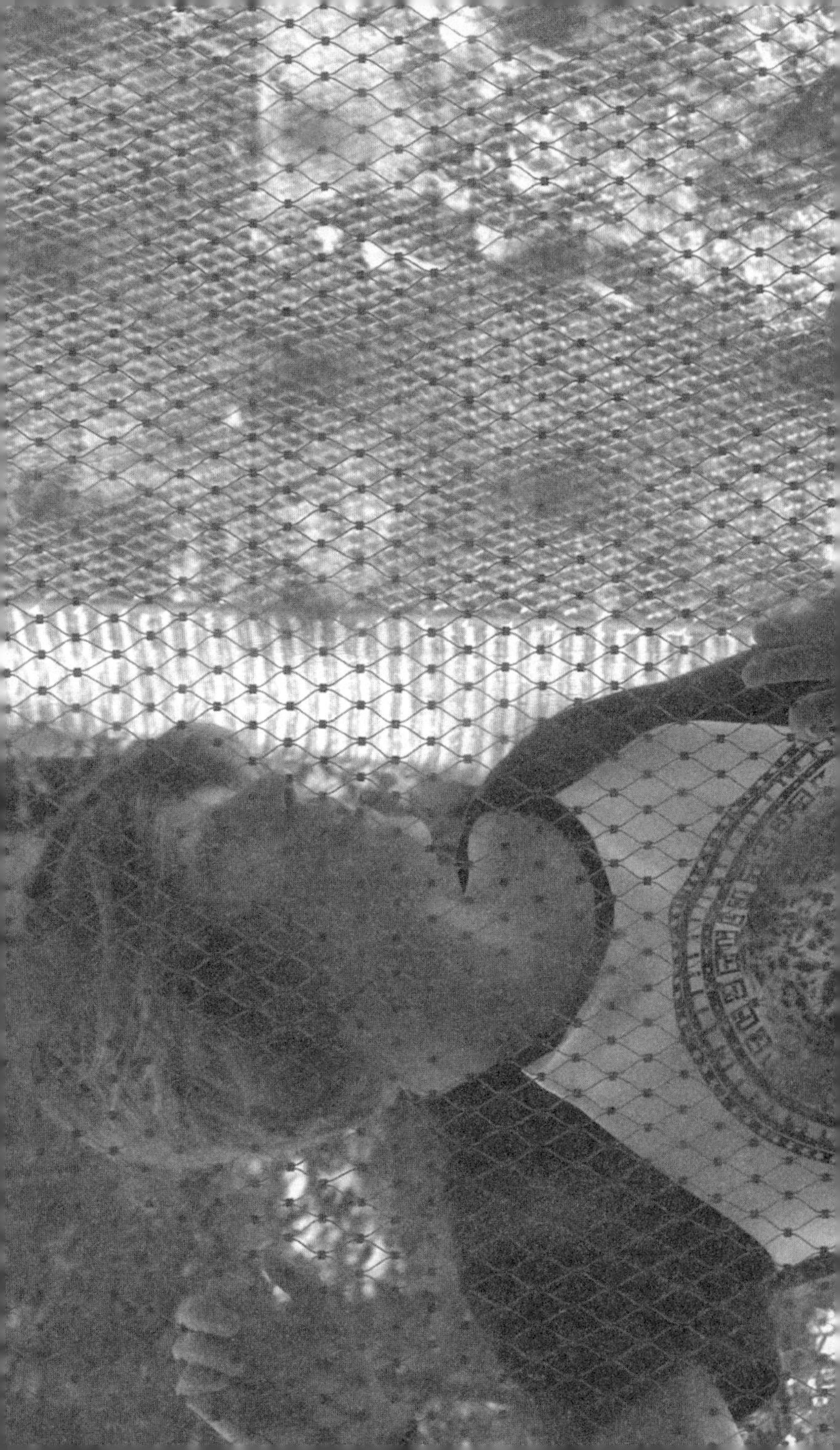

STELLA: Nor is it a simple question of transmitting knowledge.

LUCIE: The responsibility of each individual is essential. Anyone who defends educational ideals directed against responsibility, and therefore against the autonomous and conscious decision of each individual, is undemocratic.

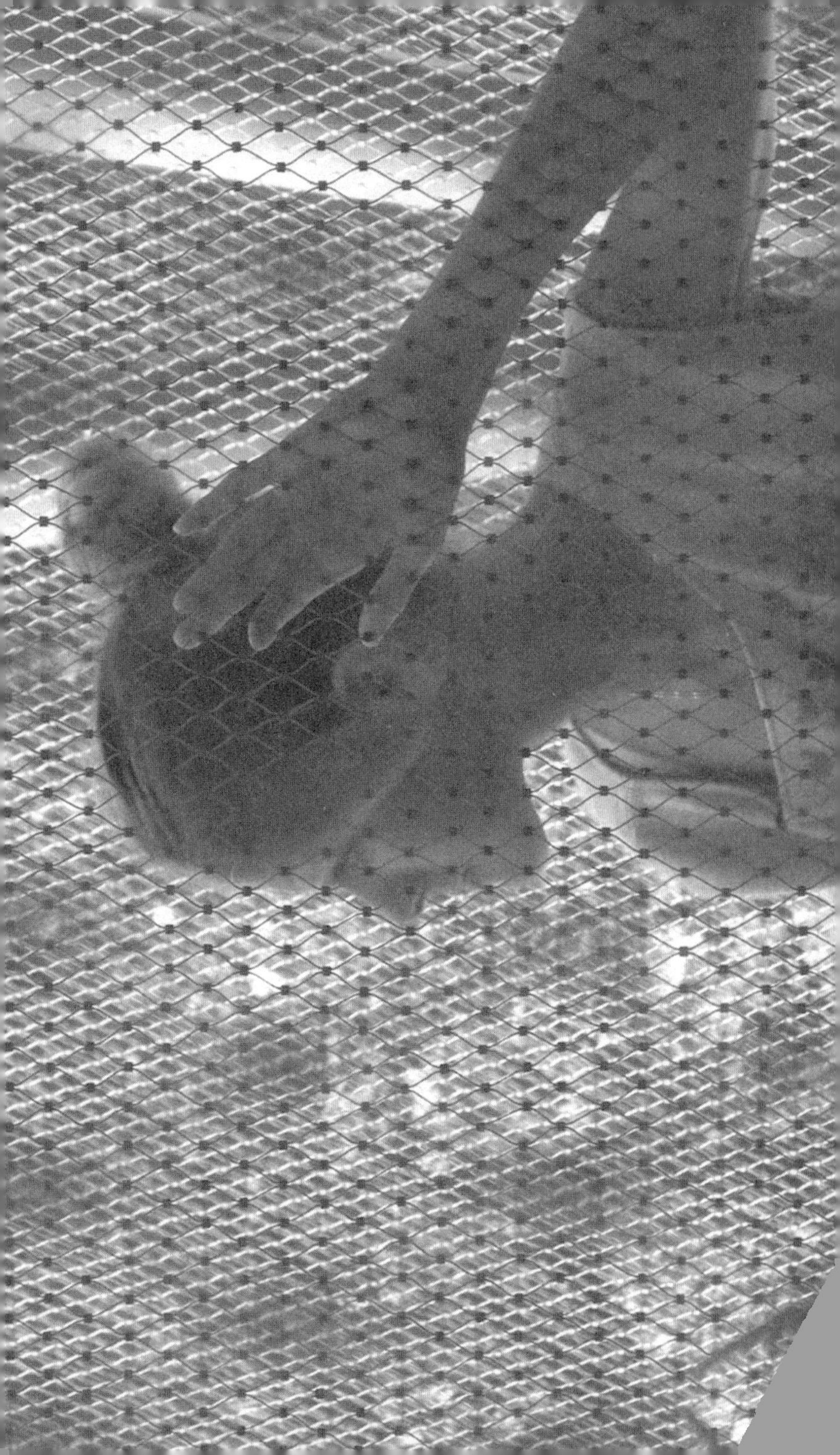

STELLA: There is another important problem in the present organization of the world, which has transformed itself into own ideology.

LUCIE: You're talking about the pressure this ideology exerts on all human beings?

STELLA: This pressure is so enormous, that it prevails over any kind of education.

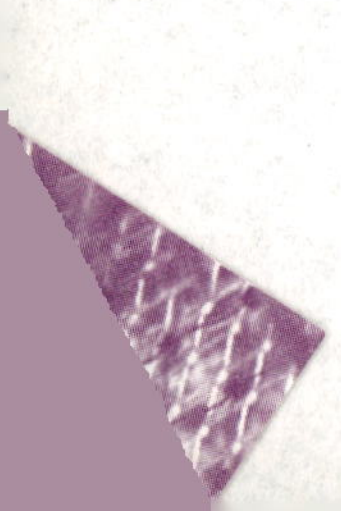

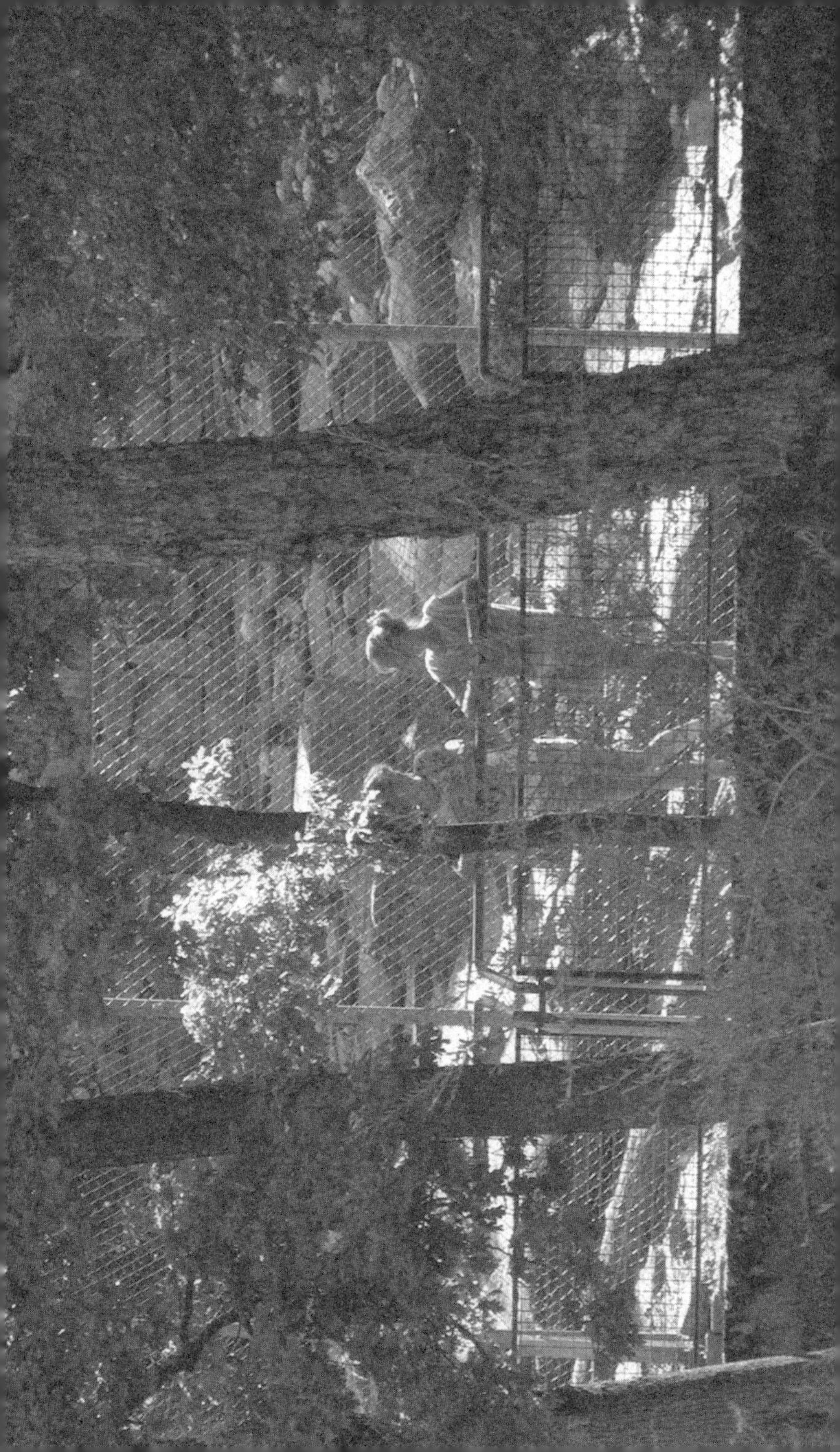

STELLA: The idea of responsibility should take into account the huge weight of the obfuscation of conscience exerted by reality.

LUCIE: And in the same vein, we should not overlook the question of adaptation. Education is powerless if it ignores the objective of adaptation.

STELLA: In other words, preparing human beings to fend for themselves in this world.

LUCIE: However, education is also questionable if it contents itself with only that, producing nothing other that "well-adjusted people."

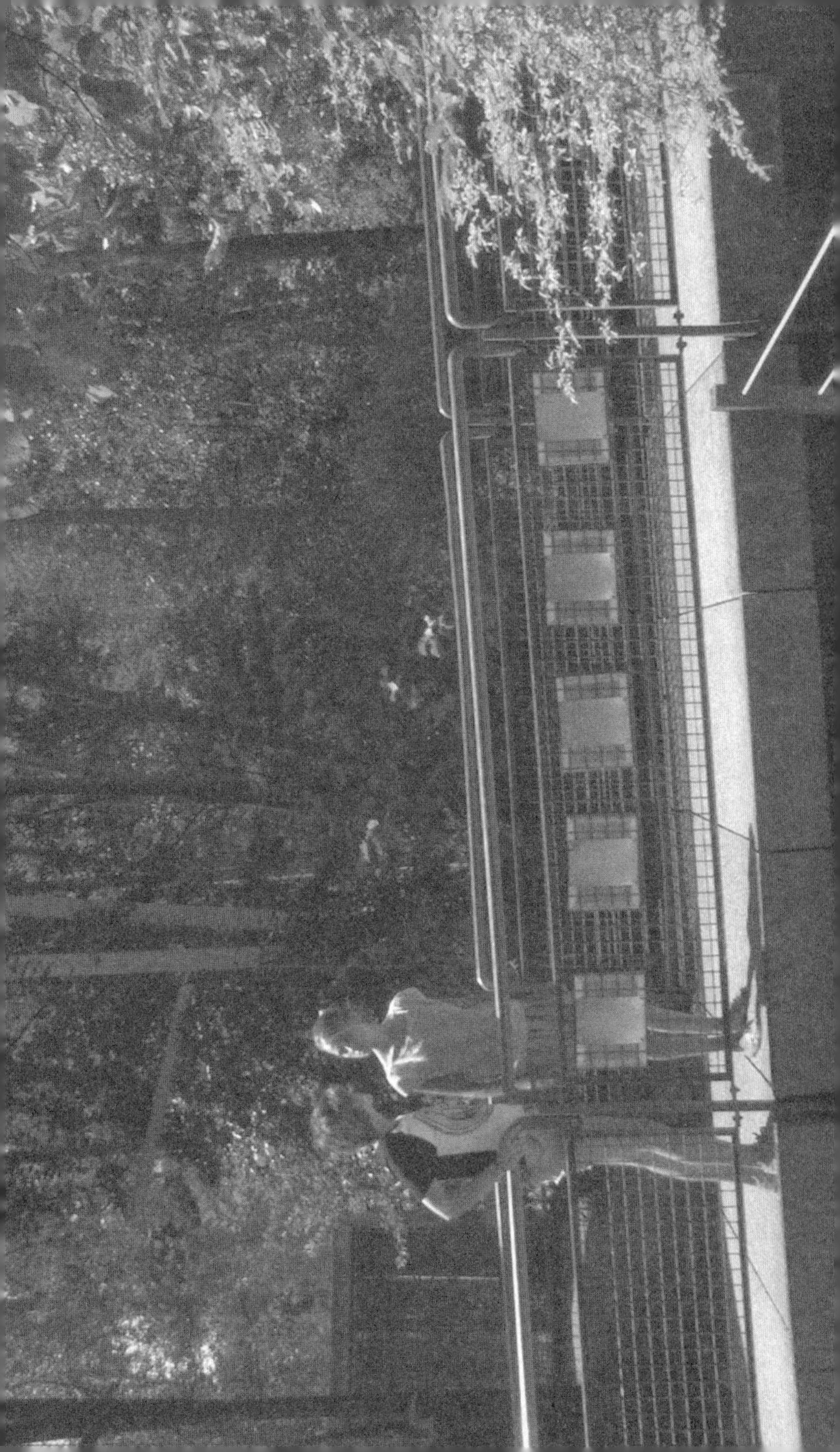

STELLA: It's important to equip an individual in such a way that he preserves his own personal qualities. Adaptation should not lead to the loss of individuality in a conformity that's destined to level everything.

LUCIE: If the task is so complicated, it's because we have to get out of an educative system that's centered only on the individual.

STELLA: On the other hand, we cannot tolerate an education that believes, in turn, that it can push the individual aside.

LUCIE: And there's the idea, it's clear now, to gather simultaneously, individual and collective principles.

STELLA: In other words, to group together, within the bounds of education, both adaptation and resistance.

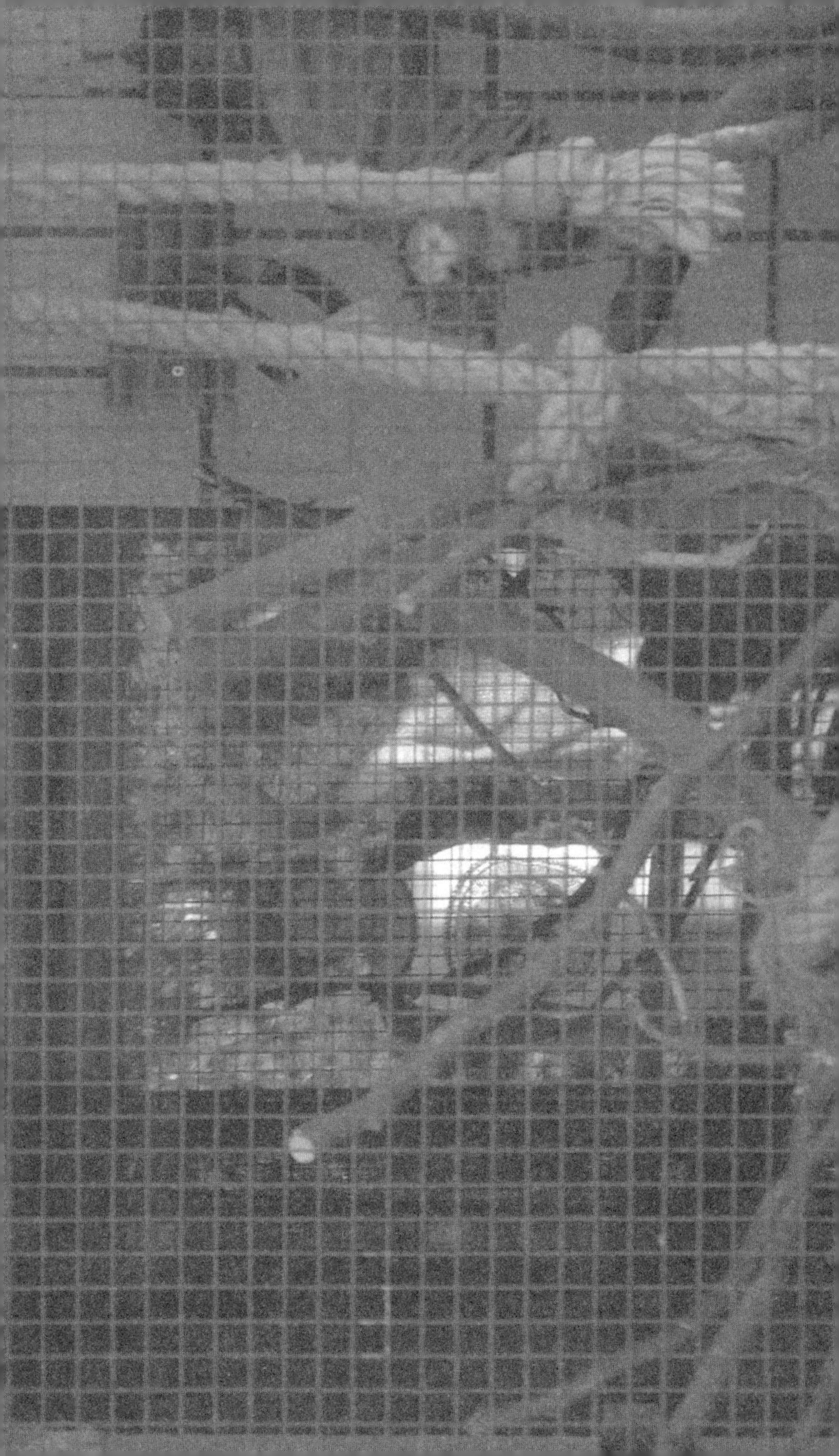

STELLA: If I trust my own observations, I would almost suppose that in young children there exists a kind of obsessive realism that's like a wound.

LUCIE: I completely agree with you. You could say that the process of adaptation is driven in such a disproportionate way by the whole environment human beings live in, that they are practically forced to inflict this adaptation painfully upon themselves.

STELLA: And even to exaggerate the hold that realism has over them, and consequently to identify with their aggressor, which is reality itself.

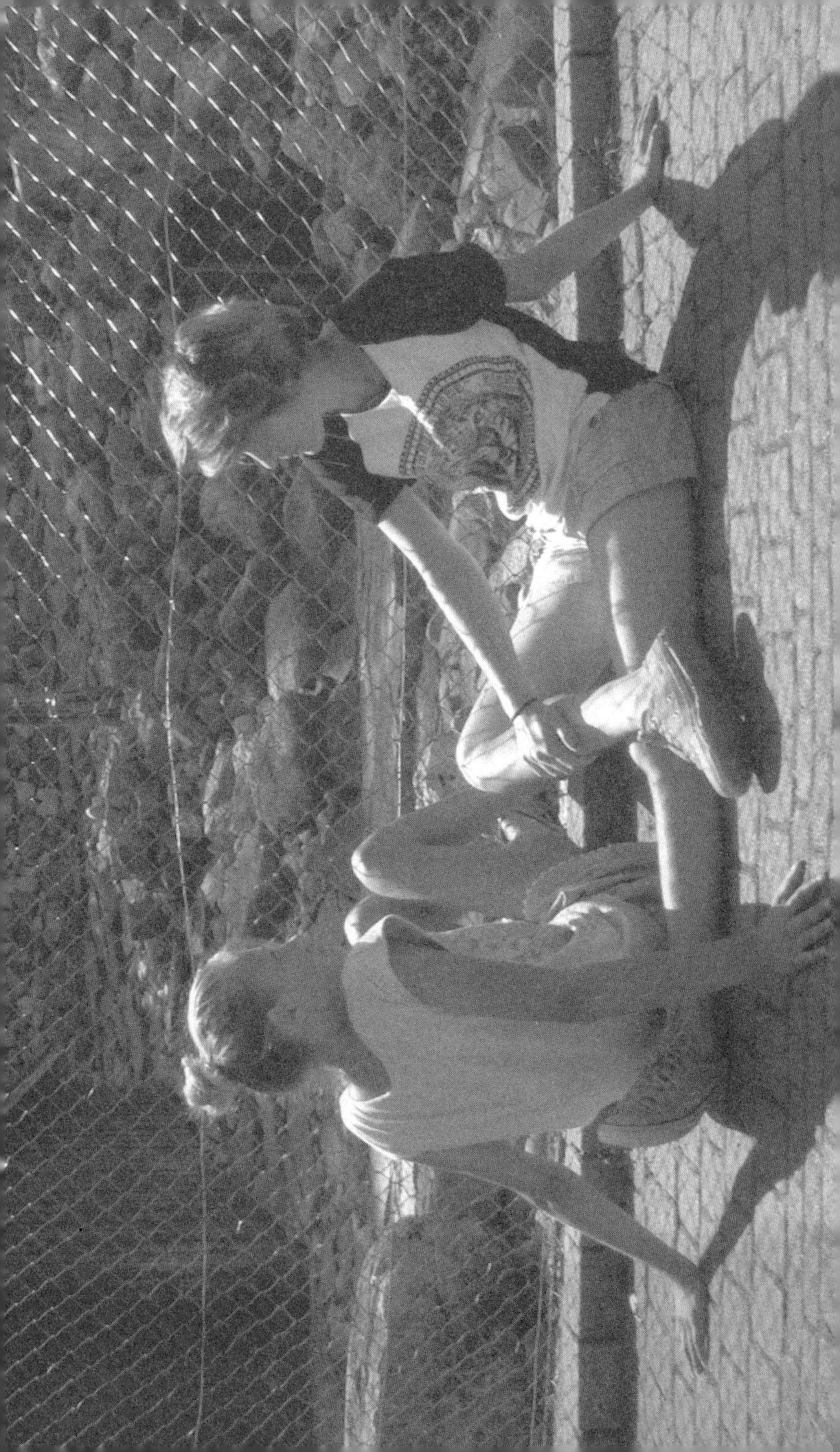

Let's Spit on Hegel

2015
10', color, sound, HD
Language: Italian, English subtitles
Format of distribution 16/9

Textual references:
Carla Lonzi, "Sputiamo su Hegel" [1970] e "Assenza della donna dai momenti celebrativi della manifestazione della cultura maschile" [1971] in *Sputiamo su Hegel e La Donna Clitoridea e la Donna Vaginale*, Scritti di Rivolta Femminile, Milano: 1978, pp. 63–65

LUCIE & STELLA: We, from Women's Revolt, refuse to take part in the celebrations of male creativity because we are aware, in a patriarchal world, that is in the world made by men for men, even creativity, which is a liberating practice, is carried out by men for men.

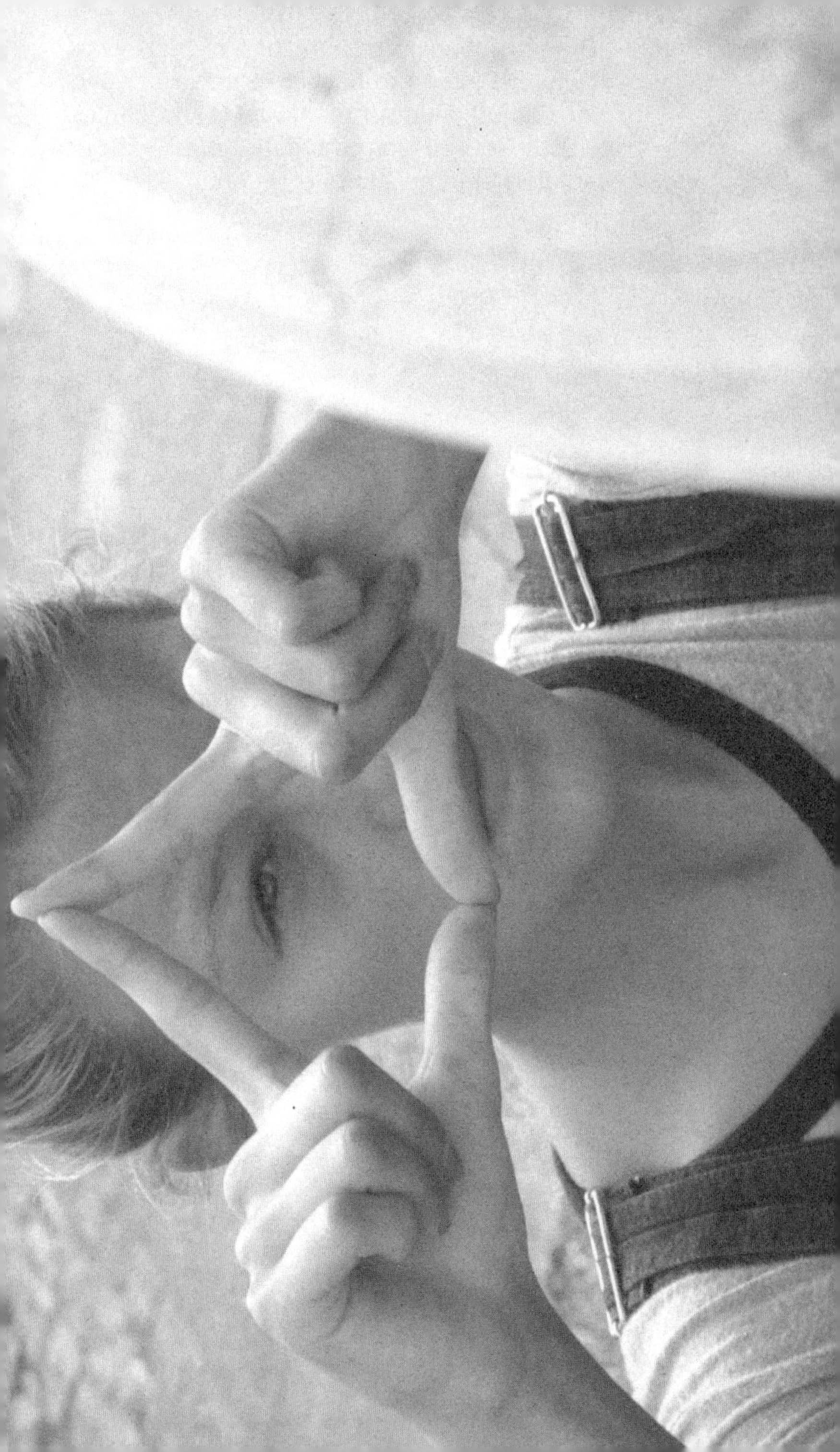

LUCIE & STELLA: By not attending celebrations of male creativity, we intend to neither to make an ideological judgment of creativity nor to contest it, but we question the idea that art can be administered as a form of pardon.

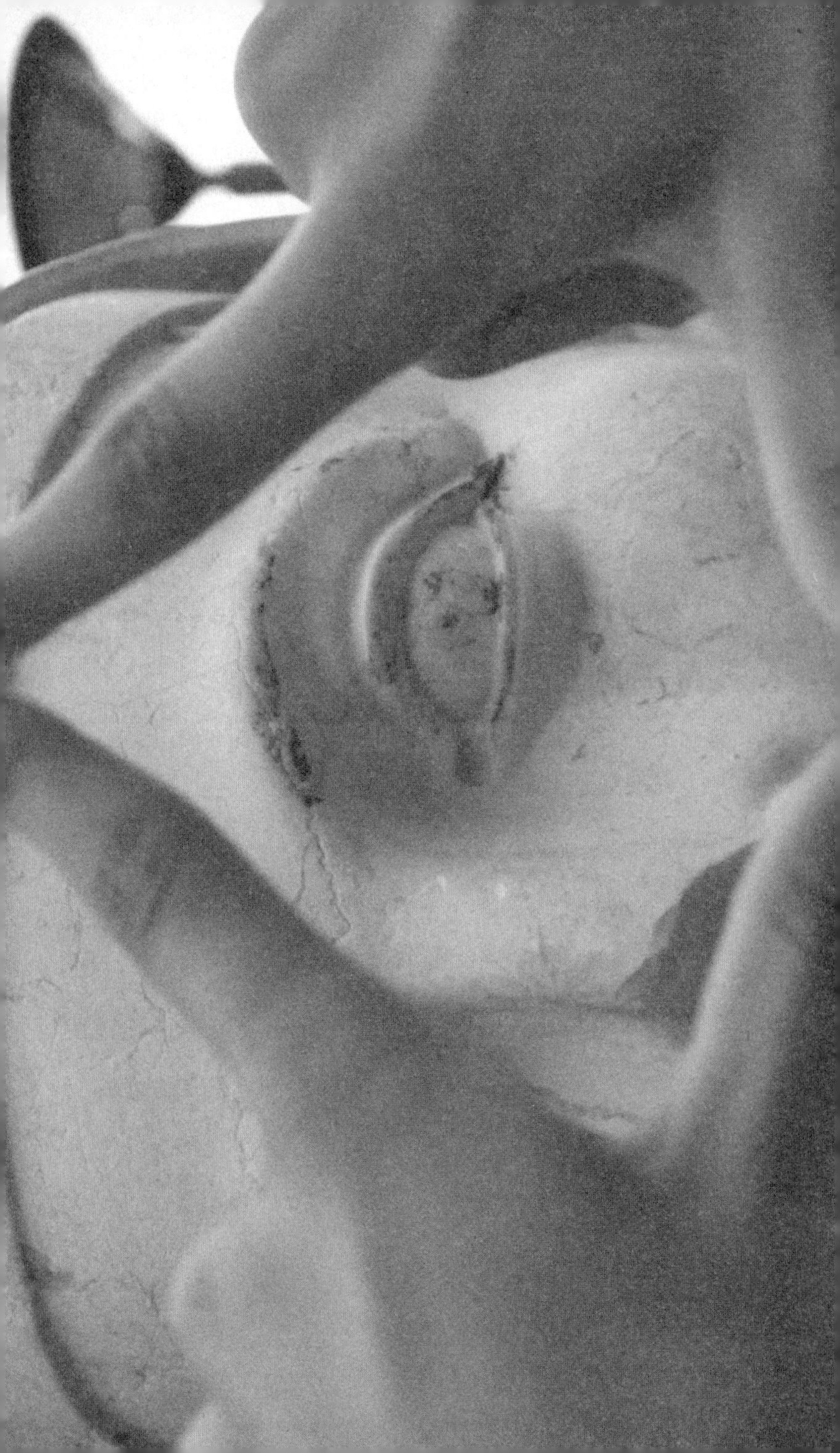

LUCIE & STELLA: To cease believing in false liberation is to release creativity from patriarchal relations. With her absence woman performs an act of awareness, liberating, and thus creative.

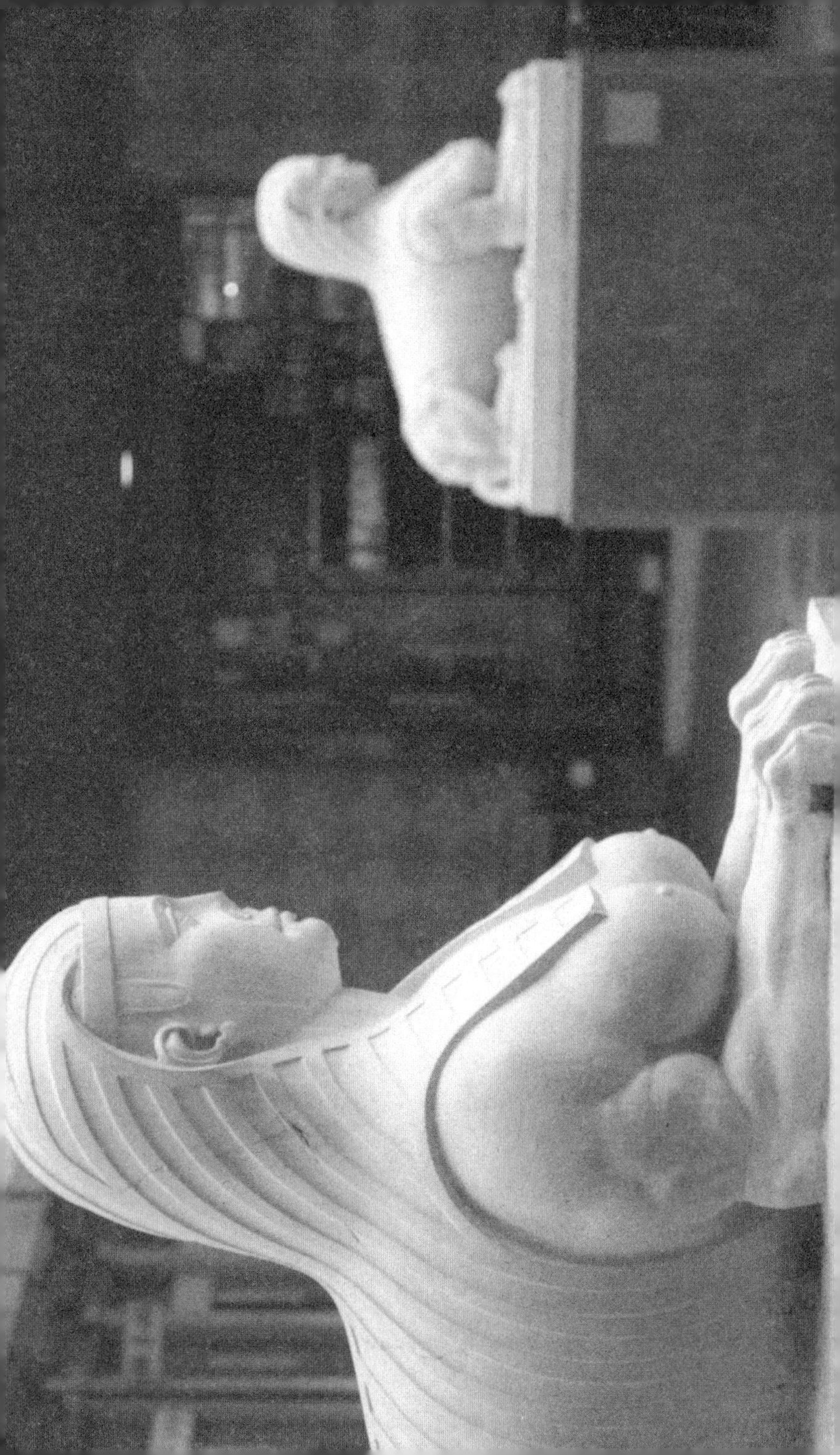

LUCIE: The Hegelian master-servant relationship is a class relationship internal to the human male world. But no solution is foreseen to the struggle between woman and man, because patriarchal culture has not defined it as a problem of humanity, but as a fact of nature. This results from the hierarchy of the sexes, whose essence is described as being a result of their opposition. The male vision of the world has found justification for the limits of its unilateral experience.

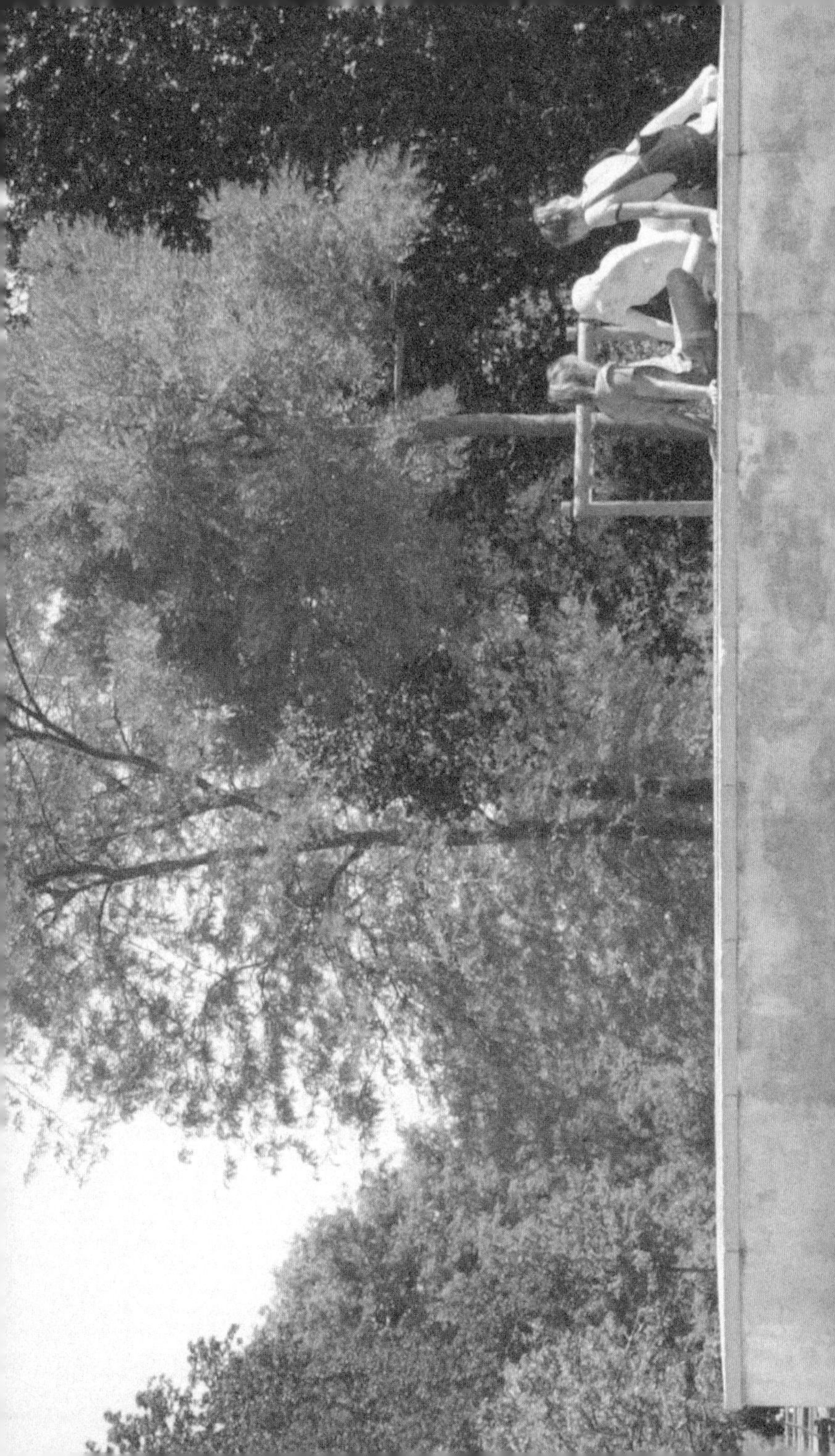

STELLA: Discussing the woman's question as part of the master-servant struggle is a historical mistake, since it springs from a culture that has excluded the essential discriminatory dynamic of humanity, the absolute privilege of man over woman, and it suggests prospects to humanity in terms of male problems that is, the only prospects it gives are for the male community. A woman is oppressed just because she is a woman, at all social levels, not on the level of class but on that of sex.

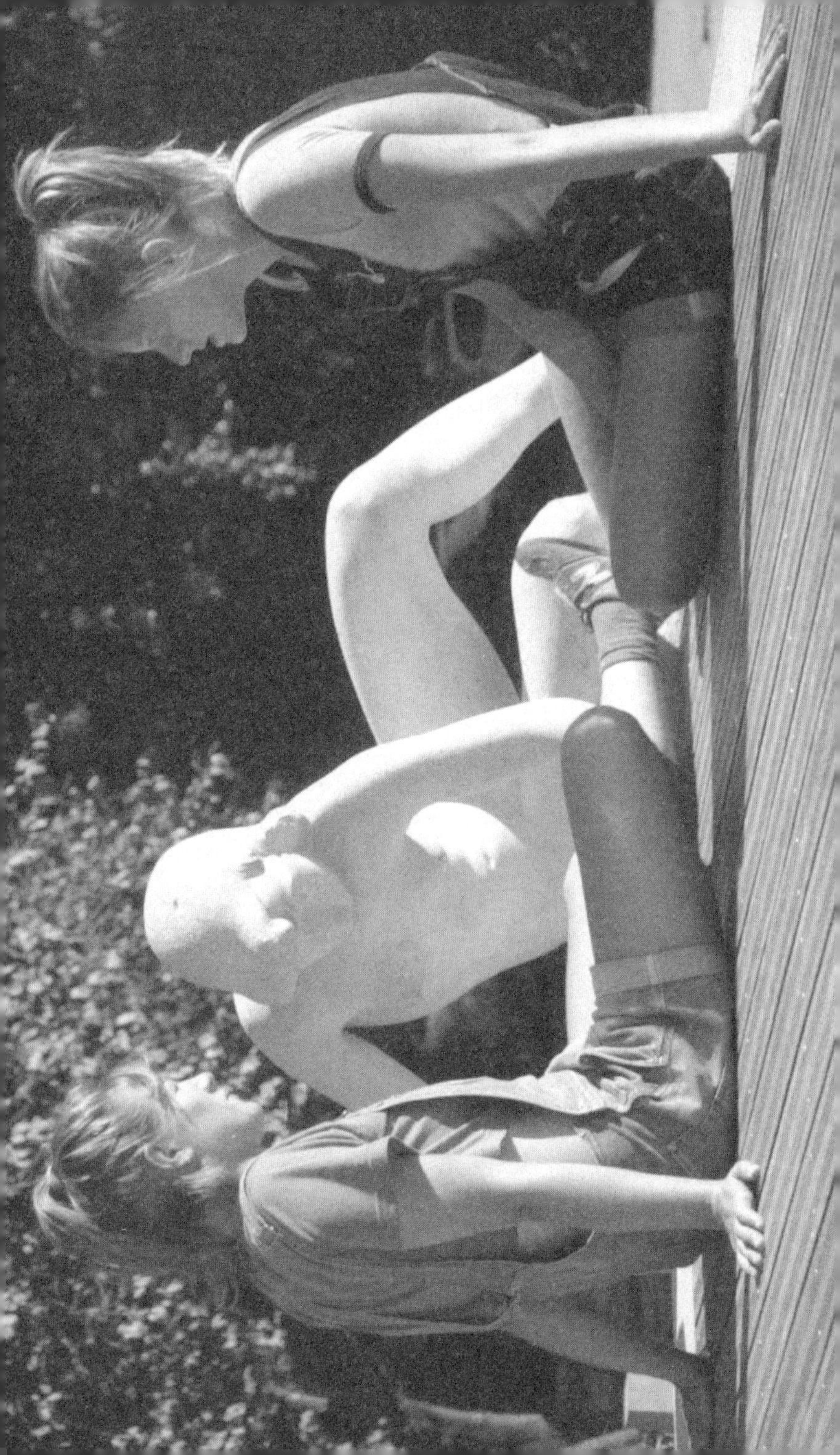

STELLA: In opposition to man's constructions, woman has opposed nothing but her existential dimension.

LUCIE: The trace of all this has disappeared because it wasn't destined to last, but our force is in refusing a mythicization of facts: action isn't a specificity of caste, but it becomes so through the power to which the action is addressed.

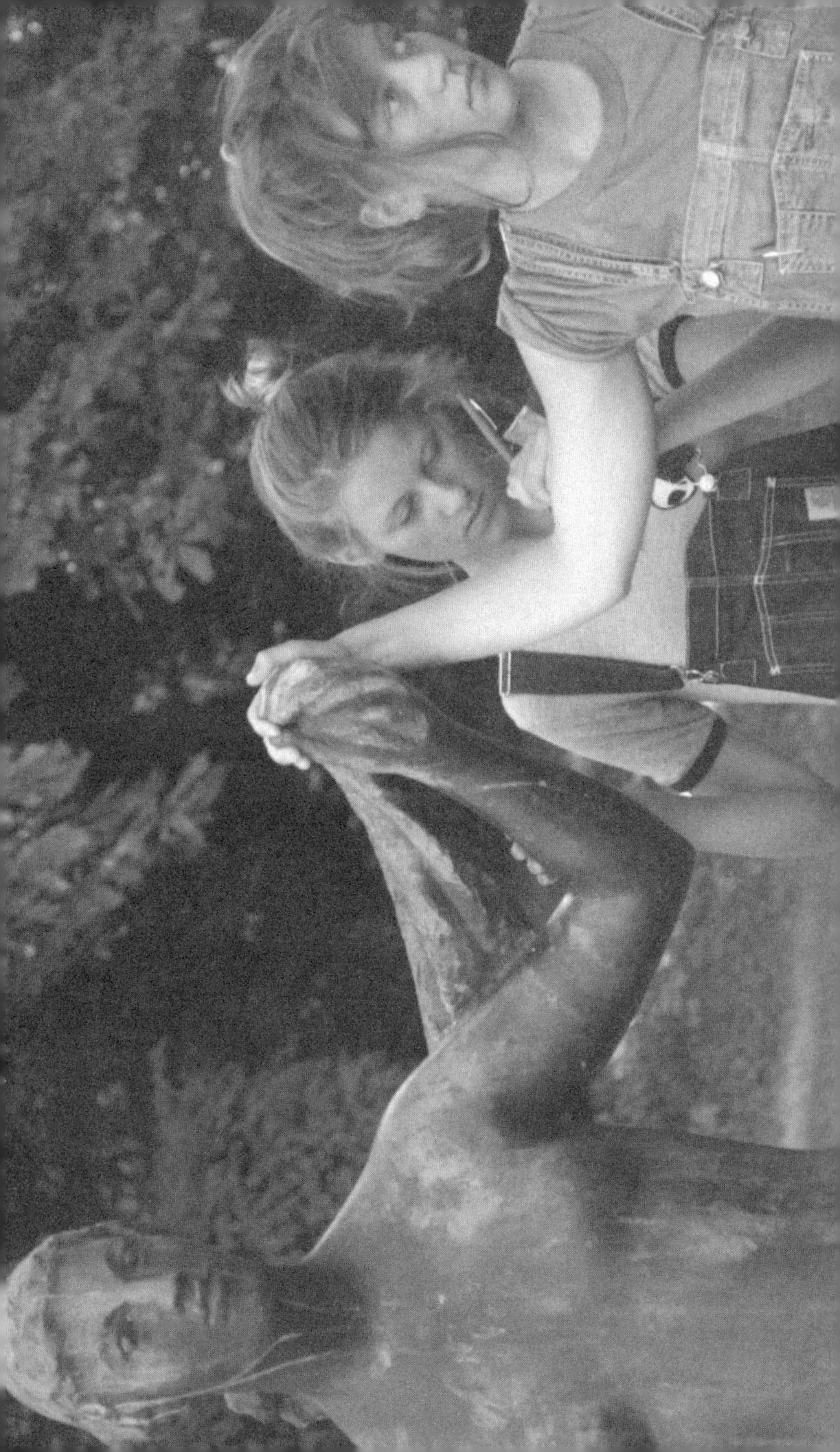

STELLA: Male humanity has taken possession of this mechanism whose justification has been culture. Denying culture means denying the evaluation of facts on the basis of power.

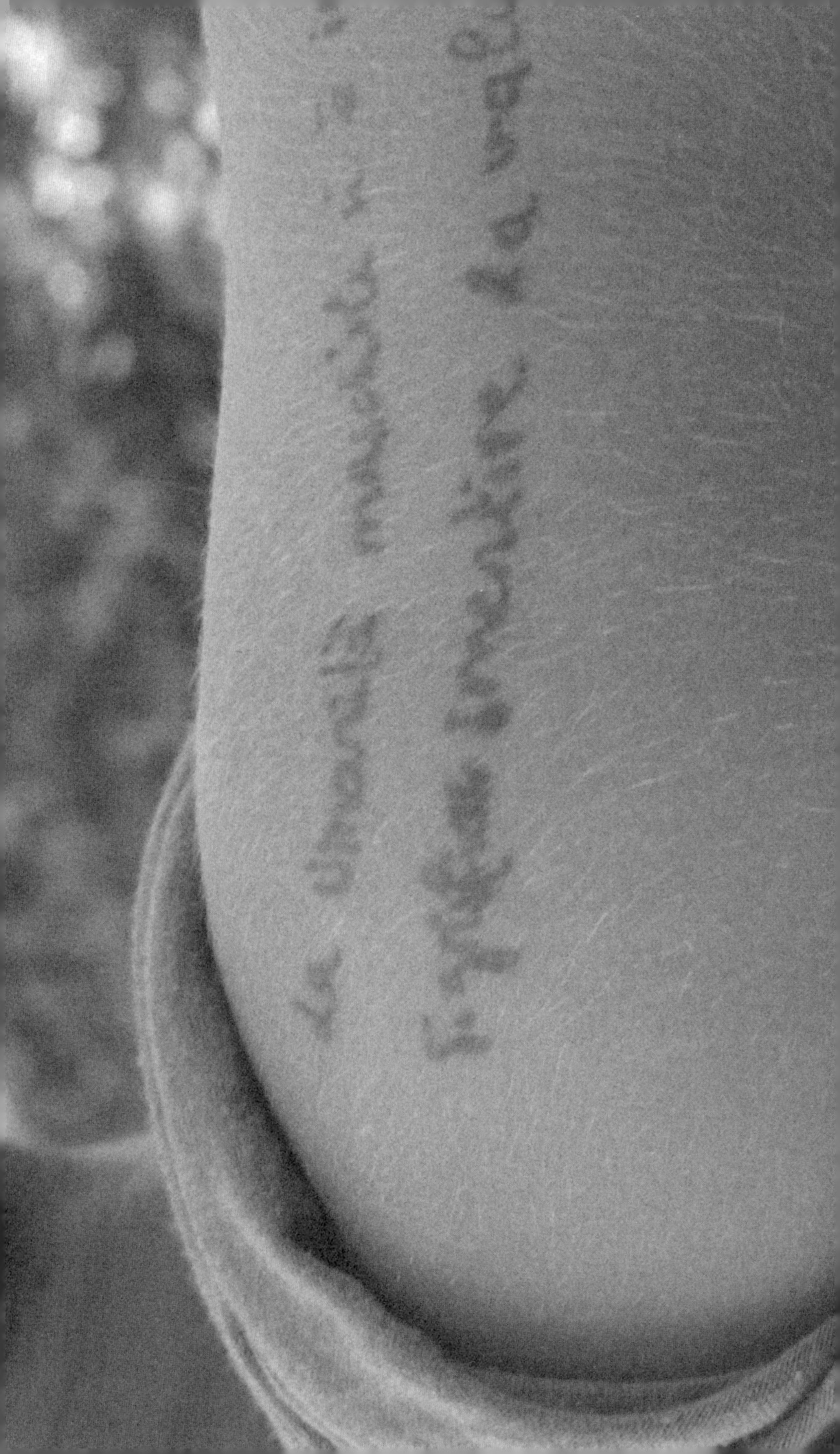

STELLA: We recognize the power we have to make this moment into a total change of life.

LUCIE: Everyone who escapes the master-servant dialectic becomes aware and enters the world of the Unexpected Subject.

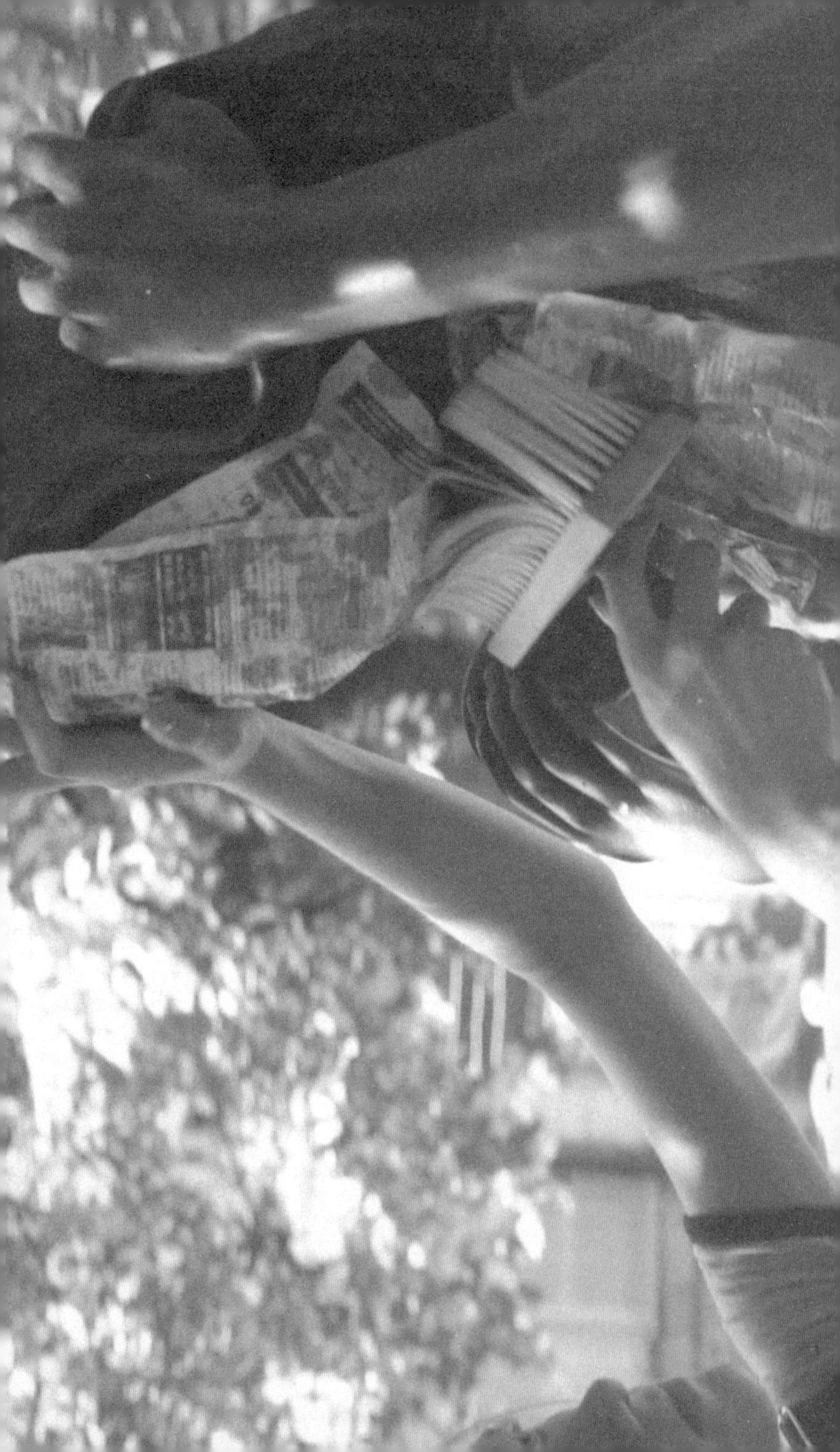

STELLA: The women's question is in itself a means and an aim of the important changes of humanity. It doesn't need a future. It doesn't make distinctions of proletariat, bourgeoisie, tribe, clan, race, age and culture. It comes neither from the top nor from the bottom, neither from the elite nor from the base. It needs neither to be directed nor to be organized, neither to be diffused nor promoted.

LUCIE: It's a new word that a new subject pronounces and entrusts to the very moment of its diffusion. Action becomes simple and elementary.

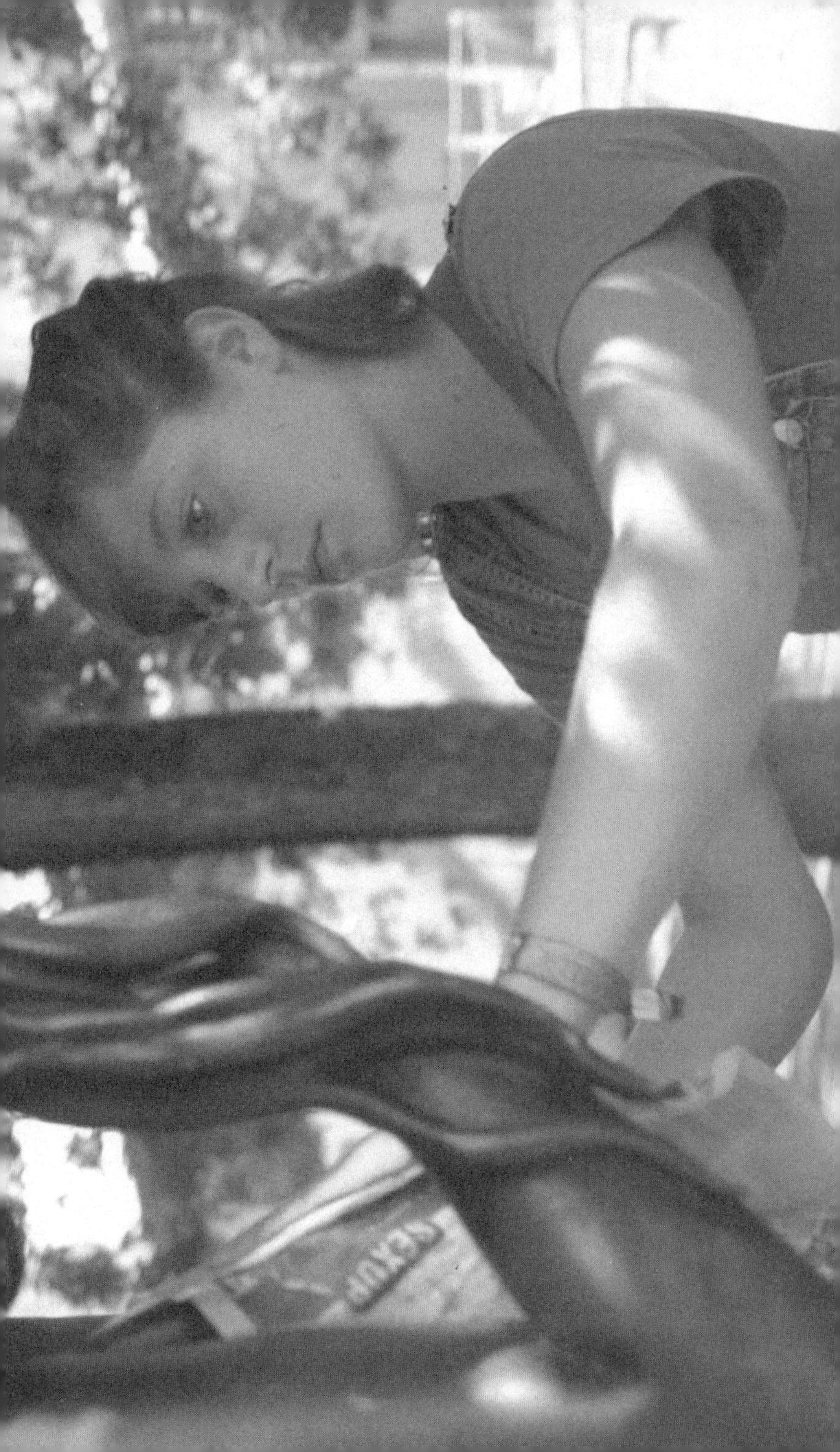

LUCIE & STELLA: We tell the man, the genius, the rational visionary, that the world's destiny is not to always forge ahead as his craving for overcoming has foretold him.

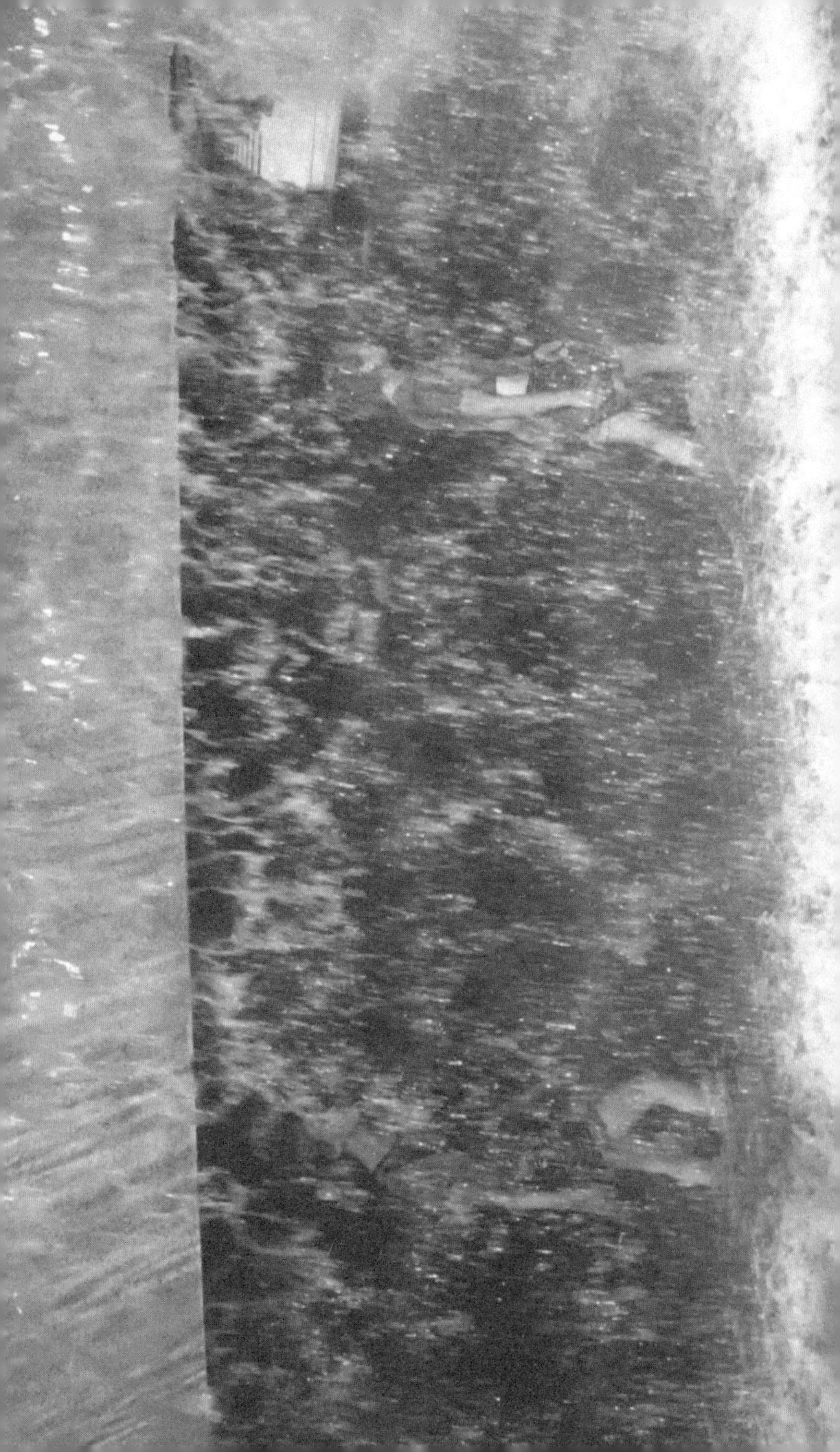

LUCIE & STELLA: The unexpected destiny of the world is in starting the journey over, together with woman as subject.

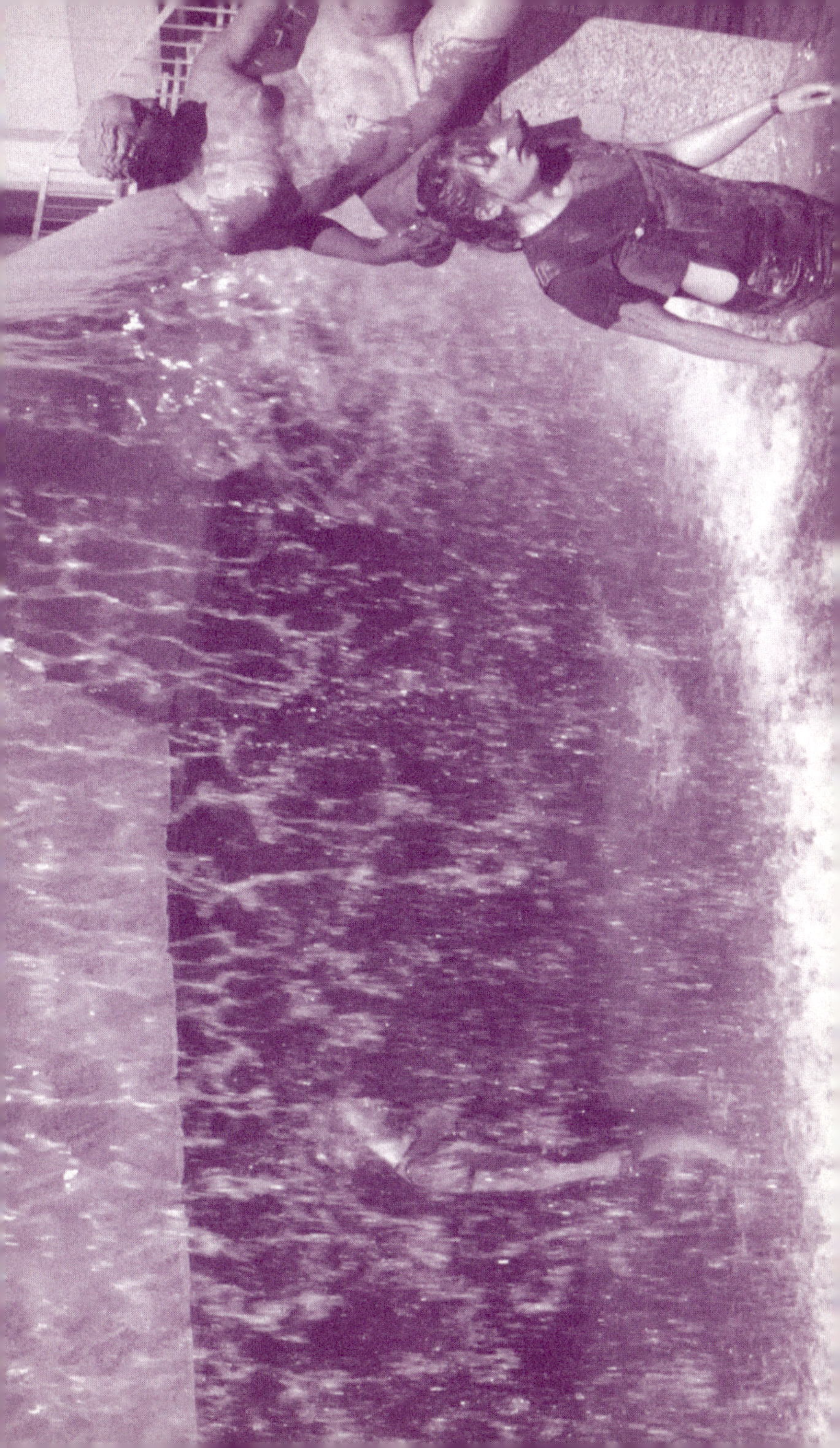

LUCIE & STELLA: There is no goal, only the present. We are the dark past of the world, we bring about the present.

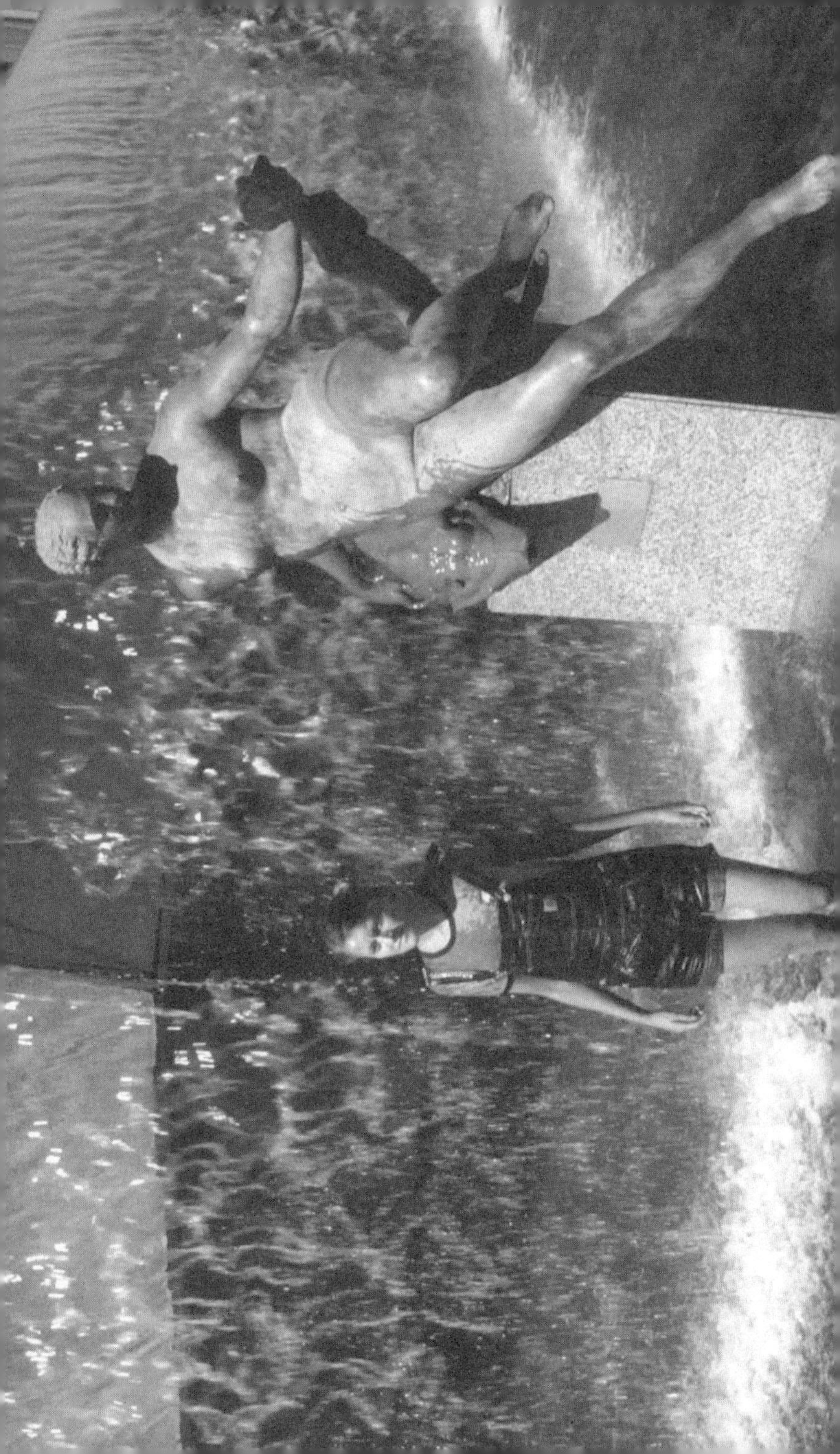

Angela Marzullo, **Homeschooling**
curated by Anna Cestelli Guidi

Super Special Thanks
Michael Hofer, Lucie Marzullo, Stella Marzullo

Special Thanks
Anna Cestelli Guidi, Francesco Ventrella, NERO Girls and Boys

Thanks
Susan Mogul, Silvie Defraoui, Moyra Davey, Stanley Brouwn, Valeria Amendolia, Nienke Terpsma, Sandra Pointet, Robert Hamelijnck, Laurent Schmid, Paola Salerno, Benedetta Cestelli Guidi, Patrick Gosatti, Martha Revuelta, Vincent Brocard, Gaspard Hirschi, Hadrien Dussoix, Jörg Bader, Noémie Etienne, Briana Berg, Karine Tissot, Valentina Sansone, Maria Rosa Sossai, Caterina Riva, Chiara Bertini, Beatrice Bertini, Benedetta Acciari, Nicole Brenez, Nadia Scheider, Hélène Fleckinger, Claudia Rampelli, Jacopo Tomassini, David Huwiler, Anna Bernardini, Lucrezia Cippitelli, Mauro Giovanni Piccinini, Serge Boulaz,Christoph Riedweg, Ellina Kevorkian, Valerio Del Baglivo, Céline Mazzon, Salvatore Lacagnina, Noah Stolz, Fanni Fetzer, Anselm Stalder, Véronique Bacchetta, Stephane Cecconi

Edited, designed, and published by
NERO

Individual orders and information
distribution@neromagazine.it

www.neromagazine.it

Photo A-Z
Sandra Pointet

Proofreading
Karen Tomatis, Erzsi Kukorelly

With the contribution of EX ELETTRO FONICA

swiss arts council
With the support of prohelvetia

ISBN 978-88-97503-86-6

Printed in December 2015
by MOS, Poznań